THE FRONTIERSMAN

Also by Mark Derr

Over Florida

Some Kind of Paradise:
A Chronicle of Man and the Land in Florida

THE FRONTIERSMAN

THE REAL LIFE
AND THE MANY LEGENDS
OF DAVY CROCKETT

———

MARK DERR

WILLIAM MORROW AND COMPANY, INC.
NEW YORK

Copyright © 1993 by Mark Derr

It is the policy of William Morrow and Company, Inc., and its imprints and affiliates, recognizing the importance of preserving what has been written, to print the books we publish on acid-free paper, and we exert our best efforts to that end.

Library of Congress Cataloging-in-Publication Data

Derr, Mark.
    The frontiersman : the real life and the many legends of Davy Crockett / Mark Derr.
        p.   cm.
    Includes bibliographical references and index.
    ISBN 0-688-09656-5
    1. Crockett, Davy, 1786–1836.   2. Crockett, Davy, 1786–1836—Legends.   3. Pioneers—Tennessee—Biography.   4.   Tennessee—Biography.   5.   Legislators—United   States—Biography.   5.   United   States.   Congress.   House—Biography.
I. Title.
    F436.C95D47   1993
    976.4'04'092—dc20
    [B]   92-41921
                                                                              CIP

Printed in the United States of America

First Edition

1 2 3 4 5 6 7 8 9 10

BOOK DESIGN BY BILL MCCARTHY

FOR MY PARENTS,
VERNON AND MARY

ACKNOWLEDGMENTS

For material on Crockett and his times, I have relied on the kindness and aid of librarians and archivists around the nation, chief among them: Alan Carter, senior librarian at the New York State Library at Albany, who tirelessly tracked down texts and provided essential books and periodicals; Ann Fears Crawford, director of the Daughters of the Republic of Texas Research Library at the Alamo, who was ready to share her knowledge and insights; Warren Stricker and Martha Utterback of the DRT Library, who also provided invaluable assistance; Ralph Elder of the Barker Texas History Center at the University of Texas at Austin; Wayne Moore, archivist at the Tennessee State Library and Archives, which also houses the Tennessee Historical Society collection, who has a talent for finding obscure information; and the staff of the Manuscripts Division at the Library of Congress. Bill Davis at the National Archives first revealed the name of the boardinghouse Crockett stayed in while in Congress, and Sandy Peterson at Yale University Library provided additional information on that score. Donnald K. Anderson, clerk of the U.S. House of Representatives, granted permission for me to review the records of Congressmen David Crockett and Thomas Chilton in the National Archives in Washington. Suzanne C. Jenkins, registrar of the National Portrait Gallery, the Smithsonian Institution;

7

ACKNOWLEDGMENTS

Elizabeth Neubauer, curatorial assistant at the Harry Ransom Humanities Research Center, the University of Texas at Austin; John Anderson, photo archivist at the Texas State Library; Karen Zakrison, photo editor at *Time,* and Gay Nemeti, librarian and archivist at the *Miami Herald,* assisted in the collection of images. Leo Cullum and *The New Yorker* kindly provided artwork. I am also indebted to David Byer and Freddy Sall for legal advice and research.

Other archives and libraries that have made material available to me are the National Archives—Mid-Atlantic Region; the East Tennessee Historical Society; the Maryland Historical Society; the Historical Society of Pennsylvania; the Maine Historical Society; the Beinecke Rare Book and Manuscript Library at Yale University; the Houghton Library at Harvard University; the Boston Public Library; the New York Public Library; the New-York Historical Society; the University of Tennessee Library and Archives; the David Crockett State Park in Lawrenceburg, Tennessee; the University of the South; the North Carolina State Library; the Buffalo and Erie County Historical Society; the Huntington Library; the Chicago Historical Society; the Pierpont Morgan Library; the Area Research Center of the University of Wisconsin at Oshkosh; the Lilly Library at Indiana University; the Southern Historical Collection at the University of North Carolina at Chapel Hill; Joyner Library at East Carolina University; and the Alabama Department of Archives and History.

This book would not exist without the unstinting support of my wife, Gina Maranto, who has kept us together, body and soul, for the more than three years of its making; and the encouragement and assistance at William Morrow of my editor, Harvey Ginsberg, and special projects manager Zachary Schisgal. My agent, Barney Karpfinger, deserves special praise for his efforts. Whatever merit *The Frontiersman* possesses belongs equally to them. The book's failings are my own.

CONTENTS

INTRODUCTION

For more than a century and a half, David—Davy—Crockett has ranked high in the pantheon of American heroes, celebrated in scores of songs, novels, children's stories, tall tales, plays, and films as a backwoods Hercules, a warrior, bear hunter, martyr to liberty. His favorite motto—"Be always sure you are right, and then go ahead!"—continues to inspire people. Yet despite his renown, he remains an enigma wrapped in paradox—an unschooled man who became a best-selling author; a man of modest achievement who metamorphosed into a legendary superman, capable of wringing the tail off Halley's comet or drinking dry the Gulf of Mexico; a poor soldier who became a celebrated warrior. As frequently as he is glorified as a hero, he is maligned as a drunkard and fraud, a fabricated man. Even in his purely fictional incarnations, he can appear as a wild man capable of loving more women, drinking more whiskey, killing more game than anyone alive or as a Lochinvar of the canebrake, a naïve and sentimental rustic.

A distant cousin of Crockett on my mother's side and an admirer of his slim autobiography, *A Narrative of the Life of David Crockett of the State of Tennessee,* I set out four years ago to find the man who gave rise to the legend and to examine both in their context. That has proved no easy task. Over the years, the invented Crocketts have been laid over the man and accepted

11

as real. The process began in Crockett's lifetime with newspaper reports from his native Tennessee when he was a state legislator in the early 1820s and, in 1827, a congressman from the Western District pledged to Andrew Jackson. In Washington, his fame became national with an 1830 play by James Kirke Paulding, *The Lion of the West,* featuring a Crockettesque "Kentuckian" named Nimrod Wildfire; continued to grow with publication in 1833 of a bogus biography, *Life and Adventures of Colonel David Crockett of West Tennessee,* which nonetheless carried factual information; and took off a year later when his own *Narrative* became an immediate success. So many tales followed that Crockett himself could not keep track of them, and after his death they multiplied again. There were comic almanacs, featuring rough woodcuts and a brawling, racist wild man; sweet melodramas; dime novels and biographies, most of which glorified him. In the main, the Crockett legends artlessly accreted until the winter of 1954–55 when Walt Disney, the master showman and creator of Mickey Mouse, brought Davy to the medium of television in a series of three programs that reaffirmed his fame and started yet another of the often contradictory characterizations.

Finding the man involves more than simply peeling back the layers of legend. The historical record is fragmentary, with gaps of many years. Even the material that does exist often amounts to little more than notices of the sale of some land or a slave child, promissory notes, a brief summary of a court case, a record of military service, a marriage license, or a census listing. With a few notable exceptions, the score or so of surviving letters from Crockett to political supporters and, in rare instances, to members of his family carry little more than tantalizing bits of information about his private life. His autobiography and works about him are silent about matters we consider of fundamental importance—the names of his wives and children, his siblings, not to mention more telling details. Dates are missing or skewed, descriptions of the players almost nil. Names are spelled with variants upon variants—even Crockett is frequently Crocket—because people who were marginally literate themselves simply transcribed what they heard.

Seeking coherence, biographers have guessed at significant dates and facts, which over the years have become received wisdom, although on close examination they are clearly incorrect.

Of necessity, I too have assigned dates that seem correct to events like Crockett's marriage to his second wife, Elizabeth, and speculated on other matters—for example, whether the marriage was a close one and why he went to Texas and, more particularly, to the Alamo, in his forty-ninth year. I have indicated where and why I have engaged in such speculation either in the text or, where appropriate, in endnotes. Despite the gaps, a fair amount is known about Crockett, his life, and the circumstances of his family, and I have drawn upon it to show how he participated fully in the creation of his various public personae, even to the extent of distorting the facts to fit his image.

The process is most apparent in *Narrative,* the primary source for most of what we know about his early life. Written as a campaign tract, preserving much of the period's customary reticence about a person's private life, it both distorted and elided facts to support the portrait of Crockett as a self-made man who had overcome potentially crushing hardships to achieve greatness. Thus, he played down the crucial importance of his second marriage, to Elizabeth Patton. A woman with sufficient means to start him on his political career, she profitably managed the family farm and enterprises while he fulfilled his official duties. Taking advantage of the public's fascination with the frontier, he trumpeted his prowess as a bear hunter and Indian scout, while so exaggerating his lack of formal education that a great many people, then and now, have wrongly assumed that he was functionally illiterate. Alexis de Tocqueville recorded the view of Crockett held by the moneyed elite around Memphis in 1831 to support his own distaste for universal male suffrage:

When voting rights are *universal,* and deputies are paid by the state, it is a strange thing how low people's choice can descend and how far it can be mistaken.

Two years ago, the inhabitants of the district of which Memphis is the capital, sent to the House of Representatives of Congress an individual called David Crockett, who had received no education, could read only with difficulty, had no property, no fixed dwelling, but spent his time hunting, selling his game for a living, and spending his whole life in the woods. His competitor, who failed, was a fairly rich and able man.[1]

Tocqueville got nearly all his facts wrong, but he captured the fear of participatory democracy current in the circles in which he traveled.

I have attempted to cull the significant details from *Narrative* and present them plainly. There is a tendency to want to use the text to psychoanalyze Crockett, especially his troubled relationship to his father. I have sought to avoid this approach on the grounds that we cannot accurately apply our theories to an early nineteenth-century backwoodsman or an autobiography ghostwritten for him. On occasion, however, I have suggested how certain patterns of behavior—turning vehemently against authority figures who are perceived to have wronged him, for example, and restlessly moving in search of financial improvement—have reverberated throughout his life, the conclusion being too apparent to ignore.

The controversy that surrounded Crockett's political career has spilled over into every study of the man, making the question of how to interpret his character more problematic than determining the details and proper chronology of his life. Do we judge him against his legend, hardly a fair comparison; against his contemporaries, like Henry Clay, Andrew Jackson, Sam Houston, all his superiors in terms of accomplishment; or in light of his own legacy as a man and fictional hero? Or—as I prefer—do we judge him in terms of his life and deeds, which, although less glamorous than those of greater men or his heroic persona, nonetheless reveal a rather extraordinary individual?

His detractors have called him a man of great fame and scant accomplishment, a sham, a buffoon, and worse. He not only failed to sponsor any successful legislation during three terms in Congress, the argument goes, but also betrayed his roots by abandoning Andrew Jackson and the Democratic Party in favor of the Whigs, the representatives of eastern industrialists and wealthy southern gentry. A political apostate, he was also a literary fraud, they claim, relying on ghostwriters to produce the four books that are ascribed to him. More recently, he has been accused of cowardice, as a number of historians have decided that he hid under a bed during the final assault on the Alamo, was captured, and then killed after trying to lie his way out of difficulty by claiming he was there by accident. A review of the record proves these to be convenient fictions that are more revealing of their authors' ideologies and the times in which they have worked than of Crockett. Still, in some circles, they are held as firmly as the image of the backwoods superman.

Harriet Martineau, a keen British observer and abolitionist touring the United States in the early 1830s, adjudged Crockett a "humorist" and true "original," in a land sadly lacking both.[2] He first entered Congress at a time when the nation's attention was fixed on the West, the place of its destiny and of opportunity, where a man—albeit a white man—could start afresh and re-create himself, unencumbered by his past failures. The popular—penny—press, which was expanding rapidly, demanded exciting stories and heroes who embodied American, not English or European, characteristics and manners.

At the same time, the political system was in ferment. Democracy was opening to that same white male. The rapid expansion of the franchise and development of politics as a mass activity left many traditional politicians, accustomed to courting the propertied class, without a constituency. The national consensus called the American system, which involved government support of manufacturing and internal improvements—public works—through a protective tariff and the sale of public lands at a relatively high price, broke down under pressure from the new democracy. Claiming the system supported moneyed interests at the expense of small farmers and artisans, its opponents rallied around Andrew Jackson, the enormously popular general who had secured the frontier from the Indians and the nation from the British in the War of 1812. Proponents of the American system, on the other hand, allied themselves with more sectional leaders, like Henry Clay of Kentucky—its chief architect—and Daniel Webster of Massachusetts.

Policy differences between the insurgent Jacksonians and the more established leaders of the dominant National Republican Party finally forced it to split in 1834 into the Whig and Democratic parties. The formation of these two groups, national in scope and intensely partisan, signaled a break from the sectional balancing act that had defined politics in the first decades of the century. Many historians have assumed that Crockett, a Tennessean, should have followed his commander, Jackson, on all issues, but from the beginning of his career the bear hunter had shown an independent streak that he would never relinquish. He would pledge allegiance, he said, to no man and no party.

Crockett was the common man, eccentric, independent, unschooled in the classical references that punctuated erudite public discourse, more familiar with the ways of livestock and hunting than with learned men and public affairs. His genius lay in his ability after a long struggle, during which he attempted to transform himself into a responsible, judicious member of Congress, to embrace what he was and adopt it as his public face. He went from being a self-conscious farmer-politician humbly representing the people of his district to being the bear hunter from the backwoods, the man who with his rustic, ungrammatical anecdotes and country witticisms could amuse any audience and demand that even President Jackson obey the Constitution—albeit to no avail. An unsuccessful legislator, he served as a vital cultural link between the "wilderness" of the frontier and the "civilization" of the East, between the poor people and their government.

The penny press created many of the tales that attached themselves to Crockett during his lifetime, treating him favorably or unfavorably according to his shifting political inclinations. Thus, early in his career Jacksonian newspapers promoted and defended him, while the anti-Jacksonians attacked, whereas later the roles were reversed. Although he was in most respects a bit player in the major dramas of his day—over the tariff, Indian removal, the Second Bank of the United States, internal improvements, and even the disposal of public lands—the Whigs found it useful to publicize his disagreements with the Jacksonians on these issues. They thought that by presenting an independent Crockett willing to sacrifice everything, including his career, for a principle, they would encourage the southwesterners to whom he appealed to break their ties to Jackson and the Democrats.

Many historians have wrongly argued that Crockett was a dupe of the Whigs (the collective, if anachronistic, name for all anti-Jacksonians in the early 1830s), as if he were a man without volition. In fact, he took an active interest in the way he was presented, enlisting ghostwriters to assist him. He wished both to guard his reputation and to profit as an author. Informing his publishers of the situation, he sought in the case of his *Narrative* to ensure that the copyright and profits were shared with his collaborator. When working on his second book, he requested that the title page state that it was a collaborative effort, but recognizing that its readers wanted only Crockett, his publisher refused. Crockett was more unique in seeking to credit his ghostwriters than in using them, the practice being as commonplace then as it is now.

Crockett's *Narrative* succeeded because his collaborator, Kentucky congressman Thomas Chilton, turned his manner of talking into literature. Written to cash in on the success of *Narrative,* the two books that followed in 1835—*An Account of Colonel Crockett's Tour to the North and Down East* and (entitled with an outrageous pun to mock his baldness and vanity) *The Life of Martin Van Buren, Hair-Apparent to the "Government," and the Appointed Successor of General Jackson*—failed to match the success of his first book not only because they were more blatantly partisan but also because they did not capture the distinctive Crockett idiom. Both, however, reflected Crockett's views—the one on the East, which he toured for his autobiography, and on such political questions as whether Jackson was attempting to assume monarchical power; the other about Martin Van Buren, for whom he, like many other westerners, had a nearly pathological hatred. The final book frequently attributed to David, *Colonel Crockett's Exploits and Adventures in Texas,* pseudonymously written shortly after his death at the Alamo, was an immediate best seller. Only its opening pages were based on material from Crockett—two letters he had written to Carey and Hart, his publisher—but the whole conveyed his flavor if not his precise tone. The ubiquitous diatribes against Jackson and Van Buren are subsumed by the fictional diary detailing the fall of the Alamo. Packaged as the "Autobiography of David Crockett," or some variation thereon, *Narrative, Tour,* and *Exploits and Adventures* have proved extremely popular over the years, remaining steadily in print from a number of publishers.

Sadly missing from the Crockett bibliography are transcripts of his stump speeches, upon which so much of his fame rested. What few remarks are reprinted, either in the records of the Tennessee legislature or the United States Congress, give only a sampling of his characteristic idiom and syntax. Occasionally, a newspaper does the same, as do the Crockett books. But the only full speeches we have were clearly written by someone else in a style devoid of his distinctive phrasing: one in support of his bill to give the occupants of public land in West Tennessee clear title to their farms; another in opposition to Jackson's plan to force the southeastern Indians to move to the west side of the Mississippi River. For reasons unknown, no reference to the speech, which was printed in a slim volume with several others on the same subject, appears in the records of the House of Representatives, although his vote against the bill is recorded. At his best, Crockett was an entertaining campaigner, drawing large crowds to hear him weave amusing tales of the hunt, of war, or of life in the backwoods into a litany of the major political issues of the day. The humor could come as often at his as at his opponent's expense, and only when it deserted him, when, feeling threatened, he became vitriolic and bitter, did he lose elections.

Playwrights, authors, and publishers of the Crockett almanacs, the popular tracts of the late 1830s, '40s, and '50s that presented Davy as the wild man from the swamp, felt no compunctions about putting outrageous speeches in their hero's mouth. The most famous and most nearly universal is Crockett's self-introduction to some tavern patrons when he is on his way to Congress:

> I'm that same David Crockett, fresh from the backwoods, half-horse, half-alligator, a little touched with the snapping-turtle; can wade the Mississippi, leap the Ohio, ride upon a streak of lightning, and slip without a scratch down a honey locust; can whip my weight in wild cats,—and if any gentleman pleases, for a ten dollar bill, he may throw in a panther,—hug a bear too close for comfort, and eat any man opposed to Jackson.

Taken here from *The Life and Adventures of Colonel David Crockett of West Tennessee,* this speech has run in various forms in nearly every Crockett book or film, including Walt Disney's. Although parts of it were used to describe him in newspapers before it even became incorporated into the fictions, we cannot determine what parts of it, if any, Crockett might have uttered himself.

Crockett could never translate his personal popularity into effective political action. Bound by his sense of duty to his constituents and his commitment to seeing government serve the poor as well as the rich, determined to follow his conscience and his notion of the Constitution, he could never master the art of compromise so necessary to the effective legislator. He failed repeatedly to gain passage of legislation favorable to his district, and lost two elections because of that. By the end of his last term in Congress, 1833–35, disgusted with the endless speeches and his inability to accomplish anything, he had become little more than an obstructionist, alienated and bitter, convinced that the democracy was headed down the road of dictatorship.

Like nearly every other politician of his day, Crockett was constantly attacked by his opponents, who charged him with corruption, drunkenness, adultery, gambling, and consorting with the enemy. Unquestionably, Crockett had a drinking problem for much of his adult life, and he doubtless bet on cards and shooting matches, losing as much as he won but not running up the massive debts common to compulsive gamblers. Some of his political foes charged that he did not always pay what he lost, but they presented no proof or witnesses and so their accusations must be treated with skepticism. Whether he indulged in the common practice among his colleagues in Congress, most of whom came to Washington without their wives, of visiting prostitutes or taking mistresses, we have no way of knowing, although he was clearly fond of women and they of him. Frequently away from home, attending sessions, hunting, or campaigning, he was not an attentive father or husband, but we can only speculate on how that affected his family, which was surrounded by relatives. On the other hand, scattered evidence indicates that, when he was home, he took an active interest in his land speculations, construction of farm buildings and mills, and the affairs of his extended family.

However one chooses to interpret him, David Crockett was an extraordinary man by virtue of having risen above his circumstances to achieve nearly universal fame. For much of his adult life, he was a full participant in that process, an increasingly self-confident manipulator of his public image who nonetheless sometimes crossed the line into self-parody. Although it was as a representative of the frontier that Crockett first achieved renown, it is as the legendary long hunter, bold warrior, narrator and hero of tall tales that he has become a cultural icon. As a legend rather than a man, he can be reinvented with each generation to embody its definition of the hero, or in recent years, the antihero. For that reason, if no other, he is an important figure in American history.

I have chosen to begin with the Crockett that many of us know—Walt Disney's Davy. The craze that sprung up with the airing of the three programs, called collectively *Davy Crockett,*

INTRODUCTION

King of the Wild Frontier, in the winter of 1954–55 and the reaction to it, reveals a great deal about our culture at the end of the first decade of the Cold War, our changing sense of heroism, and our relationship to our own history. Disney's Davy incorporates parts of the various legendary incarnations while adding new elements, especially in the depiction of his death. Similarly, the more recent and extremely negative reaction to the television character triggered a revision in the view of the man that has created distortions equal to those Disney presented. Unraveling this knot opens the way for a look at David Crockett of Tennessee.

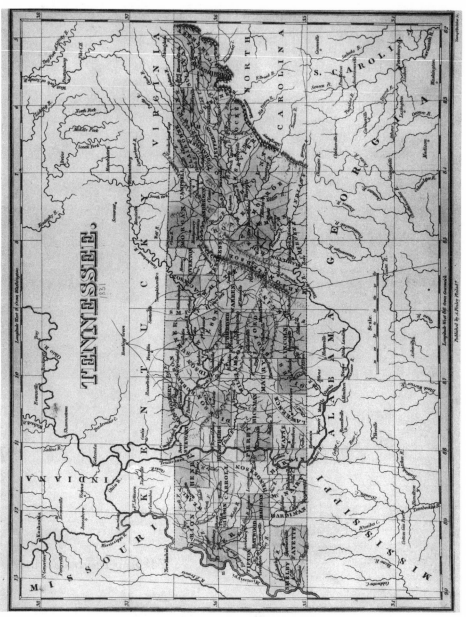

David Crockett's Tennessee in 1831

CHAPTER ONE

DISNEY MEETS DAVY

On the evening of December 15, 1954, the ABC television network, fighting to establish itself opposite CBS and NBC, broadcast Walt Disney's "Davy Crockett, Indian Fighter" and created a cultural phenomenon that transfixed the nation for nearly a year. By February the final two episodes of the trilogy—"Davy Crockett Goes to Congress" and "Davy Crockett at the Alamo"—had aired before an estimated sixty million viewers. In May, Disney released the three as a motion picture called *Davy Crockett, King of the Wild Frontier*, having shrewdly filmed the programs, which were broadcast in black and white, in color for that purpose. School halls and back yards echoed with "The Ballad of Davy Crockett."[1] By the million, children daily died and rose again from the carnage of their Indian wars, the ruins of their private Alamos. Most of those enthralled viewers—and a large number of people who never saw the programs—can today chant a verse or two of Davy's twenty-stanza ballad, and more than a few remember their first coonskin cap. Even today their children are learning the ballad in school.

Fess Parker, the six-and-a-half-foot tall, thirty-year-old Davy, overnight went from being an obscure character actor, whose sole credit was as a victim of rampaging ants in *Them*, a grade-B science-fiction thriller set in New Mexico, to an international star. In 1955, he toured forty-two cities and thirteen foreign countries, promoting the programs, the film, and an array of "Walt Disney's Davy Crockett" paraphernalia. By a contractual arrangement with Disney that was a rarity at the time, Parker received a 10 percent royalty on the sale of official clothes and toys, which totaled in the tens of millions of dollars and made him a wealthy man.[2] Huge crowds of children greeted him wherever he appeared, often creating dangerous situations. "Crowds would push out windows in store fronts," Parker said. "In Holland I had to escape in a cab because I feared for the kids' lives."[3] Parker became so thoroughly typecast that even in his starring role as Daniel Boone in the long-running television series by that title, which aired several years later, he looked and acted like Davy Crockett.

Watching Disney's Davy on videotape thirty-seven years after its debut, I was struck more by the primitive production values and stunts than by the inaccuracies in the story line, which at least serve dramatic purposes. In the wake of such recent action-adventure extravaganzas as *Star Wars, Indiana Jones,* the two *Terminator*s, even the antics of *Baron Münchausen,* the $750,000 Crockett film—not exactly low-budget for the time—resembles a home movie. Punches are clearly pulled, falls padded. The dialogue, like the action, is wooden. The Indians—white men in greasepaint—have their origins in Hollywood studios, not in life. Although the script initially parallels Crockett's biography and more or less serious legends, it departs in significant details—giving him a sidekick named Georgie Russel (Buddy Ebsen, who became more famous in *The Beverly Hillbillies*), leaving him a widower, and finally dropping his family completely. Absent altogether is Crockett the farmer, mill owner, and speculator scrambling to stay ahead of debt, the remarried man with a cabin full of children and a wife who can run the family enterprises better than he. In the third episode, Russel at last reveals that he has been writing pamphlets featuring his friend as a backwoods epic hero, and that the pamphlets have become increasingly popular. It is a clever explanation for Davy's fame, a poetic conflation of the historical process by which he became a legend.

24

Disney's Davy was the all-American manchild, the buckskin-clad paragon of the values that had won the West and was keeping the world safe for democracy—honesty, courage, and natural nobility. Able to read and write his name only with great difficulty, he was fluent in the ways of the wild, a superb tracker and hunter. The frontier, not civilization, was his true home, yet when duty summoned him to Washington to serve the people of West Tennessee, he willingly obliged. He lived for truth, justice, and liberty. He fought and killed Indians like a good scout when his country called, and then, when Justice demanded, he rode hell-bent-for-leather from Philadelphia to Washington and stalked into the House of Representatives to deliver a ringing denunciation of President Andrew Jackson's plan to force the southern Indians—the Creek, Cherokee, Seminole, Chickasaw, and Choctaw—to move west of the Mississippi.

In addition to creating the stalwart man, Disney's screenwriters paid homage to the Crockett legend, which had proved so popular over more than a century, by investing their Davy with preternatural power. Throughout the three programs, he practices grinning man and beast into submission, subjugating them by his will alone and good humor. He subdues a bear and later tries to pacify an Indian. Unfazed, his foe attacks, tomahawk raised, and Davy bests him in a bare-knuckle brawl. He wins every fight until the last one at the Alamo, where, swinging his empty gun through the final dissolve, he ascends into the pantheon of great warrior-heroes. He is a nineteenth-century Horatius, guarding the road into Texas, not the bridge to Rome.

Disney's timing was impeccable. Playing before tens of millions of viewers—nearly everyone with a television set—Davy turned ABC into the third nationwide network and did even more for Walt Disney. Davy was the star of Frontierland, one of four theme areas—the others being Fantasyland, Adventureland, and Tomorrowland—in Disneyland, the grandiose amusement park scheduled to open in July 1955 in Southern California. Featuring Crockett, Mickey Mouse, and a host of supporting characters, along with rides and displays, the park captivated the American public and established Walt Disney as the greatest showman of the age. His genius lay in his ability to blend a faith in human progress through technology with an idealized image of nineteenth-century small-town America as an idyllic place of wholesome good times, of families and friends. New machines would make the old home more real and perfect, more harmonious, as they did in Disneyland. The Disney vision offered progress without disruption or pain. His heroes might have difficulty reading and writing, but they were without major character defects that might cause one to question their motives or goodness.

Walt Disney's creations reflected and helped shape the mood of guarded optimism and self-congratulation that pervaded the nation in the mid-1950s. Having come through the Depression and emerged victorious from World War II, only to stumble into a stalemate in Korea, Americans appeared intent on pursuing prosperity and advancement. The popular press, radio, cinematic newsreels, and the fast-growing medium of television, which would collectively become the media, exuded sufficient optimism to take the edge off persistent reports of conflict, famine, a sluggish economy, and epidemics, even to make surviving a nuclear attack seem little more difficult than escaping a tornado—"duck and cover," the Civil Defense planners advised, when you hear the air-raid siren. Along with their advertisers, the media conveyed the message that business and industry would create a world richer in goods—from houses to cars to appliances—and more abundant in leisure than any imagined before. Judicious management of the national economy and control of wages, although the unions disagreed, would ensure the good life. Medical breakthroughs, like the new polio vaccine that would wipe out that scourge, promised to conquer a score of life-threatening diseases.

Political leaders in both parties and national publications like *Time* propounded the view that America's continued greatness was dependent on vigilant men, who would stand firm against Communism abroad and at home, men who not only had the capacity to harness the awesome power of the atom but also the wisdom to decide when and where to unloose it. Only with its defenses up, they argued, its institutions freed from the corrupting influence of subversives—anyone who questioned the existing system and policies—could America enjoy the fruits of its labor. Mainstream politicians who spoke out against the abuses of this red baiting were marked for defeat. In 1955, alienation was not a condition that applied to "decent" young people or professionals. What clouds there were, Davy and his fellow superheroes—strong, courageous, righteous men—could pocket and cart away.

In the first nine months of 1955, neither man nor beast escaped Davy Crockett. He was everywhere, a sudden infestation—the first of a series of "crazes" or fads that would mark the baby-boom generation, leading a number of marketing specialists, journalists, and demographers to conceive of that group of postwar children as a single monolithic entity that could be inspired to act en masse. No one had imagined that these children not only would immediately demand an object associated with the celluloid image but also could persuade their parents to go along. By some accounts, the magnitude of the response surprised even Walt Disney, who had planned the release for years and was a recognized master of the medium of television. "The Ballad of Davy Crockett," which jazz trombonist George Bruns and scriptwriter Tom Blackburn penned in twenty minutes as filler for the already completed programs—relying on rhyme, not sense—defined Davy as solidly as the film. Selling 18 million copies and recorded by no fewer than twenty crooners, including Parker himself, it was the number-one song of 1955, going away. A shelf of Crockett books—ranging from juvenile to adult fiction, biography, and autobiography—hit 14 million in sales. *The Story of Davy Crockett,* an indifferent biography by Enid La Monte Meadowcroft containing more fiction than fact—this Davy killed him a "b'ar" when he was all of ten—skyrocketed from a steady 10,000 a year in sales since its publication in 1952 to 300,000. A Crockett comic strip was syndicated in 200 newspapers. Disney distributed, under the title "Davy Crockett Says," newspaper columns featuring a picture of Fess Parker as Davy and homilies regarding honesty, trust, justice, duty, and even frugality. As the demand for coonskin caps outstripped supply, the price of pelts soared from $0.25 to $6.00 a pound. After decimating populations of raccoons, trappers turned to wolves, foxes, skunks, and opossums. Manufacturers sold the substitutes as the genuine item and also bought and recycled old fur coats.

Every child needed at minimum a coonskin cap and some semblance of a flintlock, and parents, with memories of their own Depression deprivations still fresh—many a child in the 1930s missed out on Buck Rogers toys, for example—were eager to oblige. For this Baltimore boy, aged five, a nine-iron made an enduring Old Betsy, a more sturdy long rifle than those bought for hard dollars—and it was more accurate. Parents routinely bribed their children to engage in desired behavior with a sampling of the 3,000 Crockett items—everything from the ubiquitous cap and toy gun to towels, sheets, books, records, lunch boxes, fringed shirts and pants, pajamas, moccasins, soap, balloons, and wading pools—that filled the stores.[4] Adults were not exempt: Offering a free "Davy Crockett" tent—actually a renamed pup tent—to each purchaser of a Norge appliance, Borg-Warner Corporation gave away a total of 35,000 by May.

By then, Crockett paraphernalia had reached $100 million in sales and prognosticators confidently predicted the total would soar to $300 million during the Christmas rush. In some department stores, Crockett accounted for as much as 10 percent of sales.[5] Sensing windfall profits, manufacturers and retailers began mislabeling unsold products with "Davy Crockett" and turning out vast quantities of poorly made goods. In Boston, a shoe store unloaded 3,000 moccasins after placing a "Davy Crockett" sign in front of them. Elsewhere old Daniel Boone caps, assigned a new identity, found buyers. In Albany and Rochester, New York, fake-fur hats proved easily inflammable.[6] F.A.O. Schwarz executive Philip Kirkham sounded a cautionary note, predicting that authentic Crockett toys would last on the market, because Davy was universal, but the rest of the junk would fade away.[7] No one listened.

As abruptly as it had begun, the craze went into free fall. In Washington, D.C., Crockett T-shirts that once sold by the thousand at $1.29 each gathered dust on the shelves when marked down to $0.39. From around the country came equally grim reports. In December, a number of disappointed retailers grumpily declared "kids more fickle than women."[8] *Variety* announced, "Davy was the biggest thing since Marilyn Monroe and Liberace, but he pancaked. He laid a bomb."[9]

ABC's *Disneyland* aired two new episodes—"Davy Crockett's Keelboat Race" and "Davy Crockett and the River Pirates," featuring Big Mike Fink (The King of the River), the Mississippi, and a catchy tune—in November and December. The slapdash programs cleverly played on the legends of the big river, allowing Davy, the masterful Everyman, to best the conniving, unsportsmanlike Fink—a man so locked in legend that his reality has all but vanished—in an epic keelboat race and then to destroy a den of evil thieves. The beaten Mike Fink did not tip his hat to the victor; he ate it, honoring a bet and spreading the fun. Crockett's one attempt at navigating the Mississippi in 1826 had nearly cost him his life, when his boat sank, but that accident was of no interest to Walt Disney, who presented the new programs—released to cinemas early in 1956 as *The Legends of Davy Crockett*—as nothing more than fiction. Eager to cash in on the phenomenal success of the first three episodes, he had turned fully to the tales, even having his screenwriters invent their own. But the King of the Wild Frontier and the King of the River together could not win over an audience that had lost interest. Davy had become ordinary, another program to watch or ignore. *The Wonderful World of Disney* on NBC repeated all five programs (now available on videotape) every three years into the 1970s without fanfare.

Explanations for the collapse were as diverse as those for the beginning of the fad. Some observers blamed the bad publicity attendant to problems with the production and sale of Crockett memorabilia. Others attributed the demise to critics who charged that Disney had made a hero of a reprehensible lout, a besotted liar and clown. While a number of retailers and journalists suggested that the children had grown bored or fickle and turned their short, collective attention span elsewhere, other commentators posited that they had become disaffected after learning that their hero was a fraud. Although some of the hypotheses appear somewhat silly in retrospect, the debate itself was born of genuine interest in the nature of the craze, which was the first with its origins in television. Advertisers, sociologists, marketing experts, and politicians were impressed by the power of television to influence not only public opinion but also mass behavior.

Even as hazardous merchandise drove consumers to other products, a rancorous trademark fight between Disney and a Baltimore garment maker sowed uncertainty and fear among businesses that they might be liable in a lawsuit. The dispute also prevented Disney from exercising the kind of quality control it generally enforced to protect its reputation.

On May 6, 1955, when business was booming, Walt Disney Productions went into U.S. District Court in Baltimore to file suit against Morey Schwartz, his wife Hannah, and their companies—Schwartz Manufacturing Company and Davy Crockett Enterprises, Inc., asking that their trademark, "David Crockett, Frontiersman," be declared null and void and that Disney be granted exclusive rights to its own "Walt Disney's Davy Crockett" and any permutation thereon.[10] Disney stated that its *Davy Crockett* was a fiction, conceived in 1950 "to describe the exploits of the early American pioneer and politician named David Crockett." Over the next five years, it had employed as many as 400 actors, writers, cartoonists, artists, and marketers to develop the films, the promotional material—including books and cartoons—and the merchandise. Disney considered marketing central to the financial success of the project, and so arranged for 125 licensees to produce 1,000 articles under its imprint. For all its obsession with detail, however, Disney failed to register its trademark or even have its lawyers check on other claimants to Crockett.

On the face of it, there was little reason to worry. Since the 1830s, the Crockett name had been used to sell everything from citrus to chewing tobacco and liquor. A legend of enormous proportion, Davy Crockett was fully in the public domain. A clipper ship, *David Crockett,* plied the seas from San Francisco to Wall Street during the 1850s and '60s, promising the most comfortable, fastest delivery under sail. She could make the passage in 115 days, Wm. T. Coleman and Company boasted in its advertisements, which featured a bearded Crockett riding a pair of alligators and a version of the famous Crockett motto: "Be sure you're right, then go ahead." In 1889, Betterton and Company took out a trademark on Davey Crockett Wisky, and in 1906 Union Distilling Company registered Davy Crocket Pure Copper Whiskey.[11] Both companies were playing on Crockett's notoriously poor spelling and his love for alcohol, "arden spirits," as he called it, in which he indulged much of his adult life. The registrations on both trademarks lapsed.

Then, in 1946, Morey and Hannah Schwartz registered the trademark "Davy Crockett, Frontiersman" with the U.S. Patent Office under No. 434,317. A manufacturer of military uniforms, Schwartz was inspired by his frequent visits to San Antonio, home of the Alamo, to shift production to western wear at the end of the war. But as textile mills completed the transition from military production, they began shipping their full runs of "hard-finish worsteds" to large apparel makers, leaving small companies like the Schwartzes' without access to the quality cloth they needed to compete. Their business failing, Morey and Hannah Schwartz transferred their Davy Crockett patent to Henry Kay, who produced western wear through his Advance Tailoring Company of Baltimore. When the Disney-inspired craze began, Kay, unable to raise capital to expand his business, sold the trademark back to the Schwartzes, who established Davy Crockett Enterprises, Inc., in their hometown. They began sending letters and telegrams to producers of Crockett goods demanding 5 percent of their net sales as royalties and threatening legal action if they failed to comply.

The manufacturers complained to Disney, to their associations, to each other, and to the press that they feared retaliation if they ignored the Schwartzes' demand. It was then that Walt

Disney Productions sued, seeking to appease its licensees and protect itself from charges of trademark infringement. Disney alleged that Morey and Hannah Schwartz were interfering with the production and marketing of "Walt Disney's Davy Crockett." In a countersuit, the Schwartzes portrayed themselves as small merchants victimized by a huge and powerful company from California named Disney. The press treated the whole affair with a dash of humor. "Old Davy Crockett and his winning ways have a pack of lawyers fussing and feuding and businessmen befuddled," said William E. Giles in *The Wall Street Journal* on May 11. "Hitching up his buckskins, and with his big butcher [knife] in his belt, Disney charged into Baltimore's Federal Court and brought suit against Davy Crockett Enterprises, run by an oldtime Baltimore garment maker . . . ," said *Time*.[12] For the sake of business, if not justice, the two parties settled the suit on July 12, agreeing to split the fast-growing profits through cross licensing.

After news of the settlement broke, a covey of Crockett's direct descendants filed a motion to intervene, claiming that neither Disney nor Schwartz had a right to profit from their forebear's name. Seeking royalties for themselves, the Crockett descendants had organized two groups in Illinois: the David Crockett Descendants' Fund, an educational and charitable trust; and Crockett Kids, Inc., to market the Crockett name. Lawyers for the Schwartzes and Disney united to argue that allowing the fund's trustees—Bourke C. Crockett, Margie Flowers, Pauline Flowers Tillery, Oscar Doetsch, and Albert J. Watts—to break their uneasy truce would be tantamount to bringing mass confusion and ruin on the world of Crockett merchandising. Bloodlines, they said, did not carry a right to monopolize an ancestor's name. The motion to intervene was dismissed on October 6, 1955, with the heirs unrewarded. By then, the buying frenzy was slowing, consumers having received the message that greed mattered more than quality or the safety of their children.

The great success of Disney's Davy set off an intellectual debate as intense in its way as the frenzy for Crockett products.

No sooner had the "craze" begun than a number of social critics, journalists, educators, and even politicians began to proclaim that Davy represented values ranging from anti-intellectualism to unbridled individualism that, if followed, would subvert their programs and institutions. Teachers around the country complained that their pupils were uncontrollable, spending more time singing "The Ballad of Davy Crockett" than reciting their ABCs. Invoking their fictional counterparts in a song, Fess Parker and Buddy Ebsen appealed to the kids to "do the right thing" and behave, without visible effect. Educators and journalists also engaged in a running debate over whether Davy subsumed all other frontier heroes—like Daniel Boone and Kit Carson, himself a somewhat overrated figure—thereby impoverishing the imaginations of their students, or inspired them to explore American history, thereby enriching them.

In Washington, D.C., late in the spring of 1955, a group of schoolchildren touring the Capitol asked to see the statue of their idol Davy, which they believed must be prominently displayed. Their teacher pointed to a figure dressed in buckskins, with a cap on his head and rifle in his hand, and called him Crockett. But it was Dr. Marcus Whitman, the Protestant missionary who traveled extensively through the West in the 1830s and early 1840s and helped open the Oregon country to settlement.[13] Crockett does not stand in bronze or marble in the Capitol, where he was a controversial, if colorful figure.

Teachers and students were not alone in their confusion. Texas Congressman Martin Dies asked his colleagues in the House to follow Davy's famous maxim and vote only for what was right, rather than what was expedient.[14] Other congressmen joined the fray and soon found themselves divided along party and sectional lines, with various Democrats from Tennessee and North Carolina seeking a piece of the glory by declaring Crockett a native of their states—although raised in Tennessee, he was born in the independent State of Franklin, which North Carolina considered part of its domain.

Liberal Democrats worried that the Republicans would adopt Davy and his coonskin as their campaign symbol. They overlooked the fact that Tennessee Senator Estes Kefauver, a Democrat, had been campaigning in the famous headgear since 1948, choosing instead to recall that in 1840 the Whigs, the party of the rich and privileged, had successfully, if cynically, employed the cap, the log cabin, and hard cider as symbols in order to prove themselves champions of the "common man" and place their candidate, William Henry Harrison, in the White House. If the victor at Tippecanoe could do it, the Democrats reasoned, why not the allied commander of Europe? Eisenhower hardly needed such help in 1956, but that did little to assuage the Democrats' concerns. In the pages of magazines and newspapers, on radio and television, they launched an ad hominem attack on the fictional Davy Crockett that, while sometimes farcical, had a major, negative impact on the way Crockett came to be perceived and portrayed.

Brendan Sexton, education director for the United Auto Workers in Detroit, opened the campaign soon after the Disney programs appeared. Sexton feared that Republican and anti-unionists, embracing the celluloid Crockett, would use his uncompromising individualism and martyrdom at the Alamo as a club against organized labor. He thought they would say that real Americans, like Davy, had no need or desire for a union because its emphasis on collective action and a strict seniority system for determining promotions and layoffs—the traditional "last hired, first fired" rule—was antithetical to individual opportunity. With the nation's economy in a slump and the campaign against Communism—and by extension, socialism and labor—at a fever pitch, many workers were beginning to believe that they could better serve their interests by dealing directly with management. Deciding to discredit the perceived messenger, rather than address the concerns of workers, Sexton gave a radio talk and interviews charging that Crockett was "a drunk and brawler, a wife deserter, hireling of big business, and shiftless no-account."[15]

Columnist Murray Kempton, who wrote on labor issues for the *New York Post*, picked up the refrain and charged that Crockett could be bought for the price of a drink. His diatribe inspired outraged children to demonstrate in front of his newspaper's office. John Fischer, editor of *Harper's,* one of the nation's most venerable liberal periodicals, was more caustic in his comments. After repeating Sexton's claims, he added that Crockett was "a poor farmer, indolent and shiftless. . . . He was never king of anything, except maybe the Tennessee Tall Tales and Bourbon Samplers' Association."[16] Attempting to turn anti-Communist, red-baiting sentiment against Crockett, Fischer also stated that the myth making associated with Davy most resembled that which created the benevolent image of Papa Joe Stalin.

Conservative commentator William F. Buckley, Jr., tweaked the liberals for their discomfort, announcing on his radio program that "the assault on Davy is one part traditional debunking campaign and one part resentment by liberal publicists of Davy's free approach to life. He'll survive the carpers." The liberals also found themselves criticized by the emasculated American Communist Party for attacking the nation's democratic traditions, an interesting argument grounded to some degree in Karl Marx's conception of the radical way people along the frontier organized their political and judicial institutions.[17]

Underlying the criticism of Crockett was the growing belief that the myths of America and its heroes were at variance with its history, that westward expansion was more the story of destruction of the Indians and nature for profit than of valiant white settlers struggling to survive against the elements, that slavery was a cruel and dehumanizing institution, that democracy and opportunity were not extended equally to all people. As this necessary corrective took hold, the extreme negative views of Crockett gained ascendancy over Disney's Davy. Presenting a rogues' gallery of the "Braggarts of the Backwoods," on April 11, 1960, *Life* declared Crockett "an epic boaster." *People* on January 12, 1987, ran a photo of Fess Parker with the comment that Crockett "was a flamboyant frontiersman who owed his reputation to his ability to tell tall tales. But there were a few facts that even his prodigious fibbing couldn't hide—that the king of the Wild Frontier was a drunk, a carouser, a less-than-honest politician and Army scout who'd hired someone

else to finish his term of enlistment."[18] Popular histories began
to follow suit, as did film characterizations. In the 1987 NBC
television film *The Alamo: Thirteen Days to Glory*, for example,
Brian Keith portrayed Crockett as a kindhearted, boastful, ultimately courageous drunkard.

The Disney Company engaged in revisionism of a different
sort when, in the late 1980s, it created a new five-part Davy
Crockett series, featuring a sensitive, New Age hero in tune
with nature, brave, peace-loving, and humorous in a sincere
way. One expected the backwoods stalwart to consult crystals.
The audience and critics generally nodded through the episodes, which aired on NBC's *Magical World of Disney* and now
periodically appear on the Disney Channel on cable television.

The polar images of the fictional Crockett are the negative
and positive of a freeze-frame portrait of a four-dimensional
man—fixed and predictable, the way Americans too often demand their heroes, and antiheroes, to be. Crockett the legend
is plastic enough to adjust to changing fashion and accommodate himself to those who would make him a guardian of the
environment or a wild man weaned on whiskey, a braggart, a
"screamer," or "ring-tailed roarer," in the language of the nineteenth-century comic fictions. But Crockett the man hangs
trapped between those poles, lost in the nation's ambivalence
about its past. He is a victim of a collective inability to determine
any longer how to define a brave man, by what actions or standards—those of war and exploitation or of peace and caring.
Is it necessary that a hero—or public official—be a saint, free
of earthly flaws? The only man or woman who can meet that
standard is a one-dimensional character in a poor fiction, boring
precisely because he or she is perfect. But how many and what
kind of failings are acceptable? Where is the line between
human frailty and venality? The answer to those questions can
only become clear once the individual is freed from the con-
straints of ideology and viewed in the context of his or her life,
aspirations, and accomplishments.

CHAPTER TWO

HONOR THY FATHER

Fleeing Scotland by way of Ireland, the extended Crockett family arrived in New York early in the eighteenth century, settling briefly in the vicinity of New Rochelle before beginning a southern migration that would bring parts of it to North Carolina some fifty years later. They went first to the Pennsylvania-Maryland border region—between York and Joppa—where some remained while others traveled into Virginia's Shenandoah Valley. From there, at least one branch under David Crockett, grandfather of Davy, moved to the banks of the Catawba River, near Lincolnton, North Carolina, where in 1771 it established a 250-acre farm. The traces left behind by the family suggest that its members cleared fields they then sold or abandoned because of bad luck, failed crops, unpaid debts, or the promise of land in the next county.

Around the time the first shots were fired at Lexington and Concord, David, his wife (whose name is lost), and at least four sons left their farm and crossed the Appalachian Mountains to join a hardy band of settlers along the Holston, Watauga, and Nolichucky rivers. The parents and three of the sons—William, John, and Joseph—built rough-hewn log cabins within several miles of each other, near the present site of Rogersville in the Holston valley, in the northeast corner of what is now Tennessee.

Scattered throughout the neighboring valleys were fewer than ten thousand pioneers, who had been moving into the area for half a dozen years, ignoring the King's Proclamation of 1763, which decreed the crest of the Appalachians to be the western boundary of settlement. The squatters had created their own democratic government, the Watauga Association, to deal with the Indians they had dispossessed and with British colonial authorities, who viewed them as trespassers. Although the interlopers built stockades, formed militias, and fought with the sudden brutality that marked all sides in the decades of border war that accompanied their migration, their hold on the land remained tenuous. Indian raids against isolated cabins were commonplace, as were white assaults on the towns of the natives. People were slaughtered under promises of safe passage or murdered in their homes as often as on the field of battle. Every white and Indian had at least one member of his or her family dead, wounded, or held captive.

Feeling exposed and underarmed, the Wataugans petitioned North Carolina and Virginia—the titular colonial authorities for their territory—for annexation in July 1776. At the same time, Cherokee, Creek, and Tory fighters launched a major offensive and quickly overran scattered settlements along all three rivers, forcing their occupants to take refuge in overcrowded, poorly provisioned stockades. Only the timely intervention of troops from the Carolinas, Georgia, and Virginia, who scattered the attackers, saved the colonists from annihilation. A year later North Carolina assumed administrative control of much of the region, which it called Washington County, leaving a northern section of the Holston valley to Virginia. Enmeshed in the affairs of their new community, the patriarch Crockett and his son William signed the petition of annexation to North Carolina and, along with John, the one to Virginia.

Early in 1777, Indian warriors from a number of tribes, armed and abetted by British agents and Tory militia, attacked settlements throughout Ohio, Kentucky, and the Holston valley. Because troops from the eastern colonies were too involved in defending their own homes to respond to cries from the frontier, the hard-pressed westerners had to fend for themselves. Dragging Canoe, an avowedly antisettler Cherokee, and his followers, known as Chickamauga (refugees from the Cherokee who had established towns on a creek by that name around 1776), raiding along the Holston, killed a number of settlers, including David and his wife. Of the sons, William and John were on patrol with the border rangers, Joseph suffered a broken arm from a musket ball, and James, the youngest, was taken captive. Deaf and dumb from birth, he was held for close to eighteen years until John and William Crockett, who had believed he was dead, learned that he was still alive and arranged through an Indian trader to ransom him.[1] "Deaf and Dumb Jimmy," as he was known locally, settled on Wolf Creek in Fentress County, Tennessee, and spent the rest of his life searching, diligently but unsuccessfully, for a Cherokee silver mine, which he had visited only when blindfolded. More than a few people shared his obsession.[2]

Following a peace conference late in 1777 at Long Island, North Carolina, the legislature passed a law setting a new boundary of settlement and then subverted it with another establishing offices for the sale of the state's western lands. The level of immigration and violence all along the American frontier increased dramatically, and the hard-pressed settlers gathered their reserves behind their own war leaders—George Rogers Clark in Kentucky and the Northwest; John Sevier in the Holston region—to take the battle to all who sought to block them. During three campaigns against the Cherokee, 1780–82, Sevier's mounted volunteers destroyed more than thirty-one towns as far south as Georgia, severely damaging the Indians' fighting capability.[3]

Before his opening foray against the Cherokee in December 1780, Colonel Sevier and a fellow commander, Isaac Shelby, joined their militias with that of William Campbell from neighboring Virginia and marched east across the Appalachians to confront British Major Robert Ferguson and 1,100 regulars, who had chosen to engage them from the high ground of King's Mountain, North Carolina. On the afternoon of October 7,

Sevier and Shelby's men stormed up the mountain and crushed Ferguson's force, killing 150 and taking 810 captive, at a cost of 75 casualties. Strategically, the victory broke British efforts to control the Carolinas and forced Charles, Lord Cornwallis to delay his plan for an immediate invasion of Virginia. Forestalling attack from the east, the King's Mountain victory allowed Sevier and his men to concentrate on the Cherokee and finally bring a measure of security to their farms.

Among the riders in Sevier's command was John Crockett, also listed from time to time as a member of the Lincoln County, North Carolina, militia. Although erratic record keeping makes precise dates in the lives of frontier people hard to fix, probably early in 1780—before the battle for King's Mountain—John Crockett had married Rebecca Hawkins, a native of Joppa, Maryland, who had come with her family to the Holston region a few years earlier.[4] Some local sources have argued that Rebecca was the sister of John Sevier's first wife, Sarah, although her son David's apparent failure to trade on or benefit from one of the most famous names in Tennessee politics suggests strongly that the two men were not related.

At the time David, the fifth of their nine children—six sons and three daughters, in that order—was born, August 17, 1786, John and Rebecca Crockett were living at the confluence of Limestone Creek and the Nolichucky River. The homestead was on a tract they had bought from a South Carolina land speculator named Jacob Brown, one of the ubiquitous militia colonels who acquired thousands of acres cheaply—in this case for a packhorse-load of goods—from the Indians and then parceled it out to settlers at a substantial profit.[5] It was a homestead cleared for a quick resale, where the Crocketts raised corn and hogs, perhaps a few cattle, while waiting for a buyer. The frontier having moved west and south, the region had become relatively secure from Indian attack, and it was drawing a new wave of immigrants.

The cluster of cabins along the Nolichucky and Limestone Creek occupied the center of the state of Franklin, an adventure in self-government undertaken by the former Wataugans in the politically chaotic years following the Revolution. War-weary, cash-poor, and stubbornly self-sufficient, flush with their hard-won independence from Britain but still locked in conflict with the Indians, the settlers had acted to protect their land claims and speculative ventures after North Carolina ceded its over-mountain counties to the Congress in 1784 and then reneged on the cession. It was a complicated situation tied to a struggle for power between the newly independent colonies and the central government, which was operating under the weak Articles of Confederation.

The Congress was working on a program—codified in the Land Ordinance of 1785—for creating new states from the nation's western lands, whose indigenous peoples it intended simultaneously to dispossess. The North Carolina legislature had agreed to participate in the scheme, then, after a change in its composition, reversed itself. Observing the erratic course of events, the overmountain people concluded that the distant governments in Virginia, North Carolina, and Philadelphia could not be depended on to defend their prerogatives and they would have to look after themselves. They persuaded a reluctant John Sevier to act as governor and wrote a temporary constitution for a state they called Franklin. In reality, little more than a front for the land deals of Sevier and his colleagues, Franklin collapsed into legend four years later, after ratification of the United States Constitution and North Carolina's irrevocable cession of its western territory to the central government. Born of that agreement, Tennessee completed its march to statehood in 1796, a decade after David Crockett's birth.

States and the national government regularly used land, their chief resource, to pay for services through grants or to raise money through direct sales. In relinquishing its western territory, North Carolina demanded that a large portion of Tennessee land be made available for satisfying the warrants and specie certificates it had issued to compensate its troops and fund the Revolution. Amended by law in 1806 and again in 1818, the arrangement created an aberrant situation in which, for decades after statehood, people bearing these warrants appeared as if from nowhere and, claiming prior title, forced farmers either to buy land they already considered their own or to leave it, without compensation. Because the warrants specified the number of acres alone, holders would often fill their allotments with scattered parcels selected from the most fertile grounds in an area, leaving only bits and pieces of poor and rocky soil. Virginia had made similar claims on land in Ohio and Kentucky, but the amount of land and the time for exercising warrants were fixed, whereas the situation in Tennessee remained open-ended.

Neither North Carolina nor Tennessee had a record of how many warrants and certificates had been issued, leaving them no way to determine whether those that appeared for satisfaction were counterfeit or real. But the demand was so great that in 1818 Tennessee had to petition Congress to open to claimants its Western District, an area formerly belonging to the Chickasaw and lying between the Tennessee and Mississippi rivers, which came under United States jurisdiction and was to have remained exempt from North Carolina warrants. Although David Crockett gained several hundred acres west of the so-called Congressional Reservation Line when his second wife's father exercised a North Carolina warrant, he also built his political career on defending Tennessee farmers against dispossession by warrant holders. A child of the frontier, with a legacy of debt, poverty, independence, and mutual dependence, he was so ideally matched to the battle for Tennessee lands that he could not rise above it and gain sufficient perspective to develop the sort of coherent, national program that might have helped him achieve a position of leadership to match his celebrity.

Like most people along the frontier, John and Rebecca Crockett were cash-poor and perpetually in debt, unlucky in business endeavors but not so destitute as to be called hardscrabble. In a place where many people could barely manage an X for their signature, John and Rebecca could read and write, the rudiments of which they taught their children. John Crockett served as constable of Greene County, North Carolina, in 1783, 1785, and 1789, the gap apparently coming because he supported the sovereignty of Franklin.[6] The downward spiral of poverty and creation of the territory of Tennessee brought his political career to a close. A small-scale land speculator, he kept the family on the move, making a slim profit on a 200-acre homestead—probably the one on Limestone Creek—the year following David's birth, and repeating the process at least twice more in the next half-dozen years.

Relatives and friends lived nearby, helping to clear the land and raise the buildings on the farms, which left little distinct impression on the young boy. At one homestead along the Nolichucky, he recalled, a neighbor charged from his hay lot into the river to prevent a canoe bearing one of the Crockett boys and another youth from being swept over a waterfall. Not long thereafter, on a new farm ten miles from the first, Rebecca's brother, John Hawkins, while hunting, mistook a neighbor who was gathering grapes for a deer and shot him. Young David watched in amazement as his father passed a silk handkerchief—believed to help clean the wound—through the body of the man, who, to the surprise of his friends and family, recovered.[7]

In 1794, John Crockett moved the family to nearby Cove Creek and joined with a neighbor named Thomas Galbreath to build a gristmill, only to have a flash flood sweep it away before it began to operate. Again the family packed up, and John Crockett opened an inn along the well-traveled road between Abingdon, Virginia, and Knoxville. The Crocketts ran the inn for two decades, despite a constant flirtation with bankruptcy, leaving only when they moved west to join their fifth and most successful son, David, and some of his siblings. In 1795, the sheriff of Jefferson County auctioned off a 300-acre tract to settle a $400 debt—perhaps from the mill fiasco—John could not pay. As common along the cash-starved frontier as estate sales are today, the auctions provided ample opportunity for people with ready money to increase their holdings, while providing scant return to the debtor or lien holder. For example, the sheriff received a high bid of $40 for John Crockett's 300 acres, not even enough to cover the cost of the lawsuit, although the amount cleared his debt.[8] A year after the forced sale, John Crockett was tried and acquitted for "petit larceny" of an unspecified object in Greene County, where he had once served as a constable.[9]

The Crocketts' six-room, rough-hewn wood tavern, dark and smoky inside, weathered outside, catered exclusively to wagoners. A frequently crude, filthy lot interested in little more than a stable for their teams of horses, mules, or oxen, and cheap accommodations for themselves, these teamsters formed the major overland supply line of the frontier, driving livestock and produce to eastern markets, bringing finished goods back. When fast, the wagons were slow and uncomfortable. Their nautical counterparts were the flatboats and keelboats of the hard-drinking, brawling rivermen who shared with the teamsters a predilection for obscenity, boasting, and tall tales.

Following the custom of poor frontier families, John Crockett bound his sons, as soon as they reached adolescence, to passing wagoners and drovers, to reduce the number of children he had to feed and to help satisfy his outstanding debts. When David was twelve, his father offered his labor to a Dutchman named Jacob Siler, who was heading to Rockbridge County, Virginia, with "a large stock of cattle." Never away from home before, the boy drove a stranger's herd four hundred miles, receiving at the end of the journey "five or six dollars" and praise for his work. Siler urged David to stay with him as an indentured servant, and he agreed. "I had been taught so many lessons of obedience by my father," he said, "that I at first supposed I was bound to obey this man, or at least I was afraid openly to disobey him; and I therefore staid with him, and tried to put on a look of perfect contentment until I got the family all to believe I was fully satisfied."[10]

Playing by the roadside with two other boys some five weeks later, David encountered three wagoners he recognized from his father's inn—a man named Dunn and his sons—and, relating his plight, asked that they take him home. The teamsters agreed to do so and to provide protection should Siler pursue him as a runaway, if David met them before dawn at their tavern, seven miles down the road to Knoxville. Homesick, afraid he would be caught and detained, David packed his clothes and the little money he'd saved and waited anxiously in his bed until three hours before dawn, when he sneaked out, directly into a snowstorm. In an adventure beloved by the writers of children's books, David found the road a half-mile from the house by dead reckoning, the snow blowing so hard it obscured all landmarks, and then walked through the blizzard to meet his friends, reaching them with an hour to spare. The snow, he said, stood as deep as his knees but fortunately fell so rapidly that it covered his trail, thwarting pursuit.[11]

The boy traveled with the Dunns as far as the Roanoke, Virginia, inn of John Cole and stayed the night there with them before deciding the next morning to walk ahead of the slow-moving wagons. He had not gone very far when he met a stranger, a "gentleman" returning from a livestock market in Roanoke, where he had sold all of his horses but two: the one he rode and a second, which he offered to let the boy ride. At a crossing on the Roanoke River, fifteen miles from David's home, they parted company. His benefactor rode for Kentucky and David walked to his father's tavern.[12]

The pattern of behavior David manifested during this experience was to recur throughout his life, often to his detriment. He would align himself unquestioningly with an authority figure, turn vehemently against him when he felt betrayed or abused, and then immediately seek succor from another strong man. Although one must not ascribe late-twentieth-century motivations to late-eighteenth-century boys, Crockett's actions appear to be a response to the erratic violence and cajolery of an alcoholic, passive-aggressive father. Because David barely mentioned his mother, it is not possible to speculate on their relationship, but it is clear from a variety of comments that John Crockett was a heavy drinker given to beating his sons—a common practice at the time, to be sure, but no more guaranteed to instill loyalty and love then than it is now. Like apprentices everywhere, David was also reacting to a social and legal system that placed "free" children fully under the power of adults, leaving them better off than chattel only in the sense that their servitude had a time limit.

The autumn following his flight from Siler, David enrolled with several of his brothers—John, James, William, Wilson, and Joseph, the sisters being Betsy, Jane, and Sally—in a little country school Benjamin Kitchen had recently opened near the inn. The cost of the school is unknown, but given the family's circumstances, sending even one child there would have been a burden. That several went indicates John and Rebecca Crockett's commitment to providing their children with at least the sort of basic education in reading, writing, and arithmetic such schools provided.

On his fourth day, David argued in the schoolhouse with an older, larger boy and then determined to ambush him on his way home. When the boy approached, David said, "I pitched out from the bushes and set on him like a wild cat. I scratched his face all to flitter jig, and soon made him cry out for quarters in earnest."[13] The triumphant Crockett headed for school the next morning, but fearing retaliation from the schoolmaster for trouncing a fellow student, hid in the woods. With the connivance of his brothers, he followed that routine for several days, until Kitchen sent a note to John Crockett asking why David was not in school. Intoxicated, John confronted his son and threatened to whip him with a hickory rod for his truancy—and presumably the waste of scarce money.

David fled, not to return home for three years. He joined one of his older brothers on the cattle drive of a neighbor, Jesse Cheek, to Front Royal, Virginia, by way of Lynchburg and Charlottesville. After the cattle were sold, David started home with Cheek's brother, leaving his own brother with the rest of the men. The pair broke up after David complained that his companion was not sharing time on his horse and announced that he would rather walk alone than travel with such an un-generous person. The man gave the boy four dollars to cover expenses on his four-hundred-mile journey and rode ahead.

Almost immediately, David met a Tennessee wagoner named Adam Myers and agreed to turn back with him for Gerards-town, Virginia, a community fifteen miles south of Winchester, at the head of the Shenandoah Valley. Crockett liked the man and, in any event, was afraid that if he returned home his father would beat him. After two days on the road, David encountered his brother, who pleaded with him to resume the homeward journey—to no avail. David's fear of his father's wrath over-whelmed any desire he had to return. On the road, he could see something of the world and earn some needed money as well.

Myers learned at Gerardstown that he would have to go to Alexandria to pick up a return load, and while he did that, Crockett signed on as a hand with John Gray, a local farmer, at a quarter a day. Failing to find cargo for Knoxville, the wagoner started making regular runs between Gerardstown and Baltimore, while David continued plowing for Gray and saving money. When spring arrived, he bought clothes and de-cided to travel with Myers to Baltimore, a major port and doubtless an exciting place for a young man, who, despite his travels, knew little of the world. David gave his older companion seven dollars, his entire savings, for safekeeping on the trip.

At Ellicott City, a mill town on Baltimore's outskirts, a crew of wheelbarrow men working on the road spooked the team. Bolting, the horses buckled and broke the wagon tongue. Flour barrels rolled over Crockett, who had climbed into the wagon to put on his new clothes, but he escaped unhurt. Myers flagged down another wagon, which took on their cargo and towed their wreck to Baltimore. During the wait for repairs, Crockett wandered to the docks at Fells Point where, not unlike Benjamin Franklin a generation earlier, he became enamored of the ships and the distant lands to which they might take him.

Examining one bound for London, the runaway agreed with the captain to sign on as cabin boy and went to fetch his clothes and money from Myers. But the wagoner he had found so companionable turned nasty on learning of David's plans and refused to relinquish his possessions or let him go. On the road from Baltimore, he threatened to beat the boy with his whip and otherwise mistreated him, as if David were his indentured servant. Before dawn one morning, David gathered his clothes and fled, penniless.

A few miles down the road, he encountered another teamster who kindly asked where he was going and received in response tears and the full story of his mistreatment. The stranger, Henry Myers, "a very large, stout-looking man, and as resolute as a tiger," cursed the teamster who had abused David and swore to retrieve his money or "whip it out of the wretch who had it."[14] The confrontation proved anticlimactic, as Adam Myers, who was unrelated to Henry, first said David deserved being treated badly, presumably because he had wanted to ship out to London, then confessed that he had taken and spent the money. Although broke, he said, he intended to pay David when they reached Tennessee, a long way down the road, given his inability to pick up cargo bound for there. The boy begged his protector to drop the matter, and he did.

David traveled a few days with Henry Myers before, his impatience flaring, he determined again to set out alone for home, saying he could make better time walking. The night before he left, Myers told the teamsters at the inn where they were staying that David was "a poor little straggling boy," who had been robbed, and collected three dollars from them for his trip.[15]

Running out of money in Montgomery County, Virginia, David bound himself briefly to a farmer, James Caldwell, at a shilling a day, five dollars total, and then for four years to Elijah Griffith, a hatter. Griffith went bankrupt eighteen months later, leaving David again broke and stranded. He took odd jobs until he earned enough money to buy some clothes and make his way back to Tennessee.

The vagabond nearly drowned and froze taking a canoe against all advice across the storm-tossed New River. But having accomplished the feat, he found a home where he could get some whiskey—" 'a lettle of the creater,' " which he quickly learned to enjoy—before pushing on to Sullivan County, Tennessee, home of his Uncle Joseph, where he was reunited with the brother who had accompanied him on the cattle drive nearly three years earlier.

A few weeks later, the prodigal son arrived at Crockett's tavern, crowded that day with wagoners, requested lodging, then skulked in the shadows until the family and guests sat down for dinner at the common table. Recognizing her "lost brother," his oldest sister Betsy leapt from her chair and embraced him, setting off a general celebration.[16] Gone less than three years, David, who had been immediately recognized by his brother and uncle just a few weeks earlier, had passed undetected in the small tavern for several hours. He had become a young man with a sense of drama and more than a little ambivalence about his parents.

In the absence of banks—the first one opened in East Tennessee in 1811—the people of the frontier bartered, exchanged promissory notes among themselves, or, when it was available, paid cash. John Crockett appears to have conducted much of his business on credit, for he owed money to farmers for miles around his inn. He reminded his newly arrived son that he was still bound to obey his father and then told him to work off a thirty-six dollar debt to one Abraham Wilson. John promised David that, after he had done so, he would "discharge me from his service, and I might go free."[17] David promptly signed to work six months for Wilson and, completing his term, refused to stay on because "it was a place where a heap of bad company met to drink and gamble, and I wanted to get away from them, for I know'd very well if I staid there, I should get a bad name, as nobody could be respectable that would live there."[18]

Free of his father, David sought work with a Quaker farmer named John Kennedy, who had moved recently from North Carolina. Passing a week-long trial, he learned that he could have a job, but the first six months' pay would have to go toward redeeming a forty-dollar note the man held from John Crockett. David agreed to the conditions, although he harbored enough resentment that over the next six months he never traveled the fifteen miles to the Crockett inn. After redeeming the note, he borrowed one of Kennedy's horses and rode to give the paper to his father, who assumed his son was presenting it for collection and pleaded that he had no money. When he learned that David had paid the debt with his labor, "he shed a heap of tears. . . ."[19] Satisfied, David returned to Kennedy's farm where he spent the better part of the next three years as a hired hand, living with the family.

A teenager on his own, seeking a good time after years of hard work and enamored by the prospect of love, David spent his off hours attending local frolics and hunting for a wife. Often associated with reapings, house raisings, or some other activity requiring communal effort, these backwoods bashes lasted a day or more. Drinking, dancing, contests of strength, skill, and chance, dogfights, cockfights, horse races, shooting matches, quilting bees, politicking, bartering for goods, and sexual liaisons—any and all could be on tap as people came from the surrounding countryside and stayed for several days. Among industrious people, like Kennedy, the parties were considered a waste of time and energy, gatherings for the frivolous and dissipated. David, however, was one of the boys, neither particularly dissolute nor ambitious. He was set on being a farmer or innkeeper, resigned to raising a family in relative poverty. He did not even imagine a different life, unless it was to own more property—land and slaves.

By comparison, during his late teens, the law student Andrew Jackson (nineteen years Crockett's senior) gambled profligately on horses, fighting cocks, and cards, attended parties as often as he could, drank to excess, and kept company with a series of mulatto mistresses. According to his biographer, Marquis James, the ladies of Salisbury, North Carolina, feared that he "gambled not always as a sportsman who can afford to lose, but as an adventurer who has to win."[20] Although he had spent his inheritance of close to four hundred pounds and was an orphan, Jackson was a child of privilege with the ability to move through the upper strata of society where opportunity and wealth abounded. He possessed the will and enterprise to seize every chance that came his way to increase his land holdings and fortune, while serving the desire of his fellow frontiersmen for new territory. Like most of them, he faced chronic debt, which he abhorred, because of the cash-flow problems inherent in agriculture, especially cotton, both on his plantation and the farms of those people who owed him money.

Another son of the landed gentry whose family had fallen on hard times, Sam Houston by age nineteen had lived among the Cherokee for three years and opened, for one session, a country school. His father had lost the family fortune and left debt upon his death in 1806 that forced the sale of slaves, fields, and finally the plantation house at Timber Ridge in Virginia. The widow Houston had then moved her family of six boys—seven years Crockett's junior, Sam was also the fifth son—and three girls to the East Tennessee mountains where they had relatives. Named Co-lon-neh, Raven, by the Cherokee, with whom he spent most of his time, Sam was a romantic drawn to the world beyond plantation society.[21] Like Jackson, who was a generation older, Houston had the ego to seek and attain power, greatness, or some status beyond the ordinary, to drive himself toward his goal even in those moments when, depressed, he was on one of the periodic drunks for which he was notorious.

A third of Crockett's political contemporaries and one of his political mentors, Henry Clay, joined the office of the attorney general of Virginia when only nineteen, in preparation for his law career.[22] At age twenty, he moved to Kentucky to open an office. Despite repeated claims that he was a "self-made man" who rose from poverty and hardship by his own brilliance, Henry was born into a family of well-to-do farmers. Although his father, who was also a Baptist minister, died when the boy was four, he suffered no want, his mother having then married a wealthy planter. Crockett's senior by nine years, Henry Clay was a man of tremendous appetites—a profligate gambler, hard drinker, and womanizer—and of equally monumental intellect and ego.

The teen-aged Crockett exhibited none of that freewheeling

ambition found in the young Clay, Houston, or Jackson, in large measure because he was born not to privilege but to a state of near poverty, in which securing the necessities represented a major accomplishment. No one among his family or acquaintances inspired him to use his mind or imagination to break free of his circumstances. His adventures having driven him to servitude, not fame and fortune, David was content to dream of girls and frolics, not greatness. Under the calming influence of John Kennedy, his surrogate father, he had settled into the normal routine of backwoods life.

Crockett's first love was Kennedy's niece, who was visiting her uncle from North Carolina. Smitten, so severely tongue-tied that "when I would think of saying any thing to her, my heart would begin to flutter like a duck in a puddle," the farmhand at last stammered out his affection and protested that if the young woman refused him he "would pine down to nothing, and just die away with the consumption."[23] She gently told her suitor that she was engaged to one of Kennedy's sons; instead of wasting away, David went to school, convinced that his failure stemmed from a lack of education.

He agreed with another of Kennedy's sons, who had opened a school nearby, to work for him two days each week and attend school four, learning by the end of the term "to read a little in my primer, to write my own name, and to cypher some in the three first rules of figures."[24] This exaggerated image of the barely literate young man, who must bite his tongue to sign his name, has persisted for more than 150 years and, presented in his own words, will probably linger longer. Crockett's detractors have held up to derision his lack of formal education, while his supporters have used it to portray him as a self-made man who had studied at the school of hard knocks and common sense—more truthful in his case than in Henry Clay's. Crockett consciously presented himself as a man with country wisdom, which was as useful, if not better, than book learning.

Although he would never be accused of being an intellectual or even a well-informed man, Crockett learned considerably more than he cared to reveal to the public. While lacking grammatical refinement, his letters read as well as some compositions from freshmen in college, and are no more poorly punctuated—which is to say not at all. His handwriting, which markedly improved once he became a public man, was bold and relatively legible. He read newspapers, other ephemeral publications—like almanacs—government documents, law books, and at least occasionally looked at popular books, such as Benjamin Franklin's autobiography, a copy of which he owned. In his late forties, he was working to make himself an author independent of ghostwriters.

A number of scholars have observed that in recounting his misadventures, Crockett drops a year from his childhood.[25] It is interesting to speculate—and that is all one can do—whether at least part of that lost year was spent learning to read, making his enrollment in school at eighteen a refresher rather than a new experience. He suffered most from an inability to express abstract thoughts, sustain logical arguments, or develop the sort of perspective one needs to properly conceptualize and solve problems, all of which resulted from a lack of book learning, not a deficiency of intelligence. He could have studied assiduously on his own—Abraham Lincoln, for example, had only one year of formal education in a backwoods school—but no evidence suggests he did.

After his six months of schooling, Crockett returned to work as a farm hand for the senior Kennedy and sought out a family of girls he had known years earlier. He began to court one of them, Margaret Elder. Together they were attendants at the marriage of his first love and Kennedy's son, which inspired him to redouble his efforts to gain Margaret's affections. Finally, she agreed to marry him, and on October 21, 1805, David purchased the license in Jefferson County.

Having grown attached to the rifle and having bought himself a "capital one," the self-satisfied Crockett decided to celebrate his upcoming marriage at a shooting match being held at a spot between Kennedy's farm and Margaret's house. Because Kennedy disapproved of frolics and shooting matches, Crockett would either sneak out of the house to attend—by way of a tree trunk propped outside the window of the room he shared with an indentured servant his age, who often accompanied him—or leave openly and lie about his destination. The day after securing the license, he told his employer he was going hunting, then changed course. He bought a chance at the prize beef with a partner and won, then sold his half for the hefty sum of five dollars—in coin or "the real grit"—and set off to complete the unfinished business of asking Margaret's parents for her hand in marriage.

What happened next is uncertain, but putting together several accounts, one can sketch a sequence of events. Crockett drank and danced all night at the party, then, exhausted and hung over, set out at dawn for the Elder house. Stopping along the way to visit her uncle and rest, he encountered one of her sisters, who told him that Margaret had deceived him. She planned, the sister said, to marry another suitor the next day. The sister could not persuade the dumbstruck David that her parents preferred him and would pressure Margaret to relent, if only he would go and argue his case. Too proud for that, he went home to nurse his sorrow, convinced he "was born odd," without a mate to find in the world.[26]

The jilted lover fell into depression, marked by loss of appetite and general malaise, for six to nine months before learning from a neighbor—a Dutch widow's daughter "that was well enough as to smartness, but . . . as ugly as a stone fence"—that a quite pretty girl would appear at an upcoming reaping. When the event drew near, David asked Kennedy to allow his indentured servant to go as well. Refusing, the old farmer cautioned David "that there would be a great deal of bad company there," which would besmirch his reputation.[27]

Arriving with his rifle slung over his shoulder for effect, David met first the mother and then the girl herself, red-haired Mary "Polly" Finley. She was two years his junior, a child of an Irish mother and a Scotch-Irish father, poor farmers who lived nearby. "I was plaguy well pleased with her from the word go," David said. "She had a good countenance, and was very pretty, and I was full bent on making an acquaintance with her."[28] David stayed with Polly through the frolic, dancing, talking, even enduring her mother's teasing of him as her "son-in-law." He was, he said, "salting the cow to catch the calf," an aphorism seemingly of his devise as a storyteller.[29] Like most frolics, this one lasted until dawn, night being no time to travel long miles through sparsely settled country because of the prospect of getting lost, injured, or robbed.

The next day, his depression lifting, Crockett bargained to work six months for a third Kennedy son in exchange for an old horse, his first. A little more than a month later, he traveled to visit Polly and meet her family, only to watch her arrive home with another suitor. Crockett perceived soon enough that while Polly favored him, her mother preferred the interloper, who, getting the same message, left to try another day. Crockett stayed the weekend to press his affection on the young woman.

On a wolf hunt several weeks later, Crockett became separated from the main pack of men and dogs in a section of forest that was unfamiliar to him. There were two species of wolf in that part of Tennessee—the grey, or timber, wolf and the red, sometimes called the black, wolf—both of which were marked for destruction by settlers claiming that they fed both on livestock and unwitting humans. So great was the fear that bounties were regularly paid for wolf ears and the animals were driven nearly to extinction. That day, Crockett panicked in a most unhunterly fashion and rapidly lost his bearings when the weather began to turn bad. By his calculation, he wandered six or seven miles off course until, near dusk, he espied a "little woman streaking it along through the woods like all wrath." Hoping she would lead him to safety, he pursued her. When she stopped, he realized he had been chasing Polly, who had gone looking for her father's horses earlier that day and become lost as well. Together, they found a house, where they spent the night "courting," which in that context means they could have done everything from talk to make love.[30] The next morning, the coincidental lovers discovered that they had found shelter seven miles from her home and ten miles from the Kennedy farm, distances they covered in several hours, after their separation.

Heart and mind fixed, Crockett continued to court Polly and, adding his gun to the amount he had already earned through his labor, paid off his horse in little more than a month. He and Polly then set a date for their wedding, and Crockett arranged an infare, or housewarming, for the bride at his father's tavern, choosing it because he had no home of his own. He then asked for Polly's hand in marriage. Her father consented, but her mother stoutly refused. Crockett nonetheless took out a marriage license at the Danbridge Courthouse in Jefferson County on August 12, 1806, for himself and "Polly Findley" (her name being variously spelled Findley, Findlay, Finlay on her headstone, and by current consensus, Finley). A friend, Thomas Doggett, was cosigner with David of the required bond for $1,250, to warrant that there was no cause "to obstruct the marriage. . . ."

On August 14, 1806, three days short of his twentieth birthday, David set out with his oldest brother and his wife, another brother, a sister, and two friends to collect his bride. Along the way, they encountered a large group of friends who had come to witness the event. Following custom, David's brother, sister, and his best man went ahead to the house with an empty flagon, which the family was to fill as a sign that the wedding could proceed. Although Mrs. Finley was "as wrathy as ever," Mr. Finley filled the flask, and the envoys raced back to the bridegroom with the liquor. Accompanied by his friends, Crockett then rode directly to the door of the house, leading a horse for Polly. As they left, her father blocked the gate and asked that they stay to be married there.[31]

The negotiations that followed lasted the better part of two days, ending with Mrs. Finley asking Crockett to marry in her home and apologizing for her behavior. She was, she said, distraught at the thought that her first daughter would not be properly wed. On August 16, David and Polly were married and went to the party at the Crocketts' tavern.

Close to a week later, the young couple returned to the Finley farm, where they were given two cows and two calves as a marriage portion—a meager dowry, but more than Crockett had expected. The cows were the only livestock on a small farm he rented near her parents, which Polly was able to decorate a little with a fifteen-dollar store credit from his former employer, John Kennedy. During their five years on that farm, the Crocketts had two sons, John Wesley on July 10, 1807—the precise date known only because he went on to serve in Congress—and William in 1809. But the rent was high and profits nonexistent, so, following frontier tradition, they decided to seek their fortune in "new country."

Sometime around October 1811, with the aid of Polly's father, the family moved to a five-acre parcel they bought in southern Middle Tennessee near the headwaters of the east fork of Mulberry Creek, itself a branch of the Elk River. Crockett soon leased an additional fifteen acres, but in this newly settled region he concentrated on hunting for food and pelts, not farming, and soon began to distinguish himself. "Of deer and smaller game, I killed abundance," he said, "but the bear had been much hunted in those parts before, and were not so plenty as I could have wished."[32]

In 1812, Polly gave birth to a daughter, Margaret (perhaps coincidentally named after David's first love), who became known as Polly, and early the following year, the Crocketts moved to nearby Franklin County.[33] Just a few miles north of the Alabama border, the area was still considered Indian country, and a bloody war for the entire region had already begun. The family settled on the Rattlesnake Spring branch of Bean's Creek in a cabin David called "Kentuck," thinking of the great long hunter Daniel Boone. Later several of his siblings joined him in his westward drift, but at that moment the man and his young family were on their own. Although one day he would become a famous politician, he did not own enough land—two hundred acres, minimum—to run for the state legislature.

CHAPTER THREE

SERGEANT CROCKETT

In 1800, approximately 700,000 whites lived west of the Appalachian Mountains, in a line of settlement from the Canadian border to just south of Tennessee. By rough estimates, 100,000 Indians also called the region home. In 1803, the young United States purchased the Louisiana Territory from France and immediately extended its borders south to the Gulf of Mexico and west to the Rocky Mountains, which to the Americans were terra incognita. Because they were held by Spain, Florida and Texas were left from the acquisition, but men like Andrew Jackson fervently believed that those territories and more belonged to the United States, and they devoted themselves to acquiring them by whatever means were necessary. Not even the most ardent proponents of expansion envisioned that in less than four decades more than 4.5 million people would dwell in valleys of the Mississippi and her tributaries or that the tensions and pressures arising from digesting new territories—whether to make them slave, free, or open to both—would contribute to a bloody Civil War. Seething, sometimes exploding, as social mores and economic structures clashed and groups fought for power and land, the West dominated the nation's politics by the late 1820s.

The majority of those involved with the expansion believed that removal of the Indians from their ancestral homes, by treaty or force, was the necessary first step to securing the new territory. The two men most closely identified with that program—Andrew Jackson in the Southwest and William Henry Harrison in the Northwest—rode their reputations as Indian killers to the White House, Jackson in 1828 and 1832, Harrison in 1840. Both men achieved celebrity during the bloody Creek Indian—or Red Stick—War, which finally broke the power of the trans-Appalachian tribes. An offshoot of the War of 1812, with the British arming and inciting the Indians, it was a continuation of the conflict that had begun nearly half a century earlier when the first white settlers pushed west from the coast.

The Red Stick War was instigated by the charismatic Shawnee leader Tecumseh and his brother Prophet, a self-reformed alcoholic and holy man, who dreamed of a Pan-Indian alliance of tribes from the Upper Missouri to the Gulf of Mexico that would drive the white intruders from their homes. Cultural purists, the brothers and their followers believed that a tribe's territory belonged to all of its members and, therefore, no portion of it could be relinquished without their unanimous consent. Chiefs and a few select warriors did not have the authority to sign away that birthright. Protesting a massive cession of Indian lands in 1811, Tecumseh told a gathering of Creek, Cherokee, Chickasaw, and Choctaw on the banks of the Tallapoosa River in Alabama: "Let the white race perish. They seize your land; they corrupt your women, they trample on the ashes of your dead! Back whence they came, upon a trail of blood, they must be driven."[1]

General William Henry Harrison, a native Virginian and former governor of the Indiana Territory, struck the first substantial blow in the conflict when he attacked the home of Prophet on Tippecanoe Creek in Indiana, while Tecumseh organized in the south. After rebuffing an assault they had provoked, Harrison's troops overran and burned Prophet's Town on November 7, 1811, torching as well the faith of the Shawnee and their allies in the holy man's omnipotence. Along what was then called the southwestern frontier, the battle incited both sides to greater depredations.

Tecumseh himself fell the following year in the Battle of the Thames to the Kentucky mounted volunteers of Colonel Richard Mentor Johnson, who reportedly slew the Shawnee leader in hand-to-hand combat and later boasted that his men had cut razor strops from the fallen chief's corpse. That claim is probably exaggerated, but Johnson, an innovative and courageous cavalry leader, did lead the charge that carried the battle for the Americans, during which he was severely wounded. An eccentric of the first rank—his only peer among public figures being Crockett—Johnson later established the Choctaw Academy for Indians in his native Kentucky. A congressman, senator, and vice president under Martin Van Buren, he openly carried on a series of affairs with mulatto women, including one he sold down the river after she left him and he tracked her down.

The Creek traditionalists who heeded Tecumseh eschewed all white influences and, painting their war clubs red—thus, "Red Sticks"—sought to drive from their territory the squatters who recognized no boundary and brought in their wake state officials and large-scale speculators who honored no treaty. It was a troubled situation, to be sure, for along the frontier, white and Indian intermarriage—formal and informal—was commonplace, and those men and women locked in such liaisons, as well as their children, found themselves torn by conflicting loyalties, confronted with unexpected dangers. Caught in the middle, they often were forced to choose sides and seldom could escape the cross fire. Whether they had opted for Indians or whites, they found themselves dispossessed and unwelcome in the society of the victorious Americans.

The trader and Creek mico, or chief, during the Revolutionary War, Alexander McGillivray had skillfully played to British, Spanish, and American interests to keep the southern tribes free. But after his death in 1793, no successor emerged who could keep the American colonists and their government from claiming through negotiation and land grabs ever larger pieces of Indian territory. Son of a Scotsman and a French-Creek woman renowned for her beauty, McGillivray had as a half-brother on his mother's side Charles Weatherford, who had two sons. John passed for white. William, known as Red Eagle, although generally accommodating to whites, led his warriors against Fort Mims, Alabama, on August 30, 1813, to retaliate for an ambush by white militia of a party of Creeks at Burnt Corn Creek. Fearing more trouble after that assault, people from around the region had gathered at the fort, the home of a half-white trader named Samuel Mims, for security. Some 265 militiamen—the majority belonging to a troop called the Mississippi Volunteers—under another half-breed, Major Daniel Beasley, were stationed there to defend the fort and its occupants.

Red Eagle expected to fire a few shots of intimidation against a well-defended stockade and then, after his warriors had vented their outrage, retreat—point made, damages minimal. But Beasley was playing cards that noon with his officers while his troops gamboled with the girls and the gates stood invitingly open. A young slave boy had warned the occupants that he had seen Indians, but, claiming he had misled them earlier, they refused to believe him.[2] He was being flogged for lying when the Creek warriors charged, cutting down Beasley as he belatedly tried to swing the balkish doors through the dirt, slashing and shooting their way through the garrison and refugees for three hours before temporarily retiring. The survivors barred the gates to no avail, for the returning Indians torched the walls and buildings and broke through to renew their slaughter. By evening, 500 men, women, and children lay dead. Most of the survivors—especially the slaves—were taken captive. Red Eagle subsequently disavowed the massacre and said that he had not participated, but his disclaimers mattered little.

News of the fall of Fort Mims, embellished with gruesome details and exaggerated descriptions, spread throughout the region, raising alarm and fury. The whites demanded vengeance and looked to Andrew Jackson—Sharp Knife to the Indians—in Nashville to provide it. He prosecuted the war with single-minded devotion, against Indians, British, and scheming American politicians, often driving his troops—and himself—

forward by will alone. On March 27, 1814, after six months of mutual atrocities, the two sides met at Horseshoe Bend on the Tallapoosa River, eastern Alabama. With the aid of Cherokee fighters, Jackson's volunteers smashed the Creek force, killing nearly 800 of 1,000 warriors at a loss of 49 dead and 157 wounded. Among the casualties was Ensign Samuel Houston, whose leg was pierced by an arrow when he led a successful charge against an Indian redoubt and whose arm and shoulder were shattered by musket fire during an unsuccessful assault on another position. His daring earned him a reputation for courage and the unwavering loyalty of Andrew Jackson.

The Creek were broken. Appearing in Jackson's command tent, Red Eagle declared the war over, then vanished back among his people before the Americans could react. Jackson became the most celebrated American military leader since George Washington and in May received a commission as major general in the regular army, a reward President James Madison, backed by a number of jealous politicians, had long refused to grant him. Instructed to negotiate with the defeated Creek, he demanded cession of half their territory, some 23 million acres, of which approximately half fell into the hands of Jackson's friends and political allies—speculators all. A few months after the August 9 signing of the treaty, Jackson seized Pensacola from Spain and sent his troops into the Florida Panhandle ostensibly to track down recalcitrant Indians and block British intrigue but practically to see how much territory he could take and keep.

Early in 1815, Jackson completed his defense of the union by routing the British at New Orleans, having displayed his iron determination, his disregard for any authority but his own, his willingness to assume dictatorial power in pursuit of what he deemed right. Viewed as strength by his ardent admirers, these characteristics raised equal ire among his foes, who felt he lacked proper respect for the institutions and ideals of the Republic. No one could deny, however, that after New Orleans his stature as national hero had reached epic heights.

Jackson had saved the nation and opened the West—then

western Ohio and Tennessee, Indiana, Alabama, Illinois, Missouri, Mississippi, and Arkansas—to what rapidly became a flood of settlement, as people fled the disruption of the Industrial Revolution in Europe and America, farms that had become nonproductive through misuse, and harvests that had declined because of a series of brutally cold winters. A boom in cotton prices—along with that marvelous invention the cotton gin, and the "free" labor of slaves—encouraged the movement in the Southwest, while corn and wheat profits did the same in the Northwest. In 1815, 1 million acres of federal land were sold; in 1816, 1.5 million acres; in 1817, 2 million. One year later, 2.5 million acres went for sale, and squatters were taking countless more. A year later, an economic panic damped the speculative surge but did not still the migration. In the East, the effect was seen in "abandoned farms, declining population, falling property values."[3]

The westerners exerted themselves forcefully in the War of 1812 whenever their fear of widespread border conflict became palpable. Several days before messengers brought news of the Fort Mims massacre to Jackson in Nashville, the Franklin County militia mustered in Winchester, ten miles north of the Crockett homestead. Showing the influence of his Quaker patron John Kennedy, Crockett said that, in thinking about war, he had concluded he could not fight, having no taste for the brutality or killing. But when he heard of the Creek attack, his qualms vanished and, feeling "wolfish all over," he determined to volunteer. To no avail, Polly urged him to stay home, saying "she was a stranger in the parts where we lived, had no connexions living near her, and that she and our little children would be left in a lonesome and unhappy situation if I went away."[4]

She had reason to fear his departure. He could perish in battle, come back maimed, or simply vanish without a trace, leaving her with her family to feed from a farm that was marginal. Indians were the publicized enemy, but many disreputable whites roamed the frontier, preying on isolated farms.

Communication being erratic, David and Polly, like scores of other couples, were effectively out of touch for the term of his service. The uncertainty and hardship could destroy a person's sanity and physical health, but it also could make women strongly assertive and self-sufficient, more competent at the business of farming and life than their soldier spouses.

On September 24, 1813, David Crockett was the eighteenth man to enlist in the Second Regiment of Tennessee Volunteer Mounted Riflemen for ninety days, believing, like the majority of his mates, that the war would be over before then. The company elected as its captain Francis Jones, a local lawyer who would subsequently serve three terms in Congress. Colonel Newton Cannon was regimental commander under Colonel John Coffee, who was soon promoted to brigadier general. Within ten days, the mounted riflemen were moving south.

A part-time scout and indifferent warrior more concerned with food than fighting, Private Crockett missed the war's greatest battles altogether. In his autobiography, he lengthened his brief service—one stretch of ninety days; another of six months—and generally altered his record in order to portray himself as an active, strong-minded defender of the soldier's rights (which were few), a courageous and generous comrade in arms. He also exaggerated his responsibilities as a scout to promote his celebrity as a backwoodsman and bear hunter. That politically inspired hyperbole aside, his account of his service lucidly presented the militiaman's view of the Creek campaign and the dangers of the border.

Crockett went to war in the tradition of his father—as a volunteer on horseback. The mounted frontier fighter could strike deep and fast into enemy territory, and his success in doing so created a tradition that defined him as a warrior for more than a century. The romantic heroes of the Civil War and the western Indian campaigns, for example, were the cavalry. There is a report that Crockett, on entering the Alamo, voiced his preference for "open country" where a mounted man could operate. There was also a strong belief that citizens should defend themselves through their militias and that a large, national standing army was a bad idea not only because it would deprive them of their responsibility but also because it would invest too much power in the "general government." Following form, Crockett and his neighbors insisted on riding to battle and promptly returning home when their duty was done, to tend to their farms and families. They believed their enlistments ended when the time expired or they achieved victory, whichever came first.

Outstanding fighters when the engagement was quick, the militiamen grew restive at delay. They were undisciplined garrison troops, with an extreme aversion to the tedium and incessant drilling of camp life, and indifferent foot soldiers, a condition they considered degrading. Accustomed to electing their leaders, they scorned career officers, as well as the regular troops obeying them. The disputes that inevitably arose between the two groups could wreck entire campaigns.

Traveling light, the 1,300-man troop raised at Winchester rode to Beaty's Spring south of Huntsville, Alabama, where militias were gathering from all along the frontier to await the arrival from Nashville of their commander. While there, Crockett was selected for a scouting mission into Creek territory because of his reputation as a backwoodsman—the boy of nineteen who was frightened of the forest having become by twenty-eight a skilled tracker. He chose as his companion a young neighbor named George Russell—the model for the Walt Disney character by the same name but with a single "l."

Major John H. Gibson, who was leading the excursion, immediately rejected Russell, the son of militia Major William Russell, as too young for the task. Crockett protested: "[F]or I know'd George Russell, and I know'd there was no mistake in him; and I didn't think that courage ought to be measured by the beard, for fear a goat would have the preference over a man."[5] His angry rebuttal swayed the major, and the next morning Crockett, Russell, and ten other men joined Gibson in crossing the Tennessee River at a place called Ditto's Landing for what became a sixty-five-mile reconnaissance.

Picking up a guide on their second morning out, the party

split into two groups—one under Gibson, the other under Crockett—each visiting the home of a friendly Cherokee. Crockett's patrol found a half-breed named Jack Thompson, then continued to look for Creek after Gibson failed to show up for their prearranged evening rendezvous. They stopped to feed themselves and their horses at the home of a white man named Radcliff, who was married to a Creek woman and lived on the edge of the nation's territory. He told them that a small party of warriors had passed there an hour earlier.

The scouts pushed on to the camp of some friendly Creek, meeting along the way two blacks who had been captured by the Indians and were seeking to return to their owner, for reasons not known. Perhaps they had families on the plantation; perhaps conditions were materially better than in the Indian town, where they remained slaves, albeit with some freedom of movement. The once and future chattel were brothers, bilingual, armed, and mounted; back on the farm they would lose everything. Crockett sent one to Ditto's Landing and took the other with him as an interpreter. At the camp, the Indians voiced their fear that if Red Stick warriors found the white soldiers, they would kill everyone. Crockett promised that he would stand guard all night, then fell asleep.

Shortly thereafter, a runner broke into camp screaming loudly enough to stir but not rouse the intrepid scout. Finally shaking Crockett awake, the interpreter reported that a war party intent on attacking Jackson's troops had crossed the Coosa River near Tallusahatchee, an Indian town. The scouts left immediately for Coffee's headquarters, arriving at dawn. Coffee listened politely to the report, then took no action, leading Crockett to conclude that the colonel had not treated the news with proper seriousness. After Gibson rode in the next day with confirmation and was treated as if he were a hero, Crockett became convinced that he had been slighted because of his rank. "I was no great man," he said, "but just a poor soldier."[6]

He had a point, but he also lacked any sense of perspective on his role, nor did it occur to him even after his news proved to be a lie that commanding officers acted on every unconfirmed report at their peril. Jackson had spies and scouts ranging throughout the countryside, each providing a bit of intelligence he and his officers had to filter and weigh. Intrigue having its own peculiar dynamic, many of those scouts, because they operated in constant danger, shared Crockett's sense of self-importance and belief that whatever bit of information they gained should be treated with the utmost respect. Many of them failed to take into account that their sources traded more often in rumor than in fact, working both sides of the conflict in order to survive and, in some cases, profit.

Notified by Coffee of the reported Red Stick movement, Jackson drove his troops to Huntsville in a one-day forced march of forty miles. The next morning, he dispatched the colonel and 800 men to hunt for the war party. At the headwaters of the Black Warrior River, now the site of Tuscaloosa, the Americans pillaged a large town, whose Creek inhabitants had fled their advance, taking corn and dried beef before putting it to the torch. Despite the loot, rations ran low on the return march, and Crockett volunteered as a hunter. He found a recently killed deer, which he carried back, overcoming his qualms about stealing game—an ethical violation of the worst sort—and distributed the meat, keeping only a small amount for his mess. The next evening, he flushed some hogs and in shooting one drove the others into camp, where they were slaughtered, along with a "stray" cow. The animals belonged to a group of Cherokee living nearby, who, following the custom of Indians and whites, let their livestock roam, there being no fences to contain them. The Cherokee received a government warrant for their losses, hardly a fair bargain given the difficulty they would face in converting it to food.

After rejoining Jackson, Coffee sent scouts to question Radcliff again. He confessed that he had fabricated the news of the Red Stick war party in order to scare Crockett away, because he feared retaliation if he were seen even involuntarily consorting with the enemy. The scouts showed their compassion by impressing Radcliff's sons as interpreters. The army then proceeded to Ten Islands on the Coosa River, where the imaginary warriors were crossing, and established what became Fort Strother. From there, they marched on Tallusahatchee, some eight miles distant, and encountered a small force of Creek, whom they drove back into the town. As the Americans closed in from all sides, the Indians began to surrender.

The bloodless capture turned violent when, by Crockett's count, forty-six warriors ran into a lodge guarded by one woman, who, drawing a bow against her feet, fired on the Tennesseans, killing a junior officer. In the only printed account of the massacre that followed, Crockett stated that the enraged Americans promptly killed the woman and throughout the town shot the Creek

> like dogs; and then set the house on fire, and burned it up with the forty-six warriors in it. I recollect seeing a boy who was shot down near the house. His arm and thigh was broken, and he was so near the burning house that the grease was stewing out of him. In this situation he was still trying to crawl along; but not a murmur escaped him, though he was only about twelve years old.[7]

When the slaughter finally stopped, the Americans, who lost 5 men, had killed 186 men, women, and children, and captured 80, the majority of them early in the assault. Most of the soldiers shared the view of their commander, Andrew Jackson, that they had finally "retaliated for the destruction of Fort Mims."[8]

Scavenging for food the next day, the famished Americans returned to the ruins and, finding a potato cellar under the charred lodge they had torched, turned to a form of quasi-cannibalism. "[H]unger compelled us to eat them [the potatoes]," Crockett said, "though I had a little rather not . . . , for the oil of the Indians we had burned up on the day before had run down on them, and they looked like they had been stewed with fat meat."[9]

The troops had been back at Fort Strother only four days when a runner burst in announcing that 1,100 Red Sticks had laid siege to friendly Creek in Fort Talladega. Following a forced march of some thirty miles, Jackson's army executed a pincer movement designed to encircle the attacking warriors. The Americans had begun to inflict heavy casualties when an advance troop of draftees faltered, allowing the Creek to break through the line and escape. They left some 300 of their comrades dead—more if one wishes to believe Jackson's inflated estimates—to 15 for the Americans. (Two wounded soldiers died after the battle.)

Jackson's desire for immediate pursuit, which might have shortened the war, ran afoul of rebellious East Tennessee militiamen under Generals James White and John Cocke, his political rivals, who refused to cooperate, and inadequate provisions, the troops being well ahead of their feeble supply lines. Those same East Tennessee troops on November 18, three days after the fight at Fort Talladega, massacred a settlement of Hillabee Creek, who had opened negotiations with Jackson to end hostilities. Betrayed, the Creek resumed fighting.

Although a volunteer himself, perpetually at war with his colleagues and regular army officers, Jackson had his share of trouble with his soldiers, a lot prone to desertion, disaffection, and outright mutiny under the best of circumstances. He countered with unforgiving discipline. A seventeen-year-old trooper was convicted of mutiny and shot for ignoring an order to clean up his cooking gear, but only after Jackson removed himself from the sound of the firing squad. Idled at Fort Strother, suffering from hunger and cold, a number of the men decided their tours were over and it was time to go home. When a group of Tennessee militiamen, whose ninety-day enlistments had expired, threatened to move from camp, Jackson held them in check with his United States soldiers and told them that by an act of Congress they were liable for six months of service. When the U.S. volunteers then protested that their one year enlistment was up, Jackson turned the militia against them, saying that they had not been continuously in the field for that period. At one crucial point, Jackson himself blocked a group's attempt to leave by threatening to shoot the first militiaman to cross a bridge from the fort. Tennessee Governor Willie Blount subsequently overruled his general and discharged the men, but the conflicts continued.

The following year in Mobile, Jackson—who had just been commissioned major general in the U.S. Army—crushed a mutiny of 200 Tennesseans. Condemned to death at a trial in December 1814, six ringleaders were executed following the Battle of New Orleans, after Jackson approved their sentence, a controversial decision that was to stalk him the rest of his life. Aware of that and engaged in asserting his political independence, Crockett deliberately and falsely claimed in his autobiography that he was a leader of militiamen who faced down Jackson after he denied their reasonable request to return home for fresh horses and supplies in November 1813. In fact, along with others of Coffee's riflemen, Crockett had already been furloughed for precisely that purpose. Obeying orders, he rejoined the army at Huntsville on December 8 to serve out his enlistment without incident.

Crockett also gave himself three extra months of service early in 1814, as a scout with Major William Russell, the father of the young man he had taken on his first assignment. The phantom service conferred on him an importance and standing outside the rigid military hierarchy, which he did not possess, while reinforcing his image as the great hunter and heir to Daniel Boone. It also allowed him to claim that he fought at the battles of Emuckfau Creek on January 22, 1814, and Enotachopco Creek two days later and to produce a convenient alibi for missing the decisive fight at Horseshoe Bend (Tohopeka) on March 27.[10] His horse, Crockett said, had come up lame, and with fresh recruits arriving in camp, he had accepted a generously granted and much needed leave to replace it.

According to the Records of the War of 1812, Private David Crockett was discharged on December 24, 1813, with total remuneration for his unremarkable service of $65.59, more than half of which was for his horse—$38.80—the remainder covering $8.00 a month for wages and $1.25 for traveling a total of 120 miles to and from his cabin. Crockett missed Christmas, but he had more money than he had seen before. He had a family to feed and no great love of the rigors and boredom of military life. Only years later, when it seemed politically prudent, would he feel the need for more substantial credentials.

On September 28, 1814, Crockett, declaring he wanted "a small taste of British fighting," again ignored the wishes of Polly and signed up for six months as a third sergeant in Major William Russell's Separate Battalion of Tennessee Mounted Gunmen bound for Pensacola.[11] (Farmers tried to time their enlistments so they would not interfere with planting and harvesting their crops.) A British expeditionary force under Colonel Edward Nichols had arrived during the summer and turned the old colonial city of Spanish Florida into a staging area for a planned invasion of Mobile and New Orleans as well as a bazaar of intrigue for filibusters, agents, fugitive slaves, spies, smugglers, and the extant Creole society already known for its decadence. Some 300 royal troops were agitating among those Creek who had refused to surrender to the Americans and who were finding homes in a territory settled by an earlier generation of Indian "runaways"—Seminole—who were especially hated in the American South for harboring fugitive slaves.

Jackson's 1814 foray thus was more than a preemptive strike against the British. It was also a probe into Spanish territory the Americans coveted and an early salvo in a war against the Seminole and their black allies that would continue off and on for the next fifty years. The largest collection of free blacks and fugitives in the Southeast was settled around the British-built Fort Prospect Bluff, called by Americans "the Negro fort," on the Apalachicola River. Independent, self-reliant, and armed, these free blacks served as a constant inspiration to slaves to flee or rebel, and because of that, they were feared and loathed by white southerners, who wanted them and their farms annihilated. In 1816, Brigadier General Edmund P. Gaines, on Jackson's orders, sailed up the river and destroyed the fort with bombardment from his gunboats. The shelling also killed 270 men, women, and children. Returning to the Panhandle in force in 1818, Jackson smashed Indian villages and ultimately forced Spain to cede Florida to the United States. Crockett never questioned the connections between his service and these later campaigns because he shared the opinion of Jackson and most other westerners that the business of the United States was territorial expansion.

Russell's Tennessee Volunteers arrived in Pensacola on November 8, the day after Jackson took the city more by default than by storm. Unable to mount a vigorous defense and unwilling to surrender passively, the Spanish had negotiated a temporary truce to think over their options. Just before it was to expire, they blew up the powder magazine at Fort Barrancas on Pensacola Bay, and the British war ships slipped from their anchorage, leaving the city undefended. Celebrating the victory they had just missed, Crockett and his mates caroused through town, which was renowned for its convivial ways, before returning to camp.

The next morning, they marched back into Alabama to the ruined Fort Mims, where they were assigned to a regiment commanded by U.S. Army Major Uriah Blue and charged with destroying Creek villages along the Escambia River, which drains from Alabama through the Florida Panhandle into Pensacola Bay, and Seminole towns along the Apalachicola River to the east. A detachment of Chickasaw, Choctaw, and Creek scouts accompanied the Americans in what would in a later war in Southeast Asia be called a search-and-destroy mission.

The men under Blue were left in the brackish backwash of the war and of the Gulf coast. Jackson marched rapidly to Mobile, where he strengthened the city's defenses and left in command an old compatriot, Brigadier General James Winchester, who would join him and another friend, Judge John Overton, in "founding" the city of Memphis in 1819 on land purchased under a treaty with the Chickasaw. A few years later, Crockett, who had already begun to make a reputation for himself as a politician, would move to the northwest corner of that same Chickasaw purchase and run for Congress. Winchester's son, Marcus, a leading merchant and ladies' man in the river city of Memphis, soon became his political patron, much to the dismay of Overton and Jackson.

Blue's regiment lingered several days at Fort Montgomery, two miles from Fort Mims, feeding on scrub cattle that probably had belonged to its residents. The men faced a thinly populated region of massive long-leaf pine forests, dense hammocks of moss-draped live oak; swamps, streams, rivers, and springs; some open prairies or savannas. Rich in game, insects, snakes, and alligators, it could be forbidding and inhospitable to those who did not know it, as the thousand-man troop would learn on their first march through piney woods to the banks of the Escambia. A neophyte moved in slow motion through the landscape, cursing its sand, bugs, bogs, and deadfalls in every breath, wondering whether there was any firm footing; an army crept.

Russell took a group of Indians and fifteen soldiers, including Crockett, on a reconnaissance in advance of the lurching force. Crossing the Escambia, they waded for several hours through the swamp that formed the river's east bank until they reached another stand of pine. They marched six more miles through the trees and palmetto before the Indian scouts located a Creek camp. Immediately, they stripped and painted themselves for an attack, persuading their leader, Russell, to do the same. He instructed the Indians that the white men would open fire, then leave the field to them for mayhem.

Revelatory though it is of the way whites and Indians sometimes fought together, the plan came to naught that day. As Russell's men surveyed the camp, which occupied an island, a pair of their scouts murdered and beheaded two Creek hunters and let out a war whoop that brought the Americans running. After the Indians had finished counting coup—one by one striking the severed heads with their clubs—Crockett followed suit, earning for himself the honorific "warrior." Finally, they scalped the battered heads and left them to the vultures.[12]

Refocusing on their initial target, the Creek scouts learned from a woman on the island of a canoe on their side of the river, and Russell promptly dispatched a raiding party. It quickly overran the camp, seizing the women and children, the one remaining man having fled as they approached.

Mission accomplished, Russell sent Crockett downriver to collect provisions and return by morning for an advance nine miles upriver to a redoubt the captured Creek had described before their beheading. With another white soldier and two Creek scouts, Crockett reached Blue's camp only to be told that Russell would have to return promptly so the regiment could move south. Someone else carried the order north. Several days later, part of the regiment, not including Crockett, fought with a small band of Creek on the east side of Pensacola Bay and took a number of prisoners, whom the Choctaw and Chickasaw scouts subsequently murdered with the tacit approval of Blue and his officers.

For the remainder of his time in the Panhandle, Crockett hunted food as the regiment wandered eastward toward the Apalachicola River, probably near its confluence with the Chattahoochee, looking for Seminole villages to destroy. Having left Fort Montgomery a month earlier with a twenty-day supply of flour and an eight-day supply of beef, the men were starving and justifiably enraged at the incompetence of Blue, who reinforced all of their prejudices against the regular army. Crockett said, "I had not myself tasted bread but twice in nineteen days."[13] He lived on coffee and whatever he and his messmates could scrounge on the march, no easy task since an army on the move frightens off all large animals. Hearing of a village on the Chattahoochee River, the troops made a night march and attacked at dawn only to find it deserted and stripped of provisions. Angry and frustrated, they torched the town.

Beaten by poor organization and unfamiliar country, the demoralized regiment soon divided, with one battalion under Major John Childs going through the Panhandle to Baton Rouge and joining Jackson's main army on its return from New Orleans, and that of Russell heading northwestward for Fort Decatur on the Tallapoosa River, thence to Fort Strother. Russell sent his Indian scouts and the fittest white volunteers and horses ahead to secure food and bring it back to the main force. Crockett joined a party of hunters that brought into camp everything they could kill, which amounted to all manner of small game only desperate men would take—hawks, songbirds, squirrels. Sorted from a communal pile every evening, the meat was woefully inadequate.

Crockett learned one night that officers were hoarding food for themselves and, deciding he had better "root hog or die," led his messmates out of camp the next morning, before the troops set march, so they could hunt. Although they passed the campsites of their advance party—marked by Creek corpses— and reached the Choctawhatchee River, they found no game for three days. "[W]e all began to get nearly ready to give up the ghost, and lie down and die," Crockett said, "for we had no prospect of provision, and we knew we couldn't go much further without it."[14] Pressing ahead, they came to a prairie where Crockett saw a trail made by large game, which they followed to a stream lined with wild rye. After setting the horses to graze, they went hunting and managed fortuitously to flush a flock of wild turkeys. Crockett and a companion killed two and were cooking them at camp when the advance party returned from Fort Decatur with supplies. They joined the feast and then pushed south to join the main force, arriving as Major Russell's son was preparing to slaughter and eat his horse.

Crockett killed a buck the next day, after losing one he had wounded and failing to get a shot off at a bear. He gave the venison and some honey collected the day before to the main troop, which had just rejoined his mess. At Fort Decatur, only fourteen miles away, they again found scant provisions—one ration of meat per man and no flour or corn. Deciding he had suffered enough deprivation, Crockett crossed the river and traded the Creek living there bullets and gunpowder for corn, which carried him forty-nine miles to the next fort, Williams, where the men received a ration each of pork and flour. On the way to Fort Strother, another thirty-nine miles away, the battalion once more ran out of food and abandoned thirteen horses, which they presumably could not bear to eat. Finding another Creek village, Crockett and his more enterprising fellows again traded bullets and gunpowder for corn.

Just outside the fort, the troop encountered East Tennessee militiamen heading south for Mobile. Seeing his youngest brother, Joseph, and a number of old friends among them, Crockett tarried through a night of eating and conversation before entering the fort where provisions abounded. He regained his strength and then started home on a furlough.

It was February, some six weeks before his enlistment was to expire, but he had a reason for returning to the farm, one reflecting so badly on him in retrospect that he would obscure the chronology of events, making it impossible to place them in proper sequence. But it is clear that Polly had been wasting away through much of the winter with a disease, like malaria, and that within weeks of David's homecoming, if not before, she was dead.[15] She was only twenty-seven, married less than nine years, the mother of three children, a woman who had moved into a strange country to make a new life and watched her husband twice go off to war against her wishes.

Crockett described her death as "the hardest trial which ever falls to the lot of man," and he refused to give a date for it because as a politician years after the event, he was open to charges that he had left Polly alone to die while he played soldier.[16] Accused at that time of leaving his second wife alone while he roamed—albeit practicing politics rather than waging war—he had an added incentive to conceal the facts. He was thoughtless and callous, not intentionally cruel, without the temperament or ability to take on the work of raising a family. When he confronted the difficulty after Polly's death, he found himself incapable of running the farm and caring for the children without assistance—precisely what he had demanded of Polly. He brought his brother Joseph and his wife to live with him but soon found them wanting. Although they were good with the children, the company they provided, he said, "fell short of being like that of a wife."[17]

In death, Polly had succeeded at last in keeping David from war. Called back for a final sweep along the Black Warrior and Cahaba rivers in Alabama in late February, he paid a young neighbor to fill out his term, a common practice. He knew that there were no hostile Indians in the area and had no desire to repeat his adventures of the previous five months. He had experienced far more hardship than glory and discovered that war matters "have no fun in them at all."[18] Hiring the surrogate did not prevent him from receiving his discharge and pay in Nashville on March 27, 1815, as a sergeant, third class.[19] His pay was eleven dollars a month, but without a travel and horse allowance, he made only $66.70—having served two extra days—scarcely a dollar more than during his three-month tour the year before. Ironically, when a neighbor who had been called up had approached him in September 1814 about taking his place for $100, Crockett had huffily refused, saying they both should serve. Recognizing his enthusiastic, if futile service, the Franklin County militia elected him lieutenant—his first public office—on May 22, 1815, scant consolation for his loss.

CHAPTER FOUR

AN ADVANTAGEOUS MARRIAGE

By the few descriptions and portraits that date from more than a decade later, it is possible to surmise that Crockett at the age of twenty-nine was a hardy fellow, larger than average—standing one to two inches under six feet and weighing around 190 pounds. Stoutly built, with smallish hands, he was an active, powerful man, memorable by virtue of his size but not particularly striking or handsome. He had a sharp, thin but dominant nose, a pointed chin, long brown hair, and dark blue eyes. He was vain about his ruddy cheeks, which he considered his most distinctive physical characteristic and the expression of his good health. An extroverted fellow, he was adept at telling amusing tales, always ready for a corn shucking or house raising and generous to every friend in need. An industrious farmer, setting out fruit trees and tending his corn and grain, he was nonetheless easily distracted. He also craved the companionship of women and so set out to find himself another wife.

Living in the vicinity of his Rattlesnake Spring homestead was a young widow with two small children, nearly the same ages as Crockett's second son, William, and daughter, Margaret. Born May 22, 1788, the same year as Polly, in Swannanoa, North Carolina, to a successful farmer and Revolutionary War veteran, Robert Patton—probably not quite a planter, if one takes twenty slaves as the minimum for that distinction—Elizabeth Patton had married her first cousin, James, the son of Robert's brother, Elijah, and moved with him to Franklin County, Tennessee, about the same time the Crocketts settled there.[1] James Patton had died in the Creek War at a place and time unrecorded, leaving his widow and children, George and Margaret Ann, "a snug little farm," on which they lived "quite comfortable."[2] By a number of accounts, Elizabeth was a large, industrious, and frugal woman, possessing in addition to her farm, eight hundred dollars cash, a large sum on the frontier.

No marriage license exists, but it appears that sometime early in the summer of 1815, David married Elizabeth in a ceremony at her farm attended by families and friends. This time he gained a sizable dowry, without which his subsequent career would have been impossible.[3] Through Elizabeth, he acquired far more than the two hundred acres needed to qualify for admission to the state legislature and then Congress, in addition to her cash and other possessions, the law being such that the property of the wife became that of her husband. To avoid the appearance of being a fortune hunter and to present himself publicly as the poor farmer who had risen in the world against the odds and by his own good luck, expert hunting, and industry, Crockett did no more than indirectly acknowledge his debt to her. While serving in the legislature a half-dozen years later, for example, he cast a noble light on the act, encouraging his fellow Tennesseans to marry widows in order to care for them and their children and thus keep them from becoming wards of the state, while recognizing that many of them, like Elizabeth, owned farms or businesses or had other ready assets that made them highly desirable to men seeking to improve their stations.[4] In fact, there were more reasons to act quickly, if one were courting a widow—any woman, for that matter, since they were not plentiful—than slowly.

Crockett comically affirmed his new position as head of the house at the wedding. As the guests sat in Elizabeth's cabin, awaiting her entrance, a pet pig wandered through the door. Crockett immediately herded it back out with the ribald comment: "Old hook, from now on, I'll do the grunting around here."[5] He and Elizabeth added four children of their own to their combined family—Robert Patton in 1816; Elizabeth Jane, 1818; Rebeckah Elvira, 1819; and Matilda, 1821. At various times, their immediate household would also include nephews, nieces, in-laws, farmhands, and several young slave girls, who apparently were trained as house servants and then sold.

The nature of the Crocketts' relationship can only be inferred from silence, odd scraps of information, and census data. Picking up on rumors and whispers and interpreting the bits and pieces to fit their schemes, some biographers have argued that by 1830 the marriage was an empty shell, with David and Elizabeth living in separate houses. Indeed, no correspondence between them exists, nor is any extant between David and their children, but comments scattered through the letters of Crockett to various friends, members of Elizabeth's family, and his children by Polly that have survived indicate that he felt strong affection toward her. As the family moved from Franklin County west to Shoal Creek and west again to Gibson and Weakley counties, Elizabeth helped establish and then ran their farms and mills profitably, and she raised nine children, receiving more support from relatives than from her husband. David spent most of each year campaigning, hunting, and serving his terms in the state legislature and Congress, working at the farm only on those occasions when he was home. Although it must have often been a trying situation, they both appear to have accepted it as the price for his public service. Whether they did so gladly or even with equanimity is impossible to say.

The family was not entirely blissful, to be sure, but the disagreements did not result in its dissolution. When Elizabeth objected strongly to his heavy drinking in the late 1820s, he quit, albeit belatedly. She opposed his decision to go to Texas in 1835, but could not dissuade him from the journey that led to his death. Fragments of information hint of friction between David and the children over his absenteeism, especially after he became a national celebrity. The extended family in which they were raised must have provided some compensation for his long absences. Uncles and aunts were always around, as were other children. Whatever his shortcomings as a husband and father, it is clear that David was a stalwart companion. He quickly formed and maintained through twenty often turbulent years strong friendships with members of Elizabeth's family, especially her brother George and brother-in-law Abner Burgin.

Early in the fall of 1815, Crockett left his new wife and expanded family to explore Alabama with three of his neighbors—identified only as Frazier, Robinson, and Rich. He said that his farm was sickly, and we can surmise that he was referring both to poor soil and to what at the time was called miasma, the swamp gases believed to cause malaria. The guess was close enough, because if one drained the wetlands, one killed the mosquitoes that bore the disease. The solution for the peripatetic frontiersman was to leave.

Intent on reaching the Black Warrior River near the town Coffee's troops had destroyed in the bloody attack two years earlier, the party traveled along the military road cut during that conflict through what became known as Jones Valley, after an early settler. A few Tennessee families were already scattered through the former Creek territory, making it a little less forbidding to farmers, who preferred supply lines and neighbors to absolute wilderness.[6] Near the cabin of one of Crockett's friends, where the party had stopped for food and rest, Frazier went hunting and was bitten by a poisonous snake—probably a diamondback rattlesnake or a copperhead, both of which abounded in the area. Less fatal than frequently imagined, if promptly treated, their bites nonetheless could make a person sick for several weeks. Frazier being no exception, the travelers left him behind to recover.

At the Black Warrior River, the snakebit expedition again suffered a setback when the hobbled horses crabbed off for Tennessee, bells clanging, several hours before dawn. The overconfident men waited for the sun before sending Crockett to fetch them back. Burdened with his rifle, "which was a very heavy one," he followed their tracks and bells up hill, down dale, through creeks and bogs for what he later estimated to be fifty miles without once catching sight of them. Exhausted, he spent the night at a cabin he had passed, and the next day on the way back to his companions, he suffered a full-blown attack of malaria—fever, headache, pains, weakness, and fatigue. He collapsed along the trail, unable to proceed.

A small party of Creek Indians offered him a melon and, seeing that he could not eat it, signed that they believed he was going to die. Frightened, he asked—apparently having learned sign language during his military service—that they take him to the closest cabin and then paid a half-dollar to the one who assisted him. The next day, two of his Tennessee neighbors, hearing of his illness on their way south, stopped and agreed to carry him back to his camp. When his condition worsened, Robinson and Rich took him to yet another cabin, where they purchased new horses for themselves and left him in the care of the family. Mrs. Jesse Jones nursed him for two weeks, during which he was speechless—probably semiconscious—for five days and so close to death that in desperation she fed him a bottle of Batesman's draps, a patent medicine with a large component of alcohol. The fever broke and Crockett slowly began to recover.

A passing teamster brought Crockett to within twenty miles of his home, then rented him a horse for the remainder of his journey. Crockett said, "I was so pale, and so much reduced, that my face looked like it had been half soled with brown paper."[7] To Elizabeth, he appeared a ghost, for his erstwhile neighbors upon arriving back in Tennessee had told her that her new husband was dead. In their effort to justify to themselves their bad form in abandoning their sick companion, they assured her that they had met men on the trail who had heard his last words and buried him. Crockett said, "I know'd that was a whapper of a lie, as soon as I heard it."[8]

Having lost one husband and with no reason to suspect the truth, Elizabeth had hired a man to retrieve David's horse, money, and possessions. He returned several weeks after Crockett's reappearance with the news that he lived. The events were not uncommon along the frontier where communication was uncertain and people could range from steadfast Good Samaritans, like the Jones family, to inconsistent liars like Robinson and Rich, to every variety of no-count thief and derelict. Sometimes it took a crisis to expose their character.

Rejecting Alabama as no more healthy than the area around Bean's Creek, Crockett set out the next fall for Chickasaw territory in south-central Tennessee, opened formally on September 20, 1816, by way of a treaty signed on behalf of the United States by Andrew Jackson and two other negotiators. Crockett got as far as Shoal Creek, eighty miles from his home, when he again fell ill with ague and fever from sleeping on the damp ground, he thought, although possibly it was a mild relapse of malaria. Too weak to press on, he explored the immediate countryside and was well enough pleased to settle there.

Today there is a David Crockett State Park outside Lawrenceburg with a reconstructed waterwheel of the sort used in gristmills and a rather curious display of Crockett-period memorabilia and facts. A visitor can see a stuffed black bear, which is closely identified with Crockett the hunter, although, ironically, he seems not to have focused too heavily on hunting during those years, his business enterprises and political activities consuming most of his time. More impressive than the display is the beauty of Shoal Creek, a broad, fast, fairly shallow, clear waterway, and the surrounding countryside with its rolling hills and pastures. Lawrenceburg, a several-hour drive south of Nashville, features a bronze statue of Crockett in the town square, modeled after a famous portrait by John Gadsby Chapman and erected in 1922, as well as several other plaques and markers in the surrounding area. Like the park, which opened in 1959, several of these memorials owe their existence to Disney's Davy.

The Crocketts moved either late in 1816 or early in 1817 after selling and leasing their Franklin County farms.[9] Crockett and Polly had worked approximately twenty acres, while Elizabeth and James Patton probably had held several hundred, with much of that uncleared. A man named James Penn leased thirty-eight improved acres for $2.50 an acre or $95.00 a year for two years beginning on January 1, 1817. As an incentive, the Crocketts discounted his rent to $76.00 the first year in exchange for a lump-sum cash payment in December 1816. Even that was a good price for them, given that unimproved public land was selling for $1.25 an acre.[10] If they made as much profit on the rest of the land, they would nearly have doubled Elizabeth's $800.00.

Many frontier communities were founded by small groups united by blood, marriage, and friendship, which, while not above bitter feuds, provided mutual support and assistance. The scant records that have been preserved indicate that, from the first days of their marriage, David and Elizabeth held in their orbit a sizable number of Crocketts and Pattons, which increased over the years as they moved across the state. A handful of Elizabeth and James Patton's siblings and spouses had migrated with them to Franklin County, including two sisters and their husbands: Ann and Hance McWhorter and Margaret and Abner Burgin. These couples and their children followed David and Elizabeth to Shoal Creek and then to West Tennessee six years later.

Shortly after Crockett first went to Congress in 1827, when it was clear he was a man of significant standing in the community, they were joined in West Tennessee by more of Elizabeth's sisters and their spouses; Matilda and James Trospern, Rebecca and James Edmundson, and Sarah and William Edmundson (probably brother to James). Robert Patton, the family patriarch who had divided a thousand-acre warrant to establish farms for his children and their families in that region, joined them during the last years of his life. John and William Patton, who were cousins—and perhaps brothers-in-law—of Elizabeth also had farms nearby. David referred to each of the men as "Brother," which could have been either a vestige of his years with the Quaker John Kennedy or recognition that the two were brothers of Elizabeth's first husband James, the precise genealogy being difficult to trace in the absence of documents. At least one of Abner Burgin's brothers also lived in this interrelated community.

As many Crocketts as Pattons clustered around David and Elizabeth, although, with few exceptions, he was not as close to them as he was to her relatives. Giving up the tavern, John and Rebecca Crockett trailed their prosperous son and daughter-in-law to Shoal Creek and again to West Tennessee, where they lived until their deaths with one of several of their daughters who had made the same move, as had Joseph Crockett and his family. On September 6, 1819, David guaranteed a marriage bond in Lawrence County for John Foster and Rebecca Crockett, who appears to have been a niece or cousin. David B. Crockett, a deserter from the War of 1812 who had settled in Fentress County, and several members of his family also followed their famous cousin to Gibson County sometime in the late 1820s or early 1830s. By then, David's children by Polly and Elizabeth's by James were grown and starting families of their own.

Appearing in the 1820 census for Lawrence County was a man named Yarnell Reece, who remained closely associated with Crockett for the next fifteen years. In 1831, he entered a two-hundred-acre claim in the Weakley County Occupant Entry Book on Crockett's behalf, and several times he served with him on road survey committees, or "juries of view," charged with siting roads through the unbroken country. Reece, who was probably a brother-in-law of David, is a cypher on government lists, bereft of context or family except when he enters the orbit of the famous man. Among the other names that crop up frequently in relation to Crockett is that of Olley Blakemore or Blackmore, who died in 1827, with David owing his estate $62.375—half cents being measured—from three loans in the summer and fall of 1823.

That same year, while serving his second term in the state legislature, Crockett engineered the appointment of Blakemore, Reece, Abner Burgin, and William Patton as justices of the peace in Gibson and Carroll counties, just after the entire clan had migrated to West Tennessee, a move that greatly increased its influence over local affairs. His relatives in turn provided him with a network of financial and familial support—his own backwoods political machine—working campaigns, distributing political tracts in his absence, helping with his farm and transportation as he traveled to and from Washington or around the district.

In January 1829, for example, Crockett complained to Elizabeth's brother George in Swannanoa, North Carolina, about a young man who brought his mare back from Washington to Weakley County and then charged John Patton twenty dollars for the service, an amount he considered outrageous.[11] He also described how William Patton had proposed trading a "negro boy" for the same horse and $150, a deal he considered unfair because he could purchase a slave for less than that amount in Washington and, in any event, he wanted to breed the mare and so had no intention of selling her. On other occasions, he sold small parcels of land or slaves to various of the Pattons to raise cash to pay off debts or to campaign. The McWhorters, for example, bought the first house that he and Elizabeth had occupied in West Tennessee, while George Patton bought some land and a slave girl. These transactions, together with loans and direct patronage from family and friends like Blakemore and Marcus Winchester, the Memphis merchant, helped sustain Crockett's political career through victory and defeat. His constituents expected him to serve them in return for their support, but there is no evidence that Crockett ever struck corrupt bargains with any of them.

Politics was not an activity for poor men. A congressional campaign, even the sort of shoe-string operation Crockett often conducted, cost several thousand dollars. The expense of life in Washington City, taking into consideration lodging, food, clothes, and entertainment, could easily far outstrip the eight dollars a day paid to the members of Congress. Crockett himself could be profligate—buying drinks at every opportunity, gambling, and helping out people in need—and frequently stretched his resources beyond their limit. But he also possessed a dread of debt, instilled in him from his experiences with his father, which both restrained his tendency toward profligacy and drove him always to seek more money. He complained so loudly and so frequently about his lack of resources, despite Elizabeth's frugality and excellent management of their affairs, that it is difficult ever to determine just how solvent the family was. Certainly, they began with a solid financial base, and despite some setbacks, they never faced bankruptcy because of mismanagement. Nor were they ever so poor, even during several national economic depressions, that Crockett had to abandon politics or curb his other activities.

Yet eight consecutive biennial campaigns—six of them for Congress and four of those in one of the nation's largest districts—as well as the responsibilities of office and celebrity, took their toll on what was a small farm compared with the plantations and private fortunes of many of his colleagues. A wealthy planter could own thousands of acres and upward of one hundred slaves, whereas the Crocketts owned and leased five hundred to a thousand acres and held three or four slaves at a time. They generally had an equal number of indentured and paid white farmhands. Like many of the planters they sought to become, the Crocketts speculated in land in Lawrence County and in the western counties of Gibson and Weakley. They would purchase and improve a parcel, then move to it and sell or lease their old farm. David had made the leap from tenant to yeoman through his marriage, but no matter how hard he and Elizabeth tried, they could not take the next step, from the middle to the upper, or planter, class. David's ambition to cross that elusive line led him to Texas in 1835, where he aimed to acquire a large parcel to develop for himself and sell to his friends.

Near the headwaters of Shoal Creek, three miles from the present site of Lawrenceburg, the Crocketts erected the first of the three cabins they would build, occupy, and sell over the next six years. These were rough-hewn log homes, averaging 500 to 1,000 square feet, depending on how one counted the sleeping areas upstairs, not manor houses to be sure, and crowded for a large family, but more substantial than many cabins of the period. With large fireplaces for heat and cooking, they were sparsely furnished and contained few amenities or extraneous goods. By 1820, the Crocketts owned 614 acres on thirteen different tracts, a water-powered gristmill, a gunpowder factory, a distillery, and an iron-ore mine, making them substantial players in the local economy. The mill, probably managed by Elizabeth, was one of six in the area; the distillery and gunpowder factory were without competition.

Each pound of gunpowder provided ninety-six shots for the typical muzzle-loader and brought $0.37 a pound or $0.004 a shot. Crockett's mill could produce close to 7,500 pounds of powder a year at a value of nearly $2,800.[12] His own slaves supplied most of the labor, although he also hired extra hands—either white men or slaves belonging to someone else—when necessary. He would have paid the men or the owners no more than $80.00 a piece for an entire year, leaving a tidy profit. Crockett's distillery would have cost less to operate and earned even more, the national excise tax on whiskey, levied to pay for the War of 1812, having been repealed in 1817. The mill could grind 13.5 bushels of corn a day when properly operating, most of which became whiskey.

Although the Crocketts brought substantial resources to their business ventures, they borrowed to construct them—against property, crops, or future products, making repayment little more than a matter of chance. Along the frontier debt was constant—Andrew Jackson, for example, faced chronic money problems, and he was a planter with one hundred slaves and thousands of acres. Land, slaves, timber, hides, crops, livestock, promissory notes—all served at various times in lieu of money, always in short supply.

Crockett enjoyed boasting that he and his family lived at the headwaters of Shoal Creek for two to three years "without any law at all; and so many bad characters began to flock in upon us, that we found it necessary to set up a sort of temporary government of our own."[13] They appointed constables and magistrates—Crockett among them—and set to work maintaining order through vigilante justice. "If any one was charged with marking his neighbour's hogs," Crockett said, "or with stealing any thing, which happened pretty often in those days,—I would have him taken, and if there was tolerable grounds for the charge, I would have him well whip'd and cleared."[14] Making the statements in his autobiography in 1834, Crockett was playing to the public opinion of his day rather than recounting the history of Lawrence County. His readers immediately recognized an allusion to the redoubtable "Judge Lynch," who rode in the South as a regulator, usually to beat slaves into submission or intimidate whites who supported abolition, but also to dispense vigilante justice—swift, brutal, unfettered by legal niceties. At the same time, Crockett was invoking the expired Watauga Association and the strong western tradition of independence and self-rule to show his own power and accomplishment.

He and his relatives were on Shoal Creek for less than a year before the Tennessee legislature incorporated Lawrence County in October 1817. The following month it confirmed Crockett as one of the county's first twelve magistrates. Until court sessions began in the spring of 1818, the Crockett-Patton clique, with the personable David at its head, may have run a rough form of administration to guard its interests in the newly opened country, but it certainly did not approach a self-organized government. The Crocketts and Pattons continued as powers in Lawrence County until their move west five years later, with David also serving as state representative, county commissioner, and colonel in the local militia, while acting, when needed, as court referee and juror.

As county commissioner, he performed tasks that might loosely be defined as planning and zoning. In April 1818, for example, he took depositions in an ownership dispute over four thousand acres of land on Indian Creek initially surveyed in 1784 or '85, when the area was home to Indians and North Carolina authorities were intent on awarding it to Revolutionary War veterans. In the interim, the name of the creek had changed, and the land had come into the possession of Galbreath Falls, who had in turn bequeathed it to his daughter or widow, Isabella, the records being unclear about her relationship. James Kerr protested before the will was probated that he held prior title, so John Simonton, the executor of the estate, asked the commissioners to adjudicate. Their first task involved determining whether the two tracts were, in fact, the same. The few living witnesses Crockett interviewed asserted they were, and although the final judgment is lost to history, it appears that they decided in favor of Kerr. On another occasion, Crockett was involved in selecting the site for an ironworks, probably related to the mine he owned, the line between public and private business being poorly defined.

About a year after moving to Lawrence County, Crockett made his second and boldest foray to date into electoral politics. An early settler, wealthy farmer, and former army captain named Matthews came to him one day and announced that he intended to run for colonel of the militia regiment being formed in accordance with the law and wanted David to run for first major with him. Neglecting to mention that he had been elected lieutenant in the Franklin County militia, Crockett told Matthews "that I thought I had done my share of fighting, and that I wanted nothing to do with military appointments."[15] Matthews continued to press him, however, and, finally convinced of his support in the canvass, Crockett relented.

Matthews then hosted a cornhusking and frolic at his farm to kick off the campaign. On his arrival, Crockett learned that the captain planned to renege on his agreement and endorse his son for major. When confronted, Matthews admitted that his son was running and confessed that he had come up with the ruse because he had feared that Crockett would campaign against him for colonel, which is exactly what the offended, reluctant candidate then decided to do, purely, he said, because he had gotten his "dander up high enough to see."[16] Completing his speech, Matthews informed the crowd that Crockett was his new opponent, and David "told the people the cause of my opposing him, remarking that as I had the whole family to run against any way, I was determined to levy on the head of the mess."[17] Both father and son lost, and the once-starving soldier became officially lieutenant colonel commandant in the newly formed 57th Regiment of Militia—forever Colonel David Crockett.

Crockett made a habit of filling posts for which he had no experience and then boasting of his accomplishments, masking his insecurity with bravado. Thus, he liked to proclaim that none of the judgments he made while magistrate were appealed because he was so fair and just, despite having never studied law. What scant evidence exists suggests that he handled commonplace matters well and was never challenged with more complex questions of law. His most difficult case came early in his tenure when he was asked to decide between David Welch and William White on the ownership of a number of butchered hogs. Crockett ordered Welch to compensate White for the hogs he had taken, and then declared that the two men should share the court costs because White had failed to register his brand with the county, as required by law.[18] He also issued licenses, performed marriages, certified bounties for wolves, collected money for the support of a "bastard child" from the father, and compiled a list of property owners—for taxes—and voters, which in 1819 amounted to seventy names. Unsavory characters skulked the countryside, as Crockett said, but they were seldom arrested—much less punished—for the crimes, often thefts, they committed in that jurisdiction.

Crockett resigned as justice of the peace on November 1, 1819, to focus on business. In 1817, the newly opened Second Bank of the United States, chartered by the Congress as the nation's official bank, had launched a drive to establish hard money in place of the paper scrip offered by various local banks that was fueling land speculation in the West. Within a year, banks all along the frontier were thrown into disarray, with many collapsing as full-fledged panic broke out at the beginning of 1819. The nation was thrown into a depression that lasted six years. The collapse cut short the credit that speculators like Crockett—and on a much larger scale, Andrew Jackson— needed to operate. Some people, like Jackson, were forced to call in loans in order to meet their own expenses, while others were forced to renege. Crockett scrambled against the depression and problems inherent in starting new enterprises. On October 23, 1820, he wrote to J. C. McLemore about payments he owed on two parcels of land—one of 320 acres and the other of 60 acres—asking for an extension: "I have been detained longer than I expected my powder factory have not been pushed as it ought and I will not be able to meet my contract with you but if you send me a three-hundred acer warrant by the male I will pay you interest for the money until paid."[19] As soon as the factory became operational, he thought, he would have no difficulty in repaying the debt.

He must have had some success, because by the beginning of 1821 he had decided to run for the state House of Representatives, his victorious run for militia colonel having whetted his appetite for politics. He had found his calling. Resigning as county commissioner in early March, he immediately drove a herd of horses to the Swannanoa, North Carolina, farm of his father-in-law, Robert Patton. The journey took three months and numbered among its stops one in East Tennessee to settle an outstanding debt. Passing by Morristown, Crockett visited a widow and presented the startled woman with one dollar, the amount he had borrowed from her husband more than fifteen years earlier, before his marriage to Polly. She had forgotten the loan.[20]

CHAPTER FIVE

THE CAMPAIGNER

B y June 1821, Crockett was back home and stumping for the state legislature in Lawrence and Hickman counties, trying on the role of the naïve but savvy backwoodsman he would perfect during the next fifteen years. His trademark style was an unstructured blend of outlandish boasts, amusing anecdotes, and vitriolic attacks, laced with mockery—a far remove from the stylized orations favored by the majority of candidates, who were intent on showing their erudition. The masters of the form, such as Henry Clay, Daniel Webster, and Edward Everett—the father of the Classical Revival, which, in its most visible manifestation, brought forth cities with such names as Athens, Rome, and Troy in every state in the union—regularly captivated their audiences. Lesser orators more commonly bored them into submission. Crockett's opponents, who never ignored an opportunity to impugn his character, found his style appalling. His supporters loved it.

Unfortunately, the characteristics that made him a popular campaigner militated against his being taken seriously as a public official. Later in his career, when he lost his sense of humor and let rancor rule his response to political attacks, he lost influence and elections. His bile turned him into a self-parody.

Crockett boasted when he began his first campaign that he had never read as much as a newspaper in his life and had scant idea about the government—neither what it was nor how it worked. In Hickman County, "they told me that they wanted to move their town nearer to the centre of the county, and I must come out in favour of it. There's no devil if I knowed what this meant, or how the town was to be moved; and so I kept dark, going on the identical same plan that I now find is called *'non-committal.'* "[1]

A short while later, back in Vernon, then the seat of Hickman County, the voters pressed Crockett to take a stand, demanding that he speak at a barbecue featuring all the other candidates, including those for governor and Congress, a prospect that made him "weak in the knees." The other candidates orated all day. Realizing the audience was as restive as he, Crockett, the last speaker, "got up and told some laughable story and quit."[2] From the crowd's howls of approval, the novice concluded that he had won their votes.

In Lawrence County, between forays into Hickman, candidate Crockett found himself invited to a squirrel hunt one Saturday on the Duck River. The team collecting the fewest skins, or scalps, had to pay for the barbecue and frolic that followed. A ringer brought on at the last moment because of his candidacy, he led his team to victory over that of his political opponent. Annoyed, the loser incited the crowd to demand a speech from Crockett before the dancing began. "The truth is," David said, "he thought my being a candidate was a mere matter of sport; and didn't think, for a moment, that he was in any danger from an ignorant back-woods bear hunter."[3] His performance became legendary:

> I got up and told the people, I reckoned they know'd what I come for, but if not, I could tell them. I had come for their votes, and if they didn't watch mighty close, I'd get them too. But the worst of all was, that I couldn't tell them anything about government. I tried to speak about something, and I cared very little what, until I choked up as bad as if my mouth had been jam'd and cram'd chock full of dry mush. There the people stood, listening all the while,

with their eyes, mouths, and years all open, to catch every word I would speak.

At last I told them I was like a fellow I had heard of not long before. He was beating on the head of an empty barrel near the road-side, when a traveler, who was passing along, asked him what he was doing that for? The fellow replied, that there was some cider in that barrel a few days before, and he was trying to see if there was any then but if there was he couldn't get at it. I told them that there had been a little bit of a speech in me a while ago, but I believed I couldn't get it out.[4]

The assembly roared its delight. With impeccable timing, Crockett "took care to remark that I was as dry as a powder horn, and I thought it was time for us all to wet our whistles a little; and so I put off to the liquor stand, and was followed by the greater part of the crowd."[5] It is quite possible that, as owner of the county's only distillery, he had supplied the spirits. In any event, he had succeeded not only in amusing the throng but also in carrying to the table the greater part of the audience for his competitor. Telling more anecdotes, occasionally drinking, Crockett made sure the people stayed away until his rival finished his speech.

By such tactics, the upstart won by a two-to-one margin and set out for Murfreesboro, south of Nashville, for the two-month legislative session beginning September 17.[6] He was assigned to the Committee on Propositions and Grievances, which took up issues ranging from land ownership to relief for individuals in financial distress because of a death in the family or sudden setback. Addressing everything from petitions for divorce and for the right of individual widows and divorced women to hold property and incur debt independent of a man, to propositions for a constitutional convention, taxes, and wrangles over mineral and water rights, the legislature actively intruded into nearly every aspect of social life. It also appointed local officials, set county and town boundaries, elected the state's governor and its U.S. senators, to whom it regularly sent voting instructions. Senators who could not in good conscience follow those orders often either resigned or were recalled.

Self-conscious and insecure, Crockett nonetheless made his presence known in the opening days of the session. He had just finished addressing the House on a piece of pending legislation—perhaps a bill to release landowners in the depressed Western District from paying a penalty on delinquent 1820 taxes—in his typically twisted syntax, when James C. Mitchell from East Tennessee rose and disparagingly referred to him as the "gentleman from the cane," roughly equivalent to calling someone today "Sir Redneck" or "Lord Bubba."[7] Crockett protested in the chamber and then, accosting Mitchell outside, demanded that he apologize or fight. Mitchell said he had meant no insult and left, assuming the matter was dead.

Finding a cambric ruffle, an adornment of fine fabric favored by his opponent, Crockett affixed it to his shirt and went back to the session. After Mitchell had delivered a speech, Crockett stood up and puffed out his chest, as if preparing a rebuttal. Before he uttered a sound, the legislators, seeing his garb, broke into laughter, and Mitchell fled the floor, leaving the "gentleman from the cane" victorious.

Although not a particularly active or effective legislator in his inaugural term, Crockett revealed himself to be a champion of the poor and disadvantaged, consistently voting for or introducing proposals to protect them from laws he felt were unjust or discriminatory. He considered poor farmers his people, and he sometimes so fixedly defended their interests that he lost important support from other constituents. Early in his first session, he voted for William Carroll, who was running for governor as a champion of debtors, despite the opposition of his mentor, Jackson, who as a matter of temperament feared the "undisciplined rising of the masses."[8] Continuing his support of the poor, Crockett also joined the majority in voting down a proposal to hire out insolvent debtors to recover the costs of criminal prosecutions against them.

Within two weeks of his arrival, Crockett inserted himself into the interminable debate over North Carolina claims to Tennessee land. He introduced a bill to protect the land of settlers living west and south of the Congressional Reservation Line from expropriation by holders of North Carolina warrants. Basically the Tennessee River, the reservation line initially separated territory the United States had purchased from the Chickasaw from the pool available to North Carolinians with Revolutionary War warrants. But in 1818, the state had petitioned that the Western District be opened for that purpose, and Congress agreed to release some of its territory, while retaining the rest. It had become common practice for warrant holders to piece together their thousand acres—or whatever total—from prime soils, leaving aside parcels deemed unsuitable for agriculture. As plantation slavery spread west, the practice became even more onerous, so that surveyors would place dozens of noncontiguous plots on a single warrant, whose holders would then claim prior title and move to force off the occupants. In some areas, those settlers had the "right of first refusal," but it was common practice for the claimants to set a price too high for them to match and then either turn them into tenant farmers or force them to leave.

The continued appearance of these warrants into the 1820s was due to two factors, only one of which the Tennesseans readily admitted. First, North Carolina officials were scanning the muster rolls for deceased veterans with no heirs, then issuing warrants in their names to the state university for redemption and sale. Second, speculators in Tennessee and North Carolina were gaining other warrants through fraud and deceit and exercising them with regard only to their own profit. Sometimes warrants were trumping warrants! The pressure on the Western District was exacerbated by the fact that Tennessee had bargained with the national government to keep out of the claims pool a parcel in the northeast part of the state purchased from the Cherokee in 1819. Thus, the Western District represented the last large tract of fertile land in the state.

Crockett's clever partial solution to the problem was to make it a misdemeanor for surveyors south and west of the Congressional Reservation Line to make multiple entries on a warrant or certificate—thereby forcing the holder to take a single block of land rather than several small parcels—with the penalty for violation being removal from office, a fine of $1,000 to $5,000, and imprisonment for not less than a year. He later incorporated a Tennessee Senate proposal prohibiting any existing warrant in those areas from being voided in favor of an earlier one. Penalties for violating that provision were removal from office, the same fine, but no more than a year in jail.

Both provisions alleviated the fear of expropriation among people with title to their lands, but they did not address the broader problem of providing farms for squatters, people without money or warrants who had been driven steadily westward by the endless claims. As Crockett regularly pointed out, these people were forced on to ever more marginal plots—rocky hilltops, bits and odd scraps that planters did not want.

Crockett's interest in the Western District, to which he was planning a move, directed most of his votes and activities, but in general the term hardly marked him as a major player among his colleagues. He was new, and he was distracted by the process of legislation, the social life of the politician in the capital, and major problems at home. After a twelve-day leave of absence following Carroll's election as governor, he returned in time to participate in a joint session of the House and Senate to debate calling a convention to rewrite the outdated Constitution of 1796. Those seeking a new document were concerned primarily that the Western District was seriously underrepresented and that property taxes, which assigned an equal value to all parcels, were inherently unfair. A hardscrabble farmer would pay as much for unproductive soil as the owner of a fecund plantation or a city home. The planters of East and Middle Tennessee adamantly opposed the changes and ensured that the two-thirds majority of both houses needed to convene a new convention would not be achieved. Not until 1832 did Tennessee gain a new constitution, and that one was favorable to the ruling planters.

* * *

During the second session of the Fourteenth General Assembly, called on July 22, 1822, Crockett was on the losing end of a vote to set a date after which the state would no longer honor North Carolina warrants and on the winning side of proposals to encourage ironworks; provide tax relief for Mathias, a free man of color, and other constituents; and prevent fraud in the recording of wills and testaments. He unsuccessfully opposed a measure that would have made it impossible to redeem slaves from bondage—although his sense of justice in that regard did not extend to opposition to the peculiar institution. He also voted with the minority to continue state assistance to the children and widows of veterans. He succeeded in gaining an adjustment to the boundaries of Lawrence County and having the seventh-district surveyor moved to Lawrenceburg, classic pork-barrel politics. But he failed when he finally took a stand on the great debate in Hickman County and proposed that the county seat remain at Vernon. It was moved to Centerville.

Near the close of the special session, Crockett delivered a speech against allowing magistrates to accept fees from lawsuits over which they had presided. Throughout Tennessee, unscrupulous justices of the peace and constables had been soliciting people to file civil cases in their courts and then collecting a percentage of the settlement from the successful litigants. In an effort to force those corrupt officials from office, reformers, including Crockett, had succeeded in abolishing those fees, only to face a drive to restore them. Crockett's remarks against the practice were reported in the *Nashville Whig* of August 14, 1822, marking the first time he had received press attention and indicating that he had begun to make a reputation for himself in the raucous world of Tennessee politics. The *Whig* said:

> He [Crockett] hoped the bill would not pass; he hoped it would be killed dead in its tracks. "There never had been a law repealed with so much propriety, or which resulted in so much good for the peace of society, as the repeal of the justices' out-of-door fees. It was said in favor of reviving

the fees, that under the constitution, the service of no man should, or ought, in any case, to be required without compensation. Do you pay men for performing militia duty? Magistrates are exempt from militia duty and working on roads, and this is as much compensation as they deserve. I know many of these *gentry*, who would rather serve *forty years* as a justice of the peace, than to serve one six month's tour of duty fighting the battles of their country. 'The dull pursuits of civil life' is much more congenial to the taste of some of these gentlemen than 'wild war's deadly blasts!' And then the *honor* of the office is no small consideration. I concur with the gentleman from Campbell [County], that there is no evil so great in society—among the poor people—as the management and intrigue of meddling justices and dirty constables. I have seen more peace and harmony among my constituents since the repeal of the fees, than I had seen for several years before. I do most earnestly hope that the house will be unanimous in putting the bill to instant death."

The former justice of the peace, Colonel Crockett, had the last word and carried the day.

A vote from the first session of the Fourteenth Assembly on a curious bill introduced by Felix Grundy, a surrogate for Andrew Jackson, who directed his partisans from the Hermitage, his plantation outside Nashville, parts slightly the curtain obscuring much of Crockett's personal life. He voted with the majority against a proposal to "suppress the vice of gaming," and whenever the issue arose thereafter he also cast his vote against the prohibition. Crockett was a man who liked to gamble, especially on cards—whist—and target shooting, even if he was not very successful. "At every session of the Legislature that Col. Crockett served in this state," said a pseudonymous adversary, Junius Brutus, in the Jackson *Southern Statesman* of July 9, 1831, "and at the first session of his service in Congress, he lost a part and sometimes the whole of his wages at the gaming table, and sometimes had to borrow money to bring him home, and some of that money is not paid yet." Brutus added that he could produce evidence, should Crockett wish to sue, but the man who was quick to refute every charge in that hard-fought election did not answer.

Families seldom accompanied the men to the legislature and Congress, and so they played in their off hours. They met to drink and continue debate over politics, to tell stories, to play cards, or they would visit with the ladies, including prostitutes. A good fellow, Crockett was one of the chief sources of entertainment for his friends. He drank mightily at times, but he did not gamble for the stakes of his more wealthy contemporaries. For example, until after the War of 1812, when he was drawing the salary of a brigadier general, Jackson supported the Hermitage through horse racing. The difference in scale is illustrative of the gulf between the planter and the yeoman: Jackson would bet thousands on a single match race, while Crockett appears to have played for hundreds, $273.60 being his pay for the first session of the Fourteenth General Assembly; $564.00 for both sessions of the Fifteenth. Given the size of his family and other financial obligations, those were significant amounts to earn and lose, but they were not extraordinary.

Brutus's most damaging charge was that Crockett walked away from debts he incurred to cover his gambling losses, which served both to mark him as a slacker and reaffirm the opposition of many people to the activity as one that deprived a family of much-needed money. Given Crockett's abhorrence of unpaid debt, the complaint is hard to credit. It must be seen as a case of negative campaigning. In any event, while condemning Crockett's past, Brutus implicitly confirmed that he had reformed himself considerably—he had given up drinking hard liquor and gambling—in an attempt to gain control over his life.

Crockett had been in Murfreesboro for less than two weeks of his first session when he received word from home that a flash flood had destroyed his gristmill and powder factory. Without ground corn, his distillery also had to be shut down.

Taking a leave of absence on September 29, he hurried home to survey the damage to the structures, doubtless recalling along the way the fate of his father's mill and his subsequent fall into poverty, which for David was a continual fear. Living nearby, John Crockett made that fear palpable.

Elizabeth Crockett took command of the situation. The capital and labor for their ventures being largely hers, she had suffered the greater material loss. To compound her burdens, she had an infant to care for, Matilda, their last child, as well as two-year-old Rebeckah Elvira (Sissy) and three-year-old Elizabeth Jane; in fact, of their nine children, John Wesley was the oldest at fourteen. But she would not wallow in self-pity. Recognizing that if they rebuilt on the flood-prone creek, they would merely invite another disaster, she urged that they pay off their creditors and start over someplace else. " '[W]e will scuffle for more,' " he recalled her telling him.[9]

The task of determining the Crocketts' balance sheet in 1821 is impossible, but one can say that they possessed sufficient property in terms of land, slaves, and at least the distillery to meet all outstanding debts. Nonetheless, fearing they would be shut out, a number of creditors promptly filed lawsuits claiming the land Crockett had posted as collateral for his loans. Some of them sought to attach his "securities" or guarantors as well. Nearly a year later, Crockett would vote unsuccessfully to provide relief from such actions for people who guaranteed the debt of others.

A partial accounting of the known judgments against Crockett adds up to considerably less than the $3,000.00 value he had assigned to the enterprises, suggesting that Elizabeth's family might have invested in the mills and, therefore, absorbed some of the loss. The Crocketts also sold their slaves and additional properties to meet other obligations. Among those filing suit were Pressly Ward for $71.70 plus $1.43 in interest; John R. Crisp for $55.00 plus interest, which Crockett appealed; Burwell B. Quimby for $50.00 and interest, which also drew an appeal; and William F. Cunningham for $70.00 plus $1.40 in interest.[10] John Edmundson, a brother of Crockett's in-laws

James and William, forced the sale of some land, and two men, Reubin Trip and Thomas Pryer, either bought or gained possession of the Crockett home, while the family stayed for some months with one of Elizabeth's sisters. John Crisp was the brother or father of Mansil Crisp, who represented Crockett in the last of the lawsuits resulting from the disaster and succeeded him in the Tennessee House of Representatives. Crockett's biographer James Shackford calculated that 160 acres immediately adjacent to the Crockett home went to the satisfaction of their debts, leaving some 450 acres in Lawrence County, which they must have sold or leased in subsequent transactions.

The flood forced the Crocketts, who were already suffering from the region's economic depression, to take dramatic actions to cover their debts, but did not come close to throwing them into insolvency. In fact, their situation was in most respects less grievous than that of a number of more ostensibly wealthy people. At about the same time, for example, Sam Houston, deeply in debt and recently having resigned his commission in the army, sold all his property, including his land, and still failed to clear his obligations.[11] By 1823, he was in the United States Congress. What mattered on the frontier was one's ability to bounce back from disaster. Playing on that attitude, David liked to state years later that the flood had left him with nothing and he had remade himself, a political lie that most of his listeners accepted as truth.

Ironically, a misfortune continued to plague the Crockett name in Lawrence County, even into the twentieth century. In 1969, a fire ravaged the David Crockett Museum in Lawrenceburg, destroying many pieces of memorabilia relating to his five-year residence in the county.

The disaster convinced the Crocketts and their relatives that it was time to leave Lawrence County, and so David, his son John Wesley, and a young indentured servant named Abram Henry set out in November 1821—following adjournment of the legislature—for the Obion River in northwest Tennessee.

Part of the territory Jackson had purchased for the United States from the Chickasaw in 1818, the land lay in the Western District, whose interests Crockett had championed in Murfreesboro. The multichanneled river—comprised of four forks named North, Middle, South, and Rutherford's—cut through country that a decade earlier had been devastated by the New Madrid Earthquake, estimated to have been one of the largest ever to shake North America.

With an epicenter at New Madrid, Missouri, near that state's juncture with Kentucky and Tennessee, the first temblor occurred on December 11, 1811, and was followed by others on December 16 and 17, January 23, and February 7, 1812, with intermittent aftershocks for seven years. The powerful temblors of 1811–12 rocked cities as far away as Baltimore and New Orleans, obliterated and created lakes, and caused the Mississippi River temporarily to reverse its course. Chasms opened in the earth, trees were thrown to the ground and into rivers and streams, homes destroyed. The first steamboat on those waters, the *New Orleans,* which left Pittsburgh in 1811 and arrived at its home port on January 13, 1812, had a hellish ride through a haze of gas, steam, and dirt. Exploring this country, Crockett referred to the snarled timber and undergrowth as a "harricane," synonymous in his lexicon not only with earthquake, or "airthquake" but also with a violent thunderstorm— true hurricanes rarely penetrating that far inland.

During the winter of 1831–32, a sandbar formed in the Mississippi above Memphis, threatening river traffic and setting off a heated debate among its citizens over what to do. Crockett suggested that the city fathers "send up to New Madrid for a boat load of earthquake and sink the d——d thing."[12] Having been retired from Congress by the voters in August, Crockett was visiting friends and plotting his comeback in Memphis, a city that had always supported him politically.

"It was a complete wilderness," Crockett said of the land of shakes, "and full of Indians who were hunting. Game was plenty of almost every kind, which suited me exactly, as I was always fond of hunting."[13] He had staked a claim on the east side of

Rutherford's Fork, the southernmost branch of the Obion. Records of the transaction are apparently lost, but I believe this initial claim, of several that Crockett would enter in the area, was related to a one-thousand-acre North Carolina warrant that Elizabeth's father had decided to redeem on behalf of his children.

The Western District had been open to satisfaction of those warrants barely two years and was still sparsely populated. The act Crockett had just shepherded through the legislature, which prohibited anyone with a prior warrant from taking any land the family improved, made it enticing for the patriarch to exercise one he either had held since the Revolution or had purchased from a veteran or his heirs. Subdivision immediately would have provided Crockett, who was liquidating his Lawrence County holdings to satisfy creditors, with the requisite two hundred acres for qualifying for the state legislature. Other legislation would grant Crockett, as an occupant, certain rights to additional acres he claimed for himself, but with the possibility existing that the time limit for redeeming warrants would finally expire, he would want first to act on the Patton claim. Unquestionably, he was the advance guard for his extended family, which planned to join him in West Tennessee.

Having staked his claim, Crockett, his son, and Abram Henry set out to visit their neighbor, a "man named Owens," who lived seven miles away, on the far side of the South Fork, a rain-swollen, debris-choked, cold stretch of water. After wading, swimming, and at least once fashioning a bridge from a felled tree, the soaked and exhausted travelers reached the Owens's cabin, where they warmed themselves with fire and whiskey.

Leaving John Wesley with Mrs. Owen, Crockett and Henry joined Mr. Owens on board a boat moored nearby. "We staid all night with them," Crockett said, "and had a high night of it, as I took steam enough to drive out all the cold that was in me, and about three times as much more."[14] The next morning, he volunteered to help Owens and the crew take the boat, loaded with flour, coffee, sugar, whiskey, salt, and various other articles, up the Obion to McLemore's Bluff, probably named for the same J. C. McLemore from whom he had bought land in Lawrence County. When low water forced them to abandon that effort, Crockett persuaded the men to help him construct a rough log cabin with a porch across its length and a stone fireplace—sufficient until a larger home could be built. He then bartered flour, meal, salt, and whiskey from them in exchange for continuing to crew on the boat's ascent to the bluff, while his son and Henry stayed in the cabin. Crockett proved an indifferent boatman, opting to hunt while the other men dragged the craft through the dense mass of downed wood blocking their passage. He killed six bucks and managed the next day to redeem four.

Once the boat had made its landing, the captain loaned its skiff to Crockett, who started for home with a young crewman named Flavius Harris. The newcomer joined Henry as Crockett's hired hand and together the three men and John Wesley worked through spring to start a farm. Crockett also continued his hunting, killing by his count ten bears and "a great abundance of deer."[15]

Leaving his hands in charge of the cabin, he and John Wesley returned to Lawrenceburg, stopping in Nashville where a group of political supporters awarded Crockett a .41-caliber side-lock percussion Kentucky rifle made by James M. Graham of Pennsylvania. The inscription said simply: "Presented to David Crockett at Nashville, Tenn., May 5, 1822." Apparently, this was the gun that James Strange French in his 1833 biography called "Betsy"—now often "Old Betsy"—which was also a name used for Elizabeth Crockett. David carried the rifle with him during the years he solidified his reputation as a great hunter.

Following the special legislative session in July and August, a large contingent of Crocketts and Pattons set out for Rutherford's Fork and environs, with others moving as they wrapped up their business in Lawrence County. Robert Patton had subdivided his thousand acres into five farms for his daughters' families in what was then Carroll County. As the population grew, the legislature created Gibson and Weakley counties, whose boundary with Carroll cut through the Patton-Crockett farms. David and Elizabeth also purchased additional land and built new homes in each of the jurisdictions, leaving census takers, local officials, and the Crocketts themselves confused over which county was theirs, a circumstance that over the years has led some scholars to conclude erroneously that they maintained separate residences.

At the time of their settlement, the Obion River area was a region without roads, where travel by land or water was difficult because of the debris from the earthquakes and flash floods. Although the farms of the Crocketts and their relatives lay within a ten-mile radius, they were not always readily accessible. Crockett told of traveling six miles down and across Rutherford's Fork the first December they were there to pick up a keg of gunpowder. He arrived at the end of the day soaked and suffering from hypothermia, then had to wait several days for the weather to warm up enough for him to return. In the interim a worried Elizabeth sent one of the hands in search of him.

In the first years of settlement in West Tennessee, with their farms not yet fully productive and game abundant, Crockett and his fellow pioneers embraced the culture of the rifle, taking turkey, deer, elk, and bear for food and fur. Crockett developed a fixation on black bears, *Ursus americanus*. Smaller and less ferocious than its cousin the grizzly, the black bear was still capable of instilling fear and awe in those who encountered it. Almost humanlike in posture and appearance, it was fast, intelligent, and capable of maiming a hunter and his dogs when wounded. The man who brought down a bear was considered among the elite. Relentless in pursuit of his game and unwilling to let any bear that came into his sight escape, Crockett became known as one of the finest hunters in the territory. Contrary to legend, however, he was not the best marksman: A Gibson County sheriff named McLaurin defeated him in a shooting contest for a five-hundred-dollar prize, put up by the participants themselves.[16] Around Reelfoot Lake, Crockett and his companions established and abandoned a number of hunting camps—with stands, blinds, and rustic shelters—over the years, a practice that remains common in many rural areas.

Crockett turned his hunting adventures into the amusing and harrowing anecdotes that formed the core of his stump speeches early in his career. Later, when he began to feel more confident about issues—or at least sought to prove his familiarity with them—he used the tales as adornment and metaphor, the way his more learned colleagues used classical allusions. Told in his rough country syntax and vernacular, they were consistent crowd pleasers. In more literate form, they were presented in his *Narrative* before passing into the racist grotesqueries of the almanacs, produced without his knowledge or participation by illustrators and editors seeking to cash in on his fame. The transformations of adventures from the 1820s into tales of the 1830s, '40s, and '50s points to a change in attitudes toward hunting, as the increasingly settled eastern United States turned what had been necessity into blood sport in which game was taken not for meat but for pleasure. Along the Mississippi River, for example, men fired from the decks of steamboats at any creature they saw in the water or along the banks. Crockett's contribution to this ethos came through boasts about the number of bucks or bears he slaughtered in a day, week, or season of hunting—6 bucks in two days, 105 bears during the winter of 1825–26, which might indeed have accurately reflected the kill of a hardworking and profligate fur trader.

During a prolonged hunt in that winter, with several bear carcasses already in camp, Crockett took off one evening after his hounds, following them through dense thickets, over cracks formed by the earthquakes, across creeks. Although it was a cold day, he was soon drenched with perspiration and water. After dark, his dogs treed a bear, which he shot—twice. Before he could fire a third time, the bear dropped from its poplar into the midst of his dogs. After a melee, the bear found refuge in a four-foot-deep crevice. Crockett poked his gun into the animal and fired, only to find he had hit a leg, which drove the bear back into the open and conflict with the dogs before again retreating into the crevice. After poking the wounded animal with a pole while the dogs badgered it, Crockett determined that he could sneak up on the bear from behind: "So I got down, and my dogs got in before him and kept his head towards them, till I got along easily up to him; and placing my hand on his rump, felt for his shoulder. . . . I made a lounge with my long knife and fortunately stuck him right through the heart. . . ."[17]

Aching from the struggle and cold, his clothes frozen, Crockett managed to pull the bear out and butcher it. Then, when his fire failed to warm him, he sought a way to generate heat. He yelled and jumped around without success. Finally, he said:

> . . . I went to a tree about two feet through, and not a limb on it for thirty feet, and I would climb up it to the limbs, and then lock my arms together around it, and slide down to the bottom again. This would make the insides of my legs and arms feel mighty warm and good. I continued this till daylight in the morning, and how often I clomb up my tree and slid down I don't know, but I reckon at least a hundred times.[18]

Emphasizing his hunting prowess, Crockett tapped into the fascination not only with Daniel Boone, the archetypal long hunter, who had died in 1820, but also with a group of his contemporaries whose exploits as hunters, carousers, and explorers were already legendary. These were the Rocky Mountain beaver trappers—Jedediah Strong Smith, Thomas Fitzpatrick, the brothers William and Phil Sublette, John Colter, Jim Bridger, James Beckwourth, Edward Rose, and Hugh Glass. A devoutly religious man and a nondrinker, Smith, the greatest of the mountain men, traveled over and mapped sixteen thousand miles of the West in nine years. Mauled by a grizzly, Smith had a companion stitch his ear back on and then grew his hair long to cover the crooked job. All of those who survived had harrowing tales of near escape from Indians, animals, and the elements, as well as grand descriptions of the mountains and plains. Jim Bridger, stumbling upon the Great Salt Lake, thought he had discovered the Pacific. Coming upon the geysers of the Yellowstone, he was sure he had fallen into hell.

Over the course of a dozen years, these men and their companions trapped beaver out of the western mountains to supply Europe and the eastern United States with fur for hats. Each summer, they brought their plews to rendezvous on the Green River, where they traded them for supplies, whiskey, women, and money. Gamblers, drunkards, adventurers, they were above all entrepreneurs taking their living from mountain streams. When the beaver were gone, more than a few turned to land speculation, trading, or guiding and scouting for the army and immigrants on the Oregon and Santa Fe trails.

The mountain men were themselves cultural heirs of Boone's Kentucky exploits and sometimes veterans of the transcontinental expedition of Meriwether Lewis and William Clark. Kit Carson, a young fur trapper turned Indian scout and wagon-train guide, supplanted Crockett as the star of the nation's most popular almanacs in the 1850s, as the frontier moved west. These were America's folk heroes, the embodiment of its territorial lust officially defended as Manifest Destiny. But the men and women who moved into the unknown country usually cared less about extending the nation's boundaries than about finding land and an opportunity to become rich. If anything, they wanted to be free of government until such time as they needed its force to secure their property.

Except for a few years after he and Polly first moved to Franklin County and when he and Elizabeth moved to West Tennessee, Crockett hunted more for pleasure and the companionship of his fellow hunters than for food or profit. With fruit trees, grain, hogs, cows, horses, distilleries, and mills, his farms were usually capable of sustaining the family and in good years turning some profit. Like many prosperous farmers, he conducted business with factors, or middlemen, who served as traders, bankers, and merchants. On August 6, 1824, for example, while in Nashville, he instructed his agent at C. M. McAllister and Company to send $400 from the sale of thirty bales of cotton to the firm of Major Allen and Grant of Pittsburgh and the balance of the proceeds to Major William B. Wilson and Company, another Nashville supplier. Crockett's cryptic note is short on details, but he was probably settling loans and paying for seeds, gunpowder, and other materials he had received on credit. He also asked McAllister to keep him apprised of the price of cotton, flour, and whiskey.[19] At a price of $0.08 a pound, those 30 bales—approximately 10,000 pounds—would have earned $800.00 for the Crocketts, a solid but not spectacular amount. Unknown, however, is whether Crockett was selling only his own crop or also acting on behalf of his relatives, which, given the size of the transaction, seems possible.

In February 1823—the first winter his family was on Rutherford's Fork—Crockett loaded a packhorse with furs and with his son John Wesley set off for Jackson, forty miles east-south-east, the nearest town. After selling his cache and purchasing provisions, the inveterate campaigner decided to take a "horn" or two with some fellow veterans. While they drank, three candidates for the legislature entered the tavern, looking for votes: Dr. William E. Butler, a nephew-in-law of Andrew Jackson; Major Joseph Lynn; and Duncan McIlver. They drank until a wag told Crockett he should run again for the legislature, but he demurred, saying he lived forty miles from the nearest "white settlement" and therefore had no thought of running for anything.

A visitor to the Crockett farm a week or two later told David that he was a candidate and then showed him a newspaper article to prove it. "I told my wife that this was all a burlesque on me," he said, "but I was determined to make it cost the man who had put it there at least the value of the printing, and of the fun he wanted at my expense."[20] He hired an extra hand and went hunting for votes.

Concerned that the "bear hunter" was strong enough to beat

a divided opposition, his three opponents caucused and chose Butler as the one man who would run against him. "The doctor was a clever fellow," Crockett said, "and I have often said he was the most talented man I ever run against in my life."[21] The Western District encompassed five new counties—Humphreys, Perry, Henderson, Madison, and Carroll (where Crockett lived), making it the largest in the Assembly, and the most under-represented. Politicking through it required constant travel, which suited Crockett's temperament perfectly. He wandered from farm to farm and town to town, meeting people and talking to them about their problems and desires. It was a door-to-door campaign, fundamental and effective.

On the hustings one day, he encountered Colonel Adam Alexander, a candidate for Congress, who introduced him to his audience. Soon Butler arrived and Crockett engaged him in debate, first taunting him about the caucus, which many people believed violated democratic principles because it pre-cluded electoral choice:

"Well, doctor, I suppose they have weighed you out to me; but I should like to know why they fixed your election for *March* instead of *August?* This is," said I, "a branfire new way of doing business, if a caucus is to make a representa-tive for the people!" He now discovered who I was, and cried out, "D——n it, Crockett, is that you?"—"Be sure it is," said I, "but I don't want it understood that I have come electioneering. I have just crept out of the cane, to see what discoveries I could make among white folks." I told him that when I set out electioneering, I would go prepared to put every man on as good footing when I left him as I found him on. I would therefore have me a large buckskin hunting-shirt made, with a couple of pockets holding about a peck each; and that in one I would carry a great big twist of tobacco, and in the other my bottle of liquor; for I knowed when I met a man and offered him a dram, he would throw out his quid of tobacco to take one, and after he had taken his horn, I would out with my twist and give him another chaw. And in this way he would not be worse off than when I found him; and I would be sure to leave him in a first-rate good humour. He said I could beat him electioneering all hollow. I told him I would give him better evidence of that before August, notwithstanding he had many advantages over me, and particularly in the way of money; but I told him that I would go on the products of the country; that I had industrious children, and the best of coon dogs, and they would hunt every night till midnight to support my election; and when the coon fur wa'n't good, I would myself go a wolfing, and shoot down a wolf, and skin his head, and his scalp would be good to me for three dollars, in our state treasury money; and in this way I would get along on the big string.[22]

Crockett never had such a monstrous hunting shirt made, but a surprising number of people over the years have placed it on his back and sent him beating the sticks with a plug and a dram for votes. The campaign against Butler produced other apocrypha concerning the gentleman from the cane that found print in a number of places, including the book known as *Sketches and Eccentricities of Colonel David Crockett of West Tennessee.* In one account, the backwoodsman described how on a visit to Butler's house he encountered a rug so fancy he was afraid to step on it, so he hopped from chair rung to chair rung. "Fellow citizens," Crockett said one day on the stump, "My aristocratic competitor has a fine carpet, and every day he *walks* on truck finer than any gowns your wife or your daughters, in all their lives, ever *wore!*"[23] Appearing in debate with Butler after months of campaigning, Crockett asked to go first and then delivered his opponent's standard speech verbatim from memory.

Against such a mime neither Butler nor two late entrants had a chance. By his count, Crockett, whose recollection in such matters was generally accurate, won with a majority of 247 votes. Despite changing districts, he was back in the legislature for a second consecutive term, a man with a growing reputation for eccentricity and independence.

CHAPTER SIX

MURFREESBORO TO MEMPHIS

"I am not one of those who have had the opportunities and benefits of wealth and education in my youth," Crockett told his constituents in 1824. "I am thus far the maker of my own fortunes. . . . If in the discharge of my duties as your representative, I have failed to exhibit the polished eloquence of men of superior education, I can yet flatter myself that I have notwithstanding, been enabled to procure the passage of some laws and regulations beneficial to the interests of my constituents."[1] The five counties in his district had become eleven as the population soared, but he had remained their sole representative in the state legislature. There, despite the disproportionate power of legislators representing the planters of East and Middle Tennessee, he had achieved a modicum of success fighting for the Western District's farmers. He had also manifested the independence and unpredictability that never ceased to confound both his enemies and his allies while landing him in political trouble. Thus, writing to the voters, he strongly endorsed Jackson for president, saying "the nation owes him a debt of gratitude," although he had a year earlier opposed his election to the U.S. Senate.

Early in its first session, the Fifteenth General Assembly was caught up in national politics, as Jackson's supporters sought to position him for the presidential election the following year.

One step in that process involved a purge of Colonel John Williams, the incumbent senator from Tennessee, a Knoxville native and dedicated foe of Old Hickory. The two had conducted their own skirmish during the War of 1812 when Williams refused an order to turn weapons under his command over to the forces of General Nathaniel Taylor.

Recognizing that the announced opposition candidate, Pleasant M. Miller, lacked the ability to defeat their nemesis, the Jacksonians, led by John Henry Eaton and William Berkeley Lewis, searched for a substitute. Unable to settle on a strong candidate and fearful that a loss would reflect poorly on their leader's political ability, they persuaded the Senate to ask the House for a delay in the vote. Repeatedly, the House refused. A few days before the deadline, the senators nominated Jackson, who, although he had intended to go back to Washington only as president, reluctantly agreed when he concluded that his personal popularity alone could prevent an embarrassing defeat. Led by Crockett, Williams's supporters in the House then attempted to delay the vote, but they failed. Jackson prevailed by ten votes, thirty-five to twenty-five, with Representative James Knox Polk joining the winning side at the last moment.

Somewhat disingenuously, Crockett later said he backed Williams because he felt he had performed well and should not be turned out of office. Crockett enjoyed being contrary, especially when doing so allowed him to tweak the "gentry," the privileged planter class that in Middle Tennessee was lining up behind Jackson, presenting him nationally as the man of the people. At home, the general's populism was less apparent. In the Tennessee House of Representatives, Felix Grundy led a faction aligned with Judge John Overton, Jackson's partner in land speculation and president of the state bank, while Polk, who would become Jackson's chief lieutenant in the United States House of Representatives, headed an alliance representing farmers and merchants who often found themselves opposing the Jacksonians while attempting to remain loyal to the general himself. Crockett swung between the two groups in typically unpredictable—his foes called it erratic—fashion. A better politician than his detractors like to admit, he was savvy enough in October 1824 to endorse the general, hoping to ride his long coattails to Washington. Both would fail—the first time.

Crockett announced his presence at the opening session in 1823 with a quixotic attack on the legislature's policy of hearing divorce petitions from anyone with access to a representative, which he said resulted in unnecessary, time-wasting work. He had begun the campaign two years earlier when he opposed a number of the appeals for divorce, including that of former governor Joseph McMinn, before finally introducing one himself, which his colleagues rejected in retaliation. Refusing to heed their warning, he backed a resolution from James C. Mitchell—the man who had derisively called him "the gentleman from the cane"—that the legislature consider no divorce petitions during its 1822 session and then the following year made the same proposal himself. While recognizing the political value of upholding the sanctity of marriage in the abstract, his colleagues also knew that divorces were an important constituent service. They demurred, arguing that Crockett's proposal was inherently unfair because it would keep poor people who could not afford lawyers and court fees from securing divorces. Crockett said in rebuttal that the legislature should pay their legal expenses, a radical proposition his fellow representatives ignored while voting nearly two to one not to take up divorces. Although the Senate refused to concur, the House placed no divorce petitions on its docket in 1823.

The result, which pleased no one, revealed how Crockett's good intentions often proved harmful to those he wished to help because he lacked the ability to formulate comprehensive policies and legislative strategies. He was not opposed to divorce, nor did he want to deny poor people the opportunity to dissolve a bad marriage. He was bored with the endless debates over minutiae that marked the business of the legislature, but rather than attack that problem, he picked on its more visible manifestations. He also introduced a bill "to repeal all acts and parts of acts authorizing the stay of executions on judgments had before justices of the peace," for which he cast the only affirmative vote, thirty-six of his colleagues opposing.[2] In November, he proposed a bill to "amend an act entitled 'an act more effectively to prevent duelling,'" which was rejected out of hand.[3] In all of these instances, he was more interested in forcing a confrontation than in garnering support for his proposals.

No one knew what to expect of the bear hunter, whose circuitous logic they sometimes could not ignore. Reporting on his successful opposition to a law changing the way constables were elected, the *Nashville Whig* of October 6, 1823, said, "He thought the old law on the subject would do well enough; the people all seemed to understand it and appeared satisfied, and he was not in favor of changing good *old rules,* without some good *new reason* for it." He sided with Polk in supporting a bill to increase the pay of talesmen—people summoned for trial juries—to equal that of jurors working on roads. (Men were summoned for public works, just as they were for trials, and they were called jurors.) In his inimitable fashion, he argued that men doing road work benefited materially from their labor, while those serving jury duty suffered inconvenience. Therefore, they should receive at least as much as the road builders, who, on reflection, deserved nothing.

Throughout the first session, Crockett was one of six representatives opposing a bill "to preserve the purity of elections" by forbidding candidates from treating voters to liquor during their campaign. When the bill was nearing final approval, he joined an attempt to derail it with an amendment that would outlaw the sale of "spiritous liquors by retail." He thought he would force his colleagues to recognize that they were embarking on the road to prohibition and then to drop the entire matter rather than face that unpopular prospect. But he was wrong. His amendment was defeated, 29 to 4, and the bill was passed by nearly as great a margin.[4] Crockett liked to buy rounds when he campaigned and to attend country frolics where he would stand by the whiskey barrel telling amusing stories while his opponents delivered their speeches. He also had a habit of voting against bills—Grundy introduced one in this session—designed to "suppress vice and immorality and promote virtue, . . . to put down tippling shops." The owner of distilleries, Crockett had a major economic as well as a political reason for allowing alcohol to flow freely. Of course, no law prevented liquor from being served at events the candidates were attending, or from being purchased by friends.

His eccentricities notwithstanding, Crockett's outspoken advocacy for the poor and dispossessed began to earn him bemused and respectful attention. Throughout the West, many people were suffering the lingering effects of the Panic of 1819 and in need of relief from taxes and payments for land. If they had access to legislators, they could make individual petitions, but that was a time-consuming endeavor whose results were not guaranteed. Following national trends, Crockett and other reformers sought more general redress. Early in the session, he introduced a bill to abolish imprisonment for debt and later opposed a proposal to authorize the use of convict labor to improve navigation on West Tennessee rivers, although it would have benefited his district. As finally amended, the first act required that the plaintiff in civil cases pay for the imprisonment of the debtor in fifteen-day increments. Failure to do so would result in the prisoner being set free. The convict-lease plan was tabled, but in light of the abuses the system bred in the years following the Civil War, when it was used to enslave indigents and blacks who were put to work throughout the South in turpentine camps and on railroads under brutal circumstances, it is interesting to see Crockett unalterably opposed because he considered it unjust and degrading.

He voted with the majority to reduce the state poll and property taxes, as a way to help people still suffering economically, and then in the second session successfully sponsored a $0.125-per-hundred-acre tax on property in his district to pay for channel improvements on the Obion, Forked Deer, and Hatchie rivers, which some of his colleagues had wanted convicts to perform. His logic, as reported in the September 22, 1824, *Nashville Whig* was vintage: "Mr. Crockett said that the citizens of the Western District were in favor of the bill. The large [absentee] landholders who lived in North Carolina might be opposed to it, as it would make them pay for improving the country, but the people generally were very willing to pay a small tax, in order to get all their necessary articles brought to their doors at a lower rate than they now can." He also authored an act to apply excess funds from the sale of lots in the town of Jackson to the construction of a road through the Forked Deer swamp, after municipal buildings were completed. Among the trustees appointed, with Crockett's consent, to oversee both of these projects was a Jackson lawyer, Adam Huntsman, who would later represent him in court and then become his most outspoken and successful political foe.

Looking out for his district as he prepared to wind up his career in state politics and run for Congress, Crockett also sought to have a chancery court established at Jackson. According to the *Nashville Whig* of September 22, 1824, "Mr. Crockett said that at the last session he had endeavored to get a court of Appeals, as well as of Chancery, established in the Western District; but he discovered that there was no chance of doing that without borrowing or stealing one of the other courts." The same day, he introduced "a bill to deal out justice more equally." Passed despite Grundy's opposition, the misnamed act ordered that more state money be appropriated to the Western District because the existing formula, based on inaccurate census data, understated the population and therefore awarded it too small a percentage of the state budget. Crockett also proposed legislation authorizing sheriffs in his district's counties to purchase land at bankruptcy auctions they were conducting, which would have given them the opportunity to gain considerable holdings at low prices by manipulating the bidding or not advertising the sale in order to keep prospective buyers away. His fellow representatives rejected the bill on the ground that it would encourage abuse and fraud, while Crockett either did not see the problem or did not care.

* * *

A number of battles during the Fifteenth General Assembly revolved around North Carolina land warrants and squatters' rights, as they would for another two decades. When the session opened, North-Carolina University presented a number of warrants of deceased veterans awarded to it by its state legislature and requested authorization to sell them in the Western District to raise money for its facilities and endowment. In 1822, Felix Grundy had successfully overcome opposition to approval of a set of warrants by arranging to have the proceeds split with two Tennessee colleges, but by 1825 the resistance had stiffened.

James Polk, a rigid young Presbyterian who was fast becoming a master of the legislative process, was the leader of the opposition, which included Crockett and a handful of their colleagues. Believing that many of the new warrants, totaling hundreds of thousands of acres, were counterfeit and that, in any event, Tennessee had paid enough for its independence, they demanded a deadline for recognition of new North Carolina claims. In addition, Polk wanted the U.S. Congress to award the land it retained in the Western District to Tennessee for use in the support of schools—including universities. Breaking with Polk on that point, Crockett sought to secure for squatters the right to gain title to their land, equivocating only on whether they should pay $0.125 an acre or nothing. Taking care of schools was secondary in his mind because, in general, only the wealthy benefited from them, whereas everyone could profit from owning a farm.

In November 1823, the General Assembly approved a bill that established June 1, 1825, as the deadline for filing warrants in the Western District and declared that, after that date, surveyors' offices "south and west of the Congressional reservation line" would be closed. The bill also granted occupants on parcels of between 80 and 160 contiguous acres the right of first refusal should anyone produce a warrant for their farm. Another bill extended by a year from November 1823 the deadline for filing warrants on land east and north of the Congressional Reservation Line. The legislature then sent a memorial to its congressional delegation asking that it arrange for all vacant federal lands to be turned over to the state after June 1, 1825, to be sold, with proceeds marked for education.

Although Polk had failed in an attempt to set an earlier deadline for accepting warrants in the Western District—and therefore voted against the final bill, along with Crockett—he succeeded in blocking consideration of North-Carolina University's claims to additional lands in 1823. The university marched into the second session, which Governor Carroll had called ostensibly to correct a technical problem with the selection of presidential electors, with a court order demanding that the legislature honor the warrants it had ignored the previous year.[5] Trying to appear reasonable, the university offered first to divide them once again with Tennessee colleges and then with the common school fund. Polk again used various procedural maneuvers to block any accommodation.

In 1825, with Polk in Congress and Crockett out of office, the university returned, and a more compliant legislature agreed to let it and two Tennessee colleges exercise claims in the Western District. The deadline of June 1 was voided, and no new one established. The warrants themselves were consolidated and reissued in twenty-five-acre certificates, which fell as commonly into the hands of speculators and large landholders as the people who, technically, had the right of first refusal. Feeling betrayed and bitter, Crockett spent the rest of his political life—all of it in Congress—fighting for a resolution of the aberrant and corrupt situation which affected the lives of many of his constituents.

During the tumultuous second session of the Fifteenth General Assembly, Crockett failed to persuade his colleagues to adopt a resolution banning a practice whereby a person who had exercised a warrant for land east of the Congressional Reservation Line, which was of poor quality or which he no longer wanted, could have the entry removed by paying the state of Tennessee $0.125 an acre. Then he would take the restored warrant and sell it to an occupant west of the line for $1.00 to $2.00 an acre. The *Nashville Whig* of September 27,

1824, said that Crockett "had heard much said here about frauds, &c. committed by North-Carolina speculators; but it was time to quit talking about other people, and look to ourselves. This practice was more rascally, and of greater fraud than any he had yet heard of." According to the *Whig*, he told his colleagues how the scam worked:

> The speculators . . . , pretending to be great friends of the people in saving their land, had gone up one side of a creek and down another, *like a coon,* and pretended to grant the poor people great favors in securing them occupant claims—they gave them a credit of a year, and promised to take cows, horses, &c. in payment. But when the year came around, the notes were in the hands of others; the people were sued, cows and horses not being sufficient to pay; the land itself went to pay for securing it. He said again, that warrants obtained in this way, by removal of entries for the purpose of speculation, should be as a counterfeit bank note in the hands of the person who obtained them, and die on their hands. . . .

The resolution failed to carry by two votes.

Tennessee's thorny land disputes varied from region to region. In 1823, the legislature established a graduated pricing system for land in the Hiwassee District, purchased from the Cherokee by the federal government in 1819 and given to Tennessee with the understanding that it need not be used to satisfy any North Carolina warrants. Lying in East Tennessee between the Little Tennessee and Hiwassee rivers, the land was to be sold in a range of $0.125 to $1.50 an acre, cash only. Crockett opposed that provision, saying it would cut poor people out of the process because they lacked cash, and he had not come to the legislature to serve the interests of "ready-money" men.[6] He lost. Trying to redeem something decent, he backed an amendment that would allow the district's widows to keep the plots on which they lived. He failed again.

Unexpectedly, he turned in the opposite direction when voting on a land controversy affecting the French Broad River country in East Tennessee. Squatters had been granted preemption on part of two 100,000-thousand acre tracts set aside in 1806 for education. Having regularly deferred collection of principal and interest on the $1.00-an-acre purchase price it had established, the legislature in 1823 became even more magnanimous, agreeing to forgo interest payments for the year and remit a third of the total debt, with the remaining two thirds due in seven annual installments. It voted as well to foreclose and auction the land of anyone who subsequently failed to meet his payments and give the proceeds to education. As a result of this legislative largess, a number of marginal farmers lost their homesteads.[7] Although the bill ran counter to the interests of the poor people he usually defended, Crockett voted in its favor, along with a solid majority of the legislature's more wealthy members, while Polk, his natural ally on such questions, remained firmly opposed. Crockett's position is not readily explicable, and no record of his thinking on the matter exists. He might have genuinely believed that the arrangement was not only generous but also the best that could be had and therefore ignored warnings that it was a potential disaster for the poor, who were always hard-pressed for money. He might also have felt that the people along the French Broad River had received too many special favors at the expense of those in other areas.

As soon as the legislature convened in September 1823, it was faced with a major attempt to repeal a law passed on November 13, 1821, requiring the banks of Tennessee to resume redeeming bank notes for specie—gold—by April 1, 1824. They had suspended the payments during the Panic of 1819, brought on when the newly created Second Bank of the United States decided to tighten credit in an effort to curb inflationary speculation in land and to restore value to paper money, which state banks were issuing without sufficient resources to back it up. State banks faltered, especially in the West, and many simply suspended redemption of their devalued currency. The legislative mandate to resume specie payments represented an attempt to break out of the lingering depression by restoring value to the state scrip, and Crockett opposed the effort to delay it. On September 23, he joined the debate, which the *Nashville Whig* reported in its edition of October 13, 1823: "Mr. Crockett said . . . he considered the whole Banking system a species of swindling on a large scale and it seemed to him that in all cases when any difficulty or loss was created by the Banks, that the farmers suffered most." Polk proposed a compromise allowing a more gradual return to specie, which passed. Crockett dissented, as did Polk, who was developing a habit of proposing compromises in order to break legislative logjams and then voting against the final bill. In so doing, he earned the respect of his colleagues as a compromiser while continuing to present himself to his constituents as a man of principle.

Crockett later sponsored a resolution calling on the Bank of the State of Tennessee to maintain branches in every county, including those established since 1819. Sharing with a number of his contemporaries the notion that sound economics was whatever made life more endurable and increased their wealth, he wanted the offices to loan money on favorable terms to people seeking land. Until forced to take action, the bank had refused to serve those areas, arguing that it could not decide how much money to budget for loans, which, in any event, did not return enough to cover the local agent's salary, much less produce a profit.[8]

The sixty men gathered in Murfreesboro—forty in the House, twenty in the Senate—represented the political and economic elite of Tennessee. Whatever their disagreements in session, they could not avoid each other after hours, often sharing the same boardinghouse and table and frequenting the same taverns and gaming rooms. In 1823–24, as Jackson made his first run at the presidency, the state's legislators spent hours looking beyond the state to the nation's capital. Among his surrogates and foes closely watching events from the legislature were several future congressmen and one president—Polk.

Gregarious, amusing, idiosyncratic in his manner, Crockett

was surely an arresting figure in that small community, even if not a member of the inner circle of Jacksonians or the opposition. Dressed in his Sunday best, he looked the part of a legislator, but he remained every bit the backwoodsman who had crashed the corridors of wealth and power. Bored with the legislative process and the long debates, he spent many hours—even while the House was meeting—at the taverns and card tables, blaming his absences on illness when they became a campaign issue. Despite his disaffection, he possessed an ambition for higher office—Congress.

The Ninth Congressional District of Tennessee was one of the nation's largest—with 22,000 voters by 1830, more than double the norm—because of the failure of reapportionment to keep pace with the westward rush of people. From Lawrence County in Middle Tennessee, this Western District ran to the Mississippi, encompassing virtually all of what was once the Chickasaw country and was still known as the "Jackson Purchase." Crockett had reason to feel confident as the 1825 election (congressional elections being held in odd years) approached: He had lived in and represented the district's southeastern and northwestern quadrants, and he was riding a rising crest of popularity. Additionally, he hoped to take advantage of the widespread outrage over the House of Representatives' election in February of John Quincy Adams as president. Around the nation, voters believed that Adams had struck a "corrupt bargain" with Henry Clay, awarding him the post of secretary of state in exchange for his backing after the election was thrown to the House.

The election of 1824 was a watershed in presidential politics, in which the accepted practice of courting electoral rather than popular votes was discredited, as was that of selecting candidates through party caucuses of senators and representatives. By 1824, the National Republicans formed the nation's sole functioning party—the Federalists having lost their viability after opposing the War of 1812—and they had begun to recognize the need to respond in some way to the growing agitation for

"As I recall from the last session, you were born in Tennessee and raised in the woods, so you knew every tree. Then something happened when you were only three. What was that?"

Late in 1833, Crockett sat for a portrait by Samuel Stillman Osgood, which, although now lost, served as the basis for this Albert Newsam lithograph, published by Childs and Lehman in 1834. In his own handwriting, Crockett hyperbolically declared the result "the only correct likeness that has been taken of me."

NATIONAL PORTRAIT GALLERY,
SMITHSONIAN INSTITUTION

During his distinguished career in national politics, Henry Clay served as a congressman, Speaker of the House of Representatives, senator, and secretary of state, but the prize he most sought, the presidency, eluded the Kentuckian. Author of the American System, which used revenue from tariffs and land sales to finance internal improvements, Clay was also founder of the Whig party and the arch political foe of Andrew Jackson. Endicott and Swett published this lithograph, from a portrait by William James Hubard, in 1832.

NATIONAL PORTRAIT GALLERY,
SMITHSONIAN INSTITUTION

MARTIN VAN BUREN.
Eighth President of the United States.

Old Hickory, Andrew Jackson, the Republic's most popular commander since George Washington and the champion of the Common Man, served as president from 1828 to 1836. John Henry Bufford prepared this 1830 engraving for Pendleton's Lithography Company from a highly stylized portrait made overlooking the Hermitage, Jackson's Tennessee plantation, by Ralph Eleaser Whiteside Earl.

NATIONAL PORTRAIT GALLERY,
SMITHSONIAN INSTITUTION

Crockett unloosed his most vitriolic verbal assaults on Martin Van Buren, former governor and senator from New York, secretary of state and vice president under Jackson, and president from 1836 to 1840. He was known to his friends as a master politician, to his foes as the Little Magician, the Red Fox of Kinderhook, and assorted other names. Crockett's mocking biography of Van Buren, published in 1835, verged on libel. Nathaniel Currier prepared this engraving in 1840, from a portrait by Henry Inman.

NATIONAL PORTRAIT GALLERY,
SMITHSONIAN INSTITUTION

M.r Hackett as Nimrod Wild-fire.
"Come back, Stranger! or I'll plug you like a Water-Million."

In 1831, James Hackett premiered a farce by James Kirke Paulding, which featured Colonel Nimrod Wildfire, *The Lion of the West.* The comical congressman from the Kentucky backwoods was based on Crockett, a fact that, despite Paulding's denials, escaped no one. Wildfire wore a wildcat, not a coonskin, cap. Edward W. Clay did this lithograph, which was used to promote the enormously popular play.

On June 3, 1955, Fess Parker, star of Walt Disney's hit television show and movie, *Davy Crockett, King of the Wild Frontier,* appeared in Miami, Florida, where he showed young fans his flintlock and told them to "do the right thing." Parker's promotional tour took him through much of the United States and Europe.

In his 1889 portrait, William Henry Huddle portrayed Crockett as a sincere, buckskin-clad frontiersman, holding his coonskin cap, a bit of iconography that has since become standard.

Reportedly the most popular reading matter on the frontier next to the Bible, the first Crockett almanac appeared in 1835, with additional installments—sometimes several in one year—until 1856. Produced by illustrators in the East, the almanacs featured a crude, backwoods superman—racist, violent, occasionally bumbling, and heroic. The cover of the *1836 Almanack* shows Crockett keeping his powder dry while crossing the Mississippi.

Fall of the Alamo---Death of Crockett.

The *1837 Almanack* presented one of several accounts of Crockett's death at the Alamo. Here the formally dressed former congressman falls in battle.

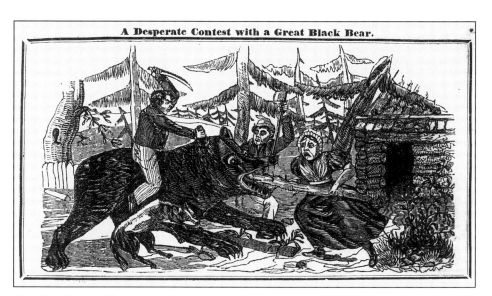

A Desperate Contest with a Great Black Bear.

Crockett boasted in his autobiography of killing a black bear with his knife during a desperate encounter, but not of requiring an assist from his wife, as portrayed in this episode from the *1837 Almanack.*

John Gadsby Chapman painted Crockett in 1834 in his typical hunting garb, with three mongrels from the streets of Washington substituting for his bear hounds. Long believed lost to fire, the portrait, also reproduced on the dust jacket of this volume, hangs in the Texas state capitol.

Sam Houston's love of costumes led him to pose in formal Cherokee Indian garb, with turban, for this portrait, made around 1830. The sword is the one he carried six years later at San Jacinto, the decisive battle in the Texas war of independence.

THE DAUGHTERS OF THE REPUBLIC OF TEXAS LIBRARY AT THE ALAMO

Wiley Martin sketched William Barret Travis in December 1835, around the time he was granted the commission in the Texas army that took him to the Alamo.

THE DAUGHTERS OF THE REPUBLIC OF TEXAS LIBRARY AT THE ALAMO

expanding democracy to include virtually all white males. Party leaders like Henry Clay, who believed that the will of the people had to be heeded, to a degree, sought a mechanism for taking selection of the party's presidential candidate out of the hands of "King Caucus," as did his chief rival in the West, Andrew Jackson.

They agreed on little else. Clay had viciously attacked Jackson in January 1819 over his invasion of Florida, comparing him to every military dictator from Julius Caesar to Napoleon Bonaparte. Although they had declared a mutual truce in 1823, they were competitors for the presidency and personal antagonists. Clay considered Jackson unfit for high political office, while Jackson thought Clay to be a conniver and poltroon, a base coward. Their differences in ability and temperament fueled their animosity. Jackson was the commander, the man of direct action who justified himself after the fact, if at all. Clay was an orator and compromiser whose domain was the legislature.[9]

Facing them as a behind-the-scenes foe was the consummate political operator Martin Van Buren, the undisputed boss of New York. Early in 1824, he organized a congressional caucus, which, attended by only 61 of the 261 senators and representatives, selected as the official National Republican candidate Virginian William Crawford. It was a cynical maneuver of the sort for which Van Buren was already famous, Crawford being near death from a stroke that left him nearly blind and mentally deficient. Van Buren, who later became secretary of state and vice president under Jackson, also tried to enlist Clay as a vice presidential candidate on the Crawford ticket and founder of a new political party. But Clay preferred to conduct his own campaign. Also joining the race was Adams, the favorite son of New England.

From the start, Clay assumed that no candidate would win a majority of the electoral vote, and thus the House of Representatives, where he presided as speaker, would select him as president. All he needed to do was finish in the top three, a task he thought easy enough. First, as a native son of Virginia and the leading politician in Kentucky, he assumed he could pick up votes in the south and hold his own in the West. Second, he counted on his partisans to carry the day in at least a few of the six states—out of twenty-eight in the nation—where the legislatures still selected their electors, leaving them unbound by the popular vote. Finally, he calculated that even if he did not draw more votes than Adams or Jackson, he could not lose to the incapacitated Crawford.

Through 1824, the candidates conducted their campaigns. Following a tradition established by George Washington which held that the office of chief magistrate should seek the man, Jackson operated largely through surrogates, preferring to keep himself and his ideas out of public scrutiny. Paying lip service to that ideal, Clay threw himself, along with his allies, into the fray. He concentrated his effort on securing electoral votes and lobbying among the powerful while Adams took a middle road between Clay and Jackson and Crawford stayed in bed. The campaign was vigorous and often brutally negative, as newspapers allied with the candidates—except Clay, who had little press backing—never shied from running any flavor of rumor and political operatives like Van Buren manipulated the ballots to their ends.

As the states voted over the course of the fall, Jackson collected a solid plurality: 152,901 popular and 99 electoral votes to 114,023 and 84 for Adams; 46,979 and 41 for Crawford; and 47,212 and 37 for Clay, who was beaten throughout the West, with the exception of Kentucky. Trounced by the man he respected least but knew to be his major obstacle to national office and shut out of the runoff in the House, Clay disregarded instructions from the Kentucky legislature to vote for Jackson and threw his support to Adams. Because he then accepted the post of secretary of state, it was widely believed that he and Adams had cut a deal, although the charge remains unproven.

That the election had been decided for Adams in defiance of a popular and electoral victory for Jackson proved to many people that the old system of choosing candidates in a closed caucus and then orchestrating the electoral vote was bankrupt.

Moreover, popular demand forced an expansion of the franchise in every state, so that the percentages of white males eligible to vote increased from 24 percent in 1824 to 75 percent in 1840.[10] Determined not to be outflanked again, Jackson concluded that the time had come to court the popular vote. Clay could never comprehend that having betrayed the people in backing Adams, he could not regain enough of their trust to be elected president. As a senator, he remained a major force in American politics, the chief nemesis of Andrew Jackson, whose popularity he consistently underestimated—to his detriment.

Crockett was unable to turn the anger over Adams's election to his advantage in his first run for Congress. The incumbent in the Western District was one of the ubiquitous colonels, Adam Alexander, a wealthy planter who also served as surveyor general of the Tenth Surveyor's District. A man with considerable influence and power, he had committed in 1824 the seemingly unpardonable sin for a southwesterner (at the time, West Tennessee was considered part of the southwestern frontier) of voting for a high tariff, a central part of Clay's national economic policy, which was viewed as a boon to manufacturers in the East and a drag on the cotton South. Two other candidates named Ferrell and Persons joined Crockett and Alexander on the hustings but appear not to have figured significantly in the outcome.[11]

Years later, Crockett would tell a story from this election to illustrate how he used cleverness to compensate for a chronic shortage of campaign funds. Dressed for a hunt, he chanced upon one of his opponents addressing a crowd outside a "ramshackle shantee," or tavern, owned by a Yankee named Job Snelling. The crowd first demanded that Crockett speak, then that he treat it to liquor at Snelling's. Seeing that the candidate lacked money, the tavern owner refused to serve drinks, and the crowd left, resentful, thirsty, ready to vote for his foe. Crockett went into the woods, shot a raccoon, and returned with its skin, which he traded to Snelling for a quart of liquor. The

131

crowd drank the whiskey and, unsated, headed back to the shantee demanding another round. Panicked, Crockett spotted the tail of his coon skin sticking between the logs as they approached the bar, surreptitiously pulled it from its storage place, and used it to pay for another round. He repeated the process ten times, he boasted, before he finally stopped.[12]

Many years later, another great southwestern humorist, Samuel Clemens, recalled the tale of the raccoon as one of those he had encountered in his youth that had influenced his art. By then, people were taking Crockett's apocrypha as fact. No one observed that his enemies, who were numerous, would have hauled him to the bar of justice had he bought drinks at Snelling's or any other shantee in violation of Tennessee's pure election laws, much less that a fresh raccoon skin was not decent barter. Crockett effectively rewrote his history with such stories.

Neither tall tales nor sincere policy speeches nor promises helped him in August, when he drew 2,599 votes to Alexander's 2,866. David attributed his loss to the fact that cotton had hit $25 per hundred pounds, damping people's concern over the tariff. Other observers have argued that Jackson's surrogate John Overton, writing under the nom de plume Aristides, had helped defeat not only Crockett but also the incumbent state senator, Thomas Williamson. Overton/Aristides had sent letters to several Western District newspapers citing Crockett's legislative proposals to add to its militia a brigade from East Tennessee and change the dates for the sessions of court as evidence that he had neglected the interests of his constituents and thus was unfit to represent them in Congress.[13] Overton had simply seized a thin reed in an effort to punish Crockett for his obstructionism during the election for U.S. senator two years earlier and his outspoken opposition to large-scale land speculators and planters, like Overton himself.

It is hard to see why such insignificant measures would be evidence of any such failure, especially since they did not pass. A change in the court's term, while inconvenient to some people, was mostly administrative, and, although adding an East Tennessee brigade to the militia of West Tennessee had political overtones and was geographically bizarre, it hardly constituted a dereliction of duty. Crockett, who was attempting to present himself as a Jacksonian and had sponsored the addition of six counties—one of those being named Fayette in honor of the Marquis de Lafayette, then on a triumphant national tour—as well as numerous towns, courts, and public facilities to the fast-growing district, said nothing of the letters. His supporters attributed the bills to clerical errors and moved on to other matters. Probably not a decisive factor in Crockett's defeat, the letters indicate that the Jacksonians viewed him less as an ally than a threat and that their mutual embrace two years later was largely opportunistic. It helped Crockett to victory and provided Jackson with another vote in the House of Representatives prior to the 1828 election.

Beaten, Crockett fell into the pattern he had followed between legislative sessions when he would join the boys in hunting, drinking, scheming to get rich, debating politics, working on roads, trying cases. Intent on winning the next congressional election, he doubtless visited various parts of the district to keep himself known. Cash was in short supply and he was more deeply in debt than usual because of the failed campaign, but the farm and other enterprises were able to provide for the extended Crockett family and keep its master on the move. By purchase and lease, he added acreage to his holdings in the Obion River country, and he received a warrant for twenty acres in Lawrence County for his service during the War of 1812, which he sold. He appears to have left the working of his own farm to his hands while improving these additional parcels for lease or sale.

During 1825–26, citizen Crockett never missed a call to join in the public-works projects or perform his other civic duties in Gibson County. In January 1825, he served on a road-building crew. In October, he posted bond for one Samuel Gordon, offense unknown, and served as a juryman. On November 8, he drew grand-jury duty, and on the ninth successfully petitioned the county court to drop a twenty-five-dollar fine it had levied against him the previous year for failing to answer a summons to serve on another grand jury, his excuse being that he was in Murfreesboro at the time. He also joined in convicting one John Gray of gaming, proof that he could play hypocrite as well as anyone. On April 24, 1826, he won dismissal of a suit that George Gibbs, a tenant, had brought against him earlier, and in June he was building roads—wagon trails—out of Trenton to the Weakley County and Obion County lines, along with his cousins Patterson and David Crockett, Jr., and other neighbors. In September, he was working out of Rutherford.[14]

Deciding that he could earn a sizable profit from the lumber business, Crockett hired a crew in the fall of 1825 to fashion wood staves at Obion Lake. He also set them to work building two flatboats, with which he planned to float his cargo down the Obion River to the Mississippi, thence to market in New Orleans. Although steamboats were becoming increasingly common on major routes, flatboats remained the most prevalent freight craft because they were easy and inexpensive to construct and could be broken up at journey's end, their timber sold along with the cargo. The men who made these trips— usually the farmers or loggers themselves—viewed them as a lark, the first time. They rapidly discovered that the barges were slow, awkward on good water, and unseaworthy in rough conditions. For rivermen, the trip Crockett contemplated was arduous; for landlubbers, it was folly.

From the start of the project, Crockett's inattention increased the danger. After the crew began work, he left for a number of prolonged bear hunts, which would occupy him until the eve of departure. The proud owner of a pack of eight hounds, he killed 105 black bears during that period, 58 of them in the fall and winter, 17 in the week after Christmas alone. He returned to his logging camp only after sating his bear lust, and by then the boats were nearly finished.[15] After loading 30,000 staves onto the untested barges, the men shoved off and drifted down the Obion without incident. But on hitting the Mississippi, the boats turned balkish, and Crockett discovered that neither he nor his pilot nor any of his hands knew the first rule of river travel: Do not overload your craft. Lacking the most rudimentary boat-handling or navigational skills, close to panic, Crockett did precisely the wrong thing. He lashed the two uncontrollable flatboats together, creating in the process a runaway block of wood.

At the mercy of the current, they drifted for part of the day parallel to some Ohio flatboats, whose crews tried unsuccessfully to tell them how to land and then advised them to run all night, keeping to the main channel. Seeing they had no other choice, Crockett unhappily agreed. The men rode the bound boats through a rough stretch called Devil's Elbow and then tried to land at several wood yards—refueling landings for steamboats—but failed, despite the attempts of lantern-waving people to instruct them. At last, they abandoned themselves to the river. Crockett retired to the cabin on one of the boats where, warming himself by the fire, he realized that he would rather be bear hunting.

While he bemoaned his fate, the inept boatmen allowed the lashed-together craft to turn broadside to the current, with Crockett's boat in the rear. Drifting toward Memphis, they came upon a collection of mid-river islands called "Paddy's Hen-and-Chickens." "The head of the Old Hen has always been considered dangerous," said James D. Davis in his *History of Memphis,* "and particularly at that time, as the river appeared undetermined on which side of it she should make her main channel, and a number of huge snags stood out as though contesting the right of way on either."[16]

Some two hundred yards above Old Hen, the flatboats ran afoul of a "sawyer," a snag formed when trees uprooted by the current undercutting a bank drift downriver until they lodge against a sandbar. The current wears trunks smooth of their limbs and causes them to bob up and down with enough force to break through a boat's hull or capsize it. The sawyer above Old Hen churned through Crockett's lead boat and began to pull his under in such a way that he was unable to escape through the deck hatch. Trying to squeeze through an opening cut in the hull for collecting water, he became stuck, with only his arms and head clear. He called to his men, "and the hands who were next to the raft, seeing my arms out, and hearing me holler, seized them, and began to pull. I told them I was sinking, and to pull my arms off, or force me through, for now I know'd well enough it was neck or nothing, come out or sink."[17]

However the dramatic rescue was made, Crockett, who had been sitting in only his shirt, found himself buck naked on a snag of downed timber with his crew outside Memphis in the middle of the night, cold and miserable, the boats and all their possessions careening down the Mississippi. In the morning, a passing boat sent a skiff, which carried them to the city, where the merchant Marcus Winchester, seeing their condition, brought them clothes from his store and took them to his home where his wife fed them. Later in the day, the rescued boaters joined the men of the town in a drinkingfest, with Crockett providing the entertainment. Because Memphis was in the Ninth Congressional District, Crockett was already known from his 1825 campaign, but that morning, seeing how the crowd responded to the tales of his adventures, Winchester not only urged him to run again but also promised to provide financial support.[18]

After receiving money from the magnanimous Winchester, all the men left for the Obion, except Crockett and one companion, who took a boat down to Natchez, where they hoped to learn the fate of their barges. People there reported that they had tried but failed to salvage one as it drifted past. Presumably, it broke up, like the other, scattering staves across the river. There is no record of how much Crockett lost on this ill-fated adventure, but, figuring in wages and supplies, it was probably around $100.

The disaster confirmed Crockett as the darling of the growing, frontier river town of Memphis, and it remained firmly in his camp until 1832, when a Jackson-controlled legislature severed it from his district to thwart his return to Congress. It was by most accounts a colorful and somewhat wild community, where interracial liaisons and marriages were relatively common and where abolitionists maintained a vocal presence into the 1830s, when a number of them represented the town at the state's Constitutional Convention. The year of Crockett's wreck, the Scottish social reformer Frances Wright, who had accompanied Lafayette on his triumphal 1824 tour of the United States, established near the city—on a site suggested by Andrew Jackson—Nashoba, her short-lived experimental community designed to provide slaves an opportunity to work for their freedom. Yet at the same time, there existed in Memphis a violently racist underclass, which, according to historian Davis, began to exercise increasing political influence in the years leading up to the Civil War.

Marcus Winchester, a prominent man in the town, was at the center of much of this ambivalence over race. Around 1818, he had begun living with a beautiful and intelligent quadroon woman named Mary, the former mistress of Thomas Hart Benton, who was eventually to become a senator from Missouri and was the granduncle of the famous early-twentieth-century painter by the same name. Two years later, Winchester, an honest and upright man, traveled with Mary to New Orleans to legitimize their union—that city being the closest one in the United States where interracial marriage was sanctioned. For a decade, the Winchesters were untroubled, but as racism became codified, he found his store boycotted and his family threatened. He survived by falling into "intemperance"—that is, alcoholism—and pandering to the prejudice of the white mob by running for the state legislature and supporting the increasingly rigid laws designed to perpetuate slavery and limit the rights of free people of color.[19]

CHAPTER SEVEN

THE BEAR HUNTER GOES TO CONGRESS

The encouragement of people like Marcus Winchester and developments during the two years he was out of office convinced Crockett that he could beat the incumbent representative, Adam Alexander. The legislature's indefinite extension for the settlement of North Carolina warrants had exposed occupants in the Western District to dispossession, and the price of cotton had fallen to a low of $6 per hundred pounds. Crockett planned to run against the tariff and for a congressional solution to the land problem. Major General William Arnold of the Western District militia and another general, John Cooke (sometimes referred to as Colonel John Cook), joined the campaign, which began in the spring of 1827.

While Arnold and Alexander debated each other, Cooke traveled around the district accusing Crockett of ignorance and moral turpitude—proclaiming him a drunkard, a gambler, and an adulterer. Crockett, as was his habit, fought back, telling ever more egregious lies about Cooke. As Sam Houston, senator of the new state of Texas, told the story twenty years later while riding a steamboat to New Orleans, Cooke decided to appear at a Crockett rally with a witness who would put the lie to every charge he was leveling.[1] Concluding a diatribe full of outrageous statements, Crockett announced that his opponent was present and planned to prove him a liar, which was unnecessary.

139

Of course he had lied, he said. Cooke had started telling false-hoods about him and so, to be fair, he had turned the tables. The truth was that they were both liars. The crowd cheered. Disgusted, Cooke quit the campaign, saying that he was too good to serve people who would applaud a liar, and two years later he rejected an opportunity to face Crockett in a rematch.[2]

Campaigning by slur and innuendo was a high art at the time. Although the presidential election was a year away, Henry Clay and John Quincy Adams through their various surrogates were involved in a vicious assault on Andrew Jackson's character, proclaiming him a drunkard, a gambler, a cockfighter, a high-stakes horse racer, and a wife-stealing adulterer. Not content with that array of charges, they went on to spread rumors that his mother had been a prostitute and his father a mulatto who had sold his oldest son into slavery. Jackson's response, espe-cially when the slurs were turned against his beloved wife Rachel—who legally had still been married when she wed Jack-son, because her husband had misled her about a Kentucky divorce—was to seek vengeance against the perpetrators, in this case Clay, Adams, and their allies. The Jacksonians attacked the morality of Clay—who had, in fact, been a notorious gam-bler, heavy drinker, and whoremonger in his younger days—and assassinated the integrity of anyone who challenged them. Where dueling was still accepted, they often pursued that course as well. Thus, Crockett's signal contribution to the art of negative campaigning was to show how to deflate it with humor and honesty, although he could not always sustain that aplomb in later elections.

The two remaining candidates in 1827 continued to treat Crockett as if he were not in the race, until they all appeared at a rally in the eastern part of the district and were asked to speak. Leading off, Crockett delivered one of his short, anec-dote-filled meanders during which he expressed his support of internal improvements—roads, bridges, and river channels—Andrew Jackson, land for squatters, and an end to the tariff. The crowd was amused and not overtaxed. Alexander followed with a long disquisition, recounting his experience and years of service to the Western District while defending his unpopular vote on the tariff. Directing his remarks at Alexander, Arnold had been speaking for a long time "when a large flock of guinea-fowls came very near to where he was, and set up the most unmerciful chattering that ever was heard. . . ."[3] Arnold interrupted his speech and asked that they be removed. After he concluded his oration, Crockett approached him and said loudly enough for the audience to hear: " 'Well, colonel, you are the first man I ever saw that understood the language of fowls.' I told him that he had not had the politeness to name me in his speech, and that when my little friends, the guinea-fowls, had come up and began to holler 'Crockett, Crockett, Crockett,' he had been ungenerous enough to stop, and drive *them* all away."[4] Crockett carried the day.

He supplemented his speeches with extensive personal campaigning in the taverns and on the farms of his large district. Although he might have treated on those rare occasions when no opponents or their supporters were watching, certainly he never declined a round. Crockett said the campaign cost him $150, with another $100 for his trip to Washington, all of which was loaned to him by Marcus Winchester of Memphis. But a campaign against an entrenched and wealthy incumbent cost considerably more, even for a candidate like Crockett, who relied on the kindness of people he met for lodging and food. Estimates have placed the price of election to the House of Representatives at $3,000 or more, with two thirds of that going for publications and postage.[5] His family and other supporters made up the difference in amounts that remain unknown.

Closely identifying himself with Jackson, Crockett took every opportunity to denounce the "coalition" of Adams and Clay that had carried the 1825 presidential vote in the House of Representatives. That group presided over the full flowering of the American system designed by Henry Clay to use income from a high tariff and land sales to support an ambitious program of internal improvements and encourage manufacturing. While the Jacksonians, including Crockett, endorsed internal improvements and cheap land, they tended to dislike industry and the tariff, because it kept high the price of manufactured goods and, when other nations retaliated, drove down the price of cotton. The first tariff was passed in 1816 to help pay for the War of 1812. The second was approved four years later in response to the Panic of 1819. The 1824 tariff was the first that was fully protective of manufacturers and the one that set off the most violent protest. Its renewal every four years precipitated repeated constitutional crises as the cotton South and industrial Northeast came to the verge of armed conflict.

Beyond policy questions, which were subject to constant re-evaluation until Jackson determined his position—often the one opposite that of Henry Clay—the Jacksonians fully supported the expansion of democracy and openly courted the vote of the "people," the "common man." Idealized as Jefferson's sturdy yeoman who was to be the backbone of the Republic, or as an independent artisan, the common man was as frequently an urban laborer or illiterate dirt farmer. Whatever his economic status, he demanded and received a role in the affairs of his community, state, and nation. By 1828, electors for the electoral college were chosen by popular vote in every state but South Carolina and Delaware, and nearly all states had removed property ownership as a condition for suffrage.

In the caldron of politics, the party label underwent a radical transformation. Jackson, Adams, Clay, and every other major politician of the mid-1820s were nominally Republicans—albeit drifting into Democratic Republican and National Republican camps. But whereas Jackson and his Democrats embraced the common man, Adams and Clay evinced a strong distaste for, if not actual fear of, the rule of the masses, which they often equated with the mob. National politics was very much the art of building coalitions between East and West, South and North, old South and the new Southwest, Southwest and Northwest, Northeast and Middle Atlantic, and between individuals with different ambitions and interpretations of the Constitution, which was regarded as nearly a sacred text. Officials and voters, who were informed and opinionated, were identified according to the person whom they supported—as Jacksonians, Adamsites, Clayites, Chiltonites, Everettites, and the like. This process of coalition building dominated the operations of the Congress until Jackson's second term, when the fight over the recharter of the Second Bank of the United States transcended sectional and personal politics to address fundamental constitutional and economic issues that were national and ideological in scope. Voters and politicians were forced to identify more closely with the emerging Whig or Democratic parties and to follow their policies.

A self-proclaimed Jackson man, Crockett won a solid plurality in the August 1827 election, collecting 5,868 votes—49 percent—to 3,646 for Alexander and 2,417 for Arnold. A disgruntled constituent, David Mitchell Saunders, asked a friend in a September 15 letter whether he had heard of the famous " 'Loco Crockett,' who could whip his weight in wild cats, jump up higher, fall down lower and drink more *liquors* than any man in the state."[6] James Erwin, a Tennessean and husband of Henry Clay's daughter Anne, told his father-in-law that Crockett was a crude, illiterate, stubbornly independent backwoodsman, "more in his proper place, when hunting a Bear in the cane Brake, than he will be in the Capital."[7] But he concluded that the bear hunter would ultimately switch his allegiance to the coalition not only because his political views were unfocused and he was notoriously contrary but also because he had already clashed with the Jacksonians over the general's election to the Senate in 1823 and over land and banking issues. Crockett was too independent, said Erwin—whose analysis proved eerily prescient—to play the good soldier.

On October 1, Crockett purchased some land—probably around two hundred acres, an amount he favored—in Weakley County, adjacent to his holdings in Gibson County, for a new farm he planned to occupy the following summer. Almost immediately thereafter he started for the nation's capital, then called Washington City, with Elizabeth and twenty-year-old John Wesley, stopping along the way to visit friends and relatives. The day after leaving the Middle Tennessee home of

James Blackburn, David fell ill with what he called bilious fever—a liver or gall-bladder infection—and later pleurisy. He managed to reach his father-in-law's farm but then was bedridden for a month.

After he had recovered enough to resume his journey, Elizabeth and John Wesley returned to their farm with three young slaves her father had given her. Arriving in Washington just before the December 3 opening of the Twentieth Congress, in company with North Carolina congressman Sam Carson, whom he had watched kill a political opponent in a duel, and probably Nathaniel Claiborne from Virginia, Crockett relapsed.[8] He was to suffer two more serious bouts of illness, during which he feared for his life, before he began to recover. His strength and his "red rosy cheeks" had deserted him, and he had missed a number of days in the opening month of the Congress.[9]

Washington City was a small but energetic town, considered by the diplomatic corps a hardship post, a place without culture or convenience. Most of the men stayed at hotels or boarding-houses near the Capitol, and Crockett was no exception, taking up quarters at Mrs. Ball's Boarding House on Pennsylvania Avenue, across the street from Brown's Hotel, with nine other representatives, including Nathaniel Claiborne, Gabriel Moore of Alabama, and Robert McHatton, Joseph Lecompte, and Joel Yancey of Kentucky. Claiborne stayed there for each of his terms, as did Crockett, their room and board probably running one to two dollars a day, depending on whether they drank liquor from the house supply. Although not in residence at that time, Henry Clay often lived in Brown's Hotel when he did not bring his family to Washington with him.

Illness aside, Crockett's personal life in Washington was chaotic, as he was swept up in the whirl of dinner parties, drinking bouts, gambling, and gossip that defined the social scene. A personable and amusing oddity, Crockett was in high demand in some quarters, and he paid the price. He missed thirty roll-call votes in the first and twenty-eight in the second session of his first term, because of his carousing, boredom with the business of legislation, and illness. On February 17, 1829, just two weeks before adjournment and Jackson's inauguration as president, Crockett borrowed $700 from his fellow boarder, Representative Robert McHatton—more than he earned for the three-month session, for which he received the standard pay of $8 a day.[10] According to rumors that have the ring of truth, he had lost heavily at the gaming tables and needed the money to get home, where he also was in debt and in arrears on the tax for his two-hundred-acre parcel in Weakley County.

Crockett's lack of manners—call it rusticity—gave rise to numerous tales of social faux pas. The most traveled story detailed how, at a state dinner sponsored by President John Quincy Adams to welcome new members of Congress, Crockett caused a scene when he accused a waiter removing his plate of trying to steal his food and later drank water from the finger bowls passed around between courses because he did not know their purpose. When the story was first publicized in 1828 by anti-Jacksonians eager to portray the general's supporters as barbarians unfit for public life, Crockett ignored it. But after it was picked up by the *Nashville Whig* and other Tennessee newspapers, he decided to respond. On January 3, 1829, he wrote to Congressmen James Clark of Kentucky, a Clayite and fellow resident of Mrs. Ball's house, and Gulian C. Verplanck of New York, who had been seated near him that evening, asking them to attest to its falsehood. "I would not make this appeal," he said, "if it were not that, like other men, I have enemies who would take much pleasure in magnifying the plain rusticity of my manners into unparalleled grossness and indelicacy." Although his letter and their responses ran in the *Whig*, the *Jackson Gazette*, and other Tennessee papers in January 1829, such was Crockett's reputation that many people refused to believe the disclaimers.[11]

Far exceeding his accomplishments, his notoriety was based on his amusing, garbled speeches, which, although ungrammatical to the point of occasional incomprehensibility, possessed a directness that people found refreshing or inane, depending on their politics. He also benefited from the glorification of both the honest yeoman farmer and the bold hunter current at the time, which increased in magnitude with the election of Jackson, the people's choice. On March 18, 1828, the *Nashville Republican* claimed that the new representative from the Western District could "wade the Mississippi, carry a steamboat on his back," and not only "whip his weight in wild-cats" but any man in the Congress as well. On January 27, 1829, the *Jackson Gazette* reported that "Col. Crockett, a member of Congress from this state, arrived at Washington City on the 8th day of Dec. and took his seat. It was reported before his arrival there, that he was wading the Ohio towing a disabled steamboat and two keels." The stories spread to newspapers around the country, whose editors gave them a positive or negative slant, depending on their political loyalties. In a sense, Crockett became a filler or comic gloss on the war between the Jacksonians and the coalition, which would not only forge the Democratic and Whig parties but also spur a proliferation of newspapers intent on converting voters.

Crockett reveled in the positive accounts, which he encouraged and, in many cases, originated with his anecdotes, but the condescending stories ate at his self-confidence, leaving him at the mercy of both flatterers seeking to use his notoriety to their advantage and opponents mocking his every action. He was caught in a trap of his own devise. During his campaigns, he had nurtured the image of the backwoods bear hunter, while seeking in Murfreesboro and, especially, Washington to fit in with his fellow legislators in his dress and, to a large degree, his manner. He wanted to be a gentleman, yet he worried that he lacked the knowledge to participate fully in the business of Congress and questioned his ability to deal equally with the "great men of the nation."[12] Although he realized almost immediately that Congress was as driven by personal jealousies and petty politics as the Tennessee legislature, he continued to feel inadequate and apologize for his lack of refinement and education throughout his first term. But when his foes turned his campaign persona on its head, mocking him as an ignorant drunkard, a bumpkin and loudmouth too crude for decent society, he bristled and fought back. He challenged the negative portrait directly and also enlisted others to write erudite speeches and letters for him. Rather than backing off, his opponents then charged that his use of ghostwriters proved his ignorance and unsuitability for office.

Primary among the handful of men who took Crockett seriously was Thomas Chilton, a representative from Kentucky, whom other members of his delegation had introduced to Crockett soon after their arrival in Washington. The two men struck up an immediate and abiding friendship, which changed the course of Crockett's life. Chilton, who moved into Mrs. Ball's Boarding House for the second session of the Twentieth Congress and subsequently stayed there whenever he was in the capital, wrote many of Crockett's speeches and formal, circular letters back to his constituents. He was also the ghostwriter for his autobiography, in which he refined the image of the amusing, self-made, self-taught bear hunter, which had become his hallmark as a campaigner.

Little is known about Chilton beyond the bare facts of his life and a few brief descriptions. Born July 30, 1798, in Lancaster, Kentucky, Chilton was a Baptist preacher and lawyer, who, like Crockett, was elected to his first term in 1827, as a Jacksonian from the state's Eleventh District. Reelected in 1829, he was beaten in 1831, and returned to the House in 1833 as an anti-Jacksonian, exactly the electoral path of his friend Crockett. Unlike David, who was defeated in 1835, Chilton chose to retire from politics. He moved to Talladega, Alabama, where he resumed his ministry and became a leader in the Alabama Baptist Convention. In 1851, he was called to be pastor of a Baptist church in Houston. He died three years later in Montgomery, Texas.

Contemporaries described him as a "physical giant," whose moral rigidity made him an outspoken obstructionist in the House. He regularly delivered orations on the need for "reform and retrenchment," the battle cry of the Jacksonians, which he turned first on their enemies, then against them after he switched allegiance. He sought across-the-board reductions in the military, in congressional pay, and in the civil and diplomatic services. Many voters in Crockett's Western District considered Chilton an evil, manipulative man who seduced their representative from the true Jacksonian path. Throughout their careers in Washington, they frequently spoke and acted in tandem.

Their names first appear together on a motion Crockett filed on January 27, 1828, asking that the Committee on Military Affairs authorize the secretary of war to sponsor an engineering survey of Big Shoal Creek and other waterways in Lawrence County, looking for suitable sites for a national armory similar to those at Harper's Ferry and Springfield. Chilton then added an amendment requesting surveys of a number of rivers in his Kentucky district, as did Gabriel Moore of Alabama, one of Crockett's neighbors in Mrs. Ball's Boarding House. On April 2, 1828, Chilton and Crockett spoke against a bill to provide a pension to the impoverished widow of a Major General Brown, arguing on constitutional grounds that special privileges should not be voted individuals; rather, Chilton said, they should go to all or none. Crockett offered to donate money from his own pocket to assist her, but no one followed his lead. The new friends had, however, provided an opportunity for their fellow Jacksonians to register a protest vote against a common form of special-interest politics.

Despite their stand on principle in Mrs. Brown's case, both men sought favors for their districts. The last seven resolutions Crockett introduced during the term sought to please particular constituents—Revolutionary War veterans William Walker and Andrew Derryberry, who desired pensions, as well as communities seeking postal routes and a military road. He also consistently demanded that the occupants in his district receive clear title to their land.

The national government owned 90 percent of the western territory, which it sold at a fixed price of $1.25 an acre, high enough to force many settlers to remain squatters. During the period 1826 to 1828, with the economy recovered from the

Panic of 1819, the number of people moving westward increased dramatically, as did the demand for more reasonably priced land. The states responded by asking the Congress to fix graduated price scales or to cede the acreage within their boundaries directly to them.

In the Senate, Thomas Hart Benton of Missouri missed no opportunity to demand a comprehensive program to sell the land cheaply and fast, while in the House the Jacksonians of the western states joined the battle. The Adamsites of the Northeast generally opposed land reform because they feared a loss not only of laborers, who were already migrating in droves, but also of political influence, as the balance of power in the Congress followed the people.[13] That concern found expression in the debate over the spread of slavery into the new territories, the South's plantation system requiring far different types of support than the North's industrial and mercantile economy. The Missouri Compromise of 1820, which brought a slave state, Missouri, and a free state, Maine, into the Union, while setting latitude 36°30′ as the northern boundary of slavery in the West, was but the most famous of a series of arrangements to forestall open conflict. In large measure, it was the work of Henry Clay, a slave owner who favored manumission and colonization of the freedmen.

In theory, the debate over public lands ideally suited the bear hunter from the canebrakes, the friend and representative of the poor farmer, but he failed to seize the opportunity to help develop a comprehensive solution. While paying lip service to the broader question, he sought special treatment for the Western District, and he stubbornly, if conscientiously, pursued his course to the exclusion of any compromise.

Ignoring the deadline it had set two years earlier for the settlement of all North Carolina claims to its territory, the Tennessee legislature had decided in 1825 to convert all land warrants owned by North-Carolina University into twenty-five-acre certificates, which would be offered first to occupants of public lands in the Western District at a price of $0.50 an acre, the proceeds being split between the university and two Tennessee colleges. Thus, a farmer with 200 acres could purchase eight warrants for $100.00 and gain clear title to land he already considered his. That same year, Polk, who had been elected to Congress, began to press Tennessee's demand that the national government cede the land it continued to control in the Western District to the state, which would then use the proceeds from its sale to fund common schools. Because the Adamsites defeated his bill in the Nineteenth Congress, Polk determined to try again in the Twentieth, where the Jacksonians formed a powerful bloc in the House and were ready for battle on every issue. Polk himself chaired the select committee to deal with the state's request, and among its members were his fellow Tennesseans Crockett and John Bell. In April 1828, the committee reported a bill providing for outright cession of land to the state, which, in turn, would set aside 444,000 acres for support of common schools, not colleges or universities.

On April 28, the debate began and the following day Crockett made his maiden speech in Congress in defense of the bill, saying that he knew the Western District better than anyone. He also echoed an argument developed the day before by Polk that the "General Government" already owed the state some 440,000 acres—the equivalent of one full section of 640 acres in each of the state's townships, which was to have been set aside for education, as it was in all other new territories.[14] Tennessee had never received the set-aside because the men who presented their North Carolina warrants had chosen their lots in such a way that it was impossible to find an undivided square-mile section in any area. He also proclaimed much of the land worthless—too heavily timbered, infertile, rocky, or too wet. "The low ground or bottoms, contiguous to the streams in this western division, are frequently from one to two miles in width; but an important reason why they neither are, nor can be valuable, is found in this, to wit, that they are usually inundated. This I know to be fact personally, having often rowed a canoe from hill to hill."[15] Crockett spoke, he said, as a farmer fully in sympathy with the cry of his colleagues to reduce the price of public land throughout the nation. "The rich require but little legislation," he said. "We should, at least occasionally, legislate for the poor."[16]

The Adamsites succeeded in tabling the entire measure, effectively removing it from consideration until the second session, beginning in December. Many of them objected to making a special law for Tennessee, especially one that might set a precedent for other states, and they pointed out that 3-to-4 million acres were to be ceded, not 444,000 as the Tennesseans claimed. The Adamsites were also eager to do anything they could to embarrass Jackson in his home state during what was already a bitter presidential campaign.

Not content to let the session end without some action, Crockett introduced on May 10 a resolution asking that the Committee on Public Lands consider giving outright to each settler in the Western District 160 acres of land, which would include any improvements he had made. The House adjourned on May 26 without taking action, and Crockett set out for home, a disappointed man. The land bill had topped his personal agenda, and he had gone to Washington expecting that the Congress, the highest legislative body in the land, would see the justice of the occupants' demands and grant them relief. He had been unprepared for the slowness with which Congress acted, the long-winded orations of its members, which were aimed more at their constituents than their colleagues, and the constant deal making and compromises.

Arriving an ardent Jacksonian, he had mouthed the party line, condemning the public printers, Gales and Seaton, who published the records of debates in both the House and the Senate, as well as the laws and official documents of the United States. The contracts to print that material, which went to publishers in various cities in every state, were highly partisan because the income from them often kept newspapers afloat. Editors would curry favor with politicians, flourishing when their candidates won and, sometimes, going out of business when they lost. As supporters of the coalition, Gales and Seaton were especially despised by the Jacksonians, and so Crockett initially applauded when the Senate voted to replace them with

Duff Green, an editor friendly to John C. Calhoun of South Carolina. Crockett had also written constituents about the growing sentiment for Jackson and his fervent hope that the general would win election in the fall. He had opposed the tariff of 1828 and cast other appropriate votes, and in return he had expected action on his land bill, telling James L. Totten of Trenton, Tennessee, "I have the subject of our vacant land under train and have but little doubt of obtaining relinquishment this session I think in a few weeks you will find that I have been successful."[17] Shortly thereafter, he told another constituent that, as soon as the tariff was voted on, the land bill would come up and pass. When it failed, he became disenchanted with his colleagues in the Tennessee delegation, thinking their support of the measure insufficiently strong.

Over the break between sessions, that disenchantment was to become a steadfast belief that the Jacksonians could deliver neither the votes nor the land. He had also become friendly not only with Chilton but also with the printers Joseph Gales and William Winston Seaton, whom he had maligned. The brothers-in-law—Seaton was married to Gales's sister, Sarah— were publishers of the Adams administration's Washington newspaper, the *National Intelligencer,* and despite losing the Senate contract, they continued to serve the House. The Jacksonians considered them archenemies, but, Washington being a small town, Seaton had met Crockett shortly after his arrival and taken an immediate liking to the "odd but warm-hearted old pioneer."[18] He cultivated Crockett socially and in *Gales and Seaton's Register of Debates in Congress* cleaned up his coarse, ungrammatical speeches. Crockett welcomed the opportunity to have his comments on the page look congressional—to impress his constituents. Crockett also formed a cordial relationship with Mathew St. Clair Clarke, the clerk of the House, who was loyal to the coalition and an accomplished raconteur who enjoyed trading stories with him.[19] By the time David left Washington for Tennessee, these personal relationships were beginning to play an important role in the formulation of his political positions.

* * *

In June, he sold his house in Gibson County to Hance and Ann McWhorter and moved his family one farm over, to Weakley County, which served as his home for the next several years. Almost immediately, Crockett increased his debt by ordering construction of a horse-powered gristmill. In the fall, he set out for Washington, arriving on December 8, a week after the start of the second session. He may have lingered in Nashville for news of Jackson's progress in the presidential election and then stopped to visit the Pattons in North Carolina. Whatever his excuse, his opponents seized on his tardiness as one more proof of his dereliction of duty.

Within a month, Crockett was in open conflict with the rest of the Tennessee delegation over the land bill, which had been reintroduced. Dominating the House during the second week in January, the debate centered on states' rights and general government policy with regard to public lands, while having as a subtext the continuation of an argument over power and privilege as old as the Republic. Conservatives viewed any move to provide land to squatters as tantamount to a social revolution, because it would not only entice working men and women to march West in greater numbers than ever but would also empower them.

On December 27, 1828, the *Jackson Gazette* had printed a petition to Congressman Crockett from the citizens of Haywood County, asking him to press for direct cession of land to the occupants in the Western District. They complained that the profits from previous sales of federal land ceded to the state had benefited only people in its eastern and middle sections and nothing short of a direct grant would prevent that from happening again. On January 5, 1829, he formally introduced as an amendment to Polk's land bill, held over from the previous session, his resolution that the General Government grant up to 160 acres to anyone who had settled on vacant land in the Western District and improved it prior to April 1, 1829. The grants would be available to men and women and required only that the occupants pay for the surveys, which would be performed by Tennessee officials. Similarly, the state would be required to record and certify the titles.

The resolution was consistent with positions Crockett had taken during his term as representative from the Western District in the state legislature, and he defended it on the same grounds in a speech to the House, which his new friends Gales and Seaton cleaned up and published as a circular letter he sent to his constituents. It was an erudite, if uncharacteristic, speech, invoking his responsibility to the people whom he represented and appealing to a benevolent General Government to take care of the

> hardy sons of the soil; men who entered the country when it lay in a state of native wilderness; men who had broken the cane, and opened in the wilderness a home for their wives and children. If most of these enterprising and industrious settlers had once possessed other and better homes than they now enjoyed: they had entered on fertile lands, under titles which they believed to be good, and were successfully pushing their humble independent fortune, when they were unexpectedly driven from their improvement by the appearance of a stranger, bringing a warrant of older date than theirs.[20]

Furthermore, he said, when those warrants were sold for cash, which the occupants were often hard-pressed to find, the profits went to colleges and universities, which existed for the rich, not the poor.

Crockett loved the speech, but his amendment came under immediate fire, from Adamsites who denounced the precedent, North Carolinians who saw their land business slipping away, and more subtly but no less forcefully from the Tennesseans who saw it as a threat to state sovereignty, education, and lucrative speculations. Polk, as leader of the delegation and author of the bill, sought to incorporate Crockett's concerns by stating that occupants would be given preference on up to 160 acres of their land, with improvements, without charge. But the amendment he offered required that the lands first be ceded to the state, so it could properly exercise power within its borders.

The delegation fell into line, with John Blair and Pryor Lea from East Tennessee taking especially aggressive and belligerent stances toward Crockett. Revealing his low opinion of the "poor farmers," Lea said that granting land to the occupants was tantamount to unloosing a swarm of locusts, who would devour all of the government's property. He also invoked the trauma that might come to suffering widows and orphans in North Carolina, should their warrants not be valid.[21] After a long diatribe, in which he echoed the delegation's line that Crockett had insulted his native state, Blair announced, "He was not sent here to indulge in acts of humanity and benevolence, nor could he do so on any other basis than his individual resources."[22] He certainly would not support free land for West Tennessee's squatters.

On the last day of debate, Polk reminded the House that the Tennessee delegation was merely obeying a memorial from the legislature, and even Crockett had supported the original bill, only to turn around and call it a "trap." He had then proposed his own amendment, which Polk dismissed as absurd. Polk said that he

knew his colleague did not at all times speak in measured language, and, therefore, he concluded that he did not fully comprehend the import of . . . many [remarks] that he had made against his own State. His colleague . . . was co-operating by his course with the enemies of this bill, and contributing to its defeat. He had opposed himself to the Legislature of the State; to their instructions; to the whole Tennessee delegation; and it was painful to see him joining our enemies, and abusing the Legislature, and the State from which he comes.[23]

Crockett held firm, convinced that Polk's land bill had no chance of success while his, even if it did not carry, would create a situation in which it would become too difficult for the General Government to sell any land in his district because of the possibility of future legislation. He also had a healthy distrust for the Tennessee General Assembly and feared that, if the Western District lands were given to the state for disposal, it would charge exorbitant amounts or otherwise shut out the occupants, as it had so many times before. Those explanations aside, he was, on the whole, confident that his amendment would carry because it was right. Although he had a core of people sympathetic to his cause—including a number of Kentuckians—either because they believed as he did or simply wanted to badger the Jacksonians on the eve of Jackson's inauguration, he never had a chance of convincing a majority to give away government land.

On January 14, after nine days of acrimonious and tedious debate, the bill was tabled for the remainder of the session, with the entire Tennessee delegation united in its opposition to the move—albeit for different reasons. In a small, ironic twist showing how public policy and personal interests were intertwined, two months later Crockett wrote to a friend and vocal opponent in the House, John H. Bryan of North Carolina, asking him to grant leases to two men, one of whom was a squatter, then living on some Weakley County land that Bryan owned.[24] Bryan honored his request.

Crockett's titular colleagues from Tennessee were less helpful. In a bitter letter to a constituent, dated January 16, Polk, after admitting the chances for success had not been great, blamed Crockett for the defeat of the land bill. "He associated himself with our political enemies, and declared . . . he would vote for any measure any member wished him to vote for, provided he would vote for his foolish amendment and against the original Bill."[25] The Adams men, he continued, had seduced Crockett in order to embarrass the Tennesseans politically. "Gales and some of the *Adamsites* during the whole discussion were nursing him, and dressing up and reporting speeches for him, which he never delivered as reported, & which all who know him, know he never did. Rely on it he can be and has been opporated [*sic*] on by our enemies. We can't trust him an inch." Confirming Crockett's tergiversation, in Polk's mind, were the rumors that he would vote soon for Gales and Seaton to remain as public printers rather than for John Calhoun's mouthpiece, Duff Green.

Polk, whose district included a number of people who stood to benefit from Crockett's amendment, had a secretary write and sign his letter, so he could disavow it should it become public. As an excuse for his secretiveness, he said he did not want to make Crockett seem a significant political figure. He then encouraged Pryor Lea to send an anonymous letter to Duff Green's *United States Telegraph* in early February condemning Crockett in much the same language and accusing him of dining with Joseph Gales—later changing that to William Seaton—and otherwise trading his vote for the advancement of his bill, while disregarding the feelings of his state and fellow representatives.

During the next two months, from Washington to Jackson, newspapers ran all or parts of the spirited exchange between Lea and Crockett, each intent on insulting or impugning the integrity of the other. Lea hammered on the theme that Crockett had betrayed his party and state by selling his vote, although the charge was patently absurd given the amount of vote trading that occurred daily. Crockett called Lea a "poltroon" and "a puppy" while intimating that he would challenge him to a duel or fisticuffs when they met again. The *National Intelligencer* of Gales and Seaton moved to open the rift further by asserting that Crockett had not dined with either of its publishers and therefore could have struck no bargains with them. The paper also suggested to Lea that it would print his speeches, as it had Crockett's, if he asked. The entire exchange disintegrated into an unpleasant sideshow that reflected well on no one.

The Jacksonians felt their outrage was justified. On December 22, 1828, on the eve of what was to be his triumphal journey to Washington, Rachel Jackson died, and the heartbroken general nearly failed to make it to the capital in time for his inauguration. In his grief and forever after, he blamed Clay,

Adams, and their henchmen, who had savaged the Jacksons during the presidential campaign, for her death. Their political feud had turned dangerously personal, and for someone like Crockett to consort with the enemy was tantamount to treason.

If Crockett knew the consequences, he did not care because he believed his duty was to serve his constituents by promoting their rights and also because he was engaged in fighting his own battles. Throughout the term, he was struggling to keep his drinking in check; given the intensity of the debate, he was remarkably successful. He was also proud enough to tell his family. Even on receiving news from his son John Wesley that his young niece, Rebecca Ann Burgin, had died at the Crockett farm when a brace of oxen crushed her head against a post, he stuck to a pledge he had made upon his arrival in Washington in December. Informing his brother-in-law George of the accident in a letter on January 27, Crockett said, "I thought almost as much of her as one of my own I hope she is this day in eternal happiness whare I am endeavoring to make my way."[26] In this, his most introspective letter to survive to the present, he continued:

> I have altered my cours in life a great deal sence I reached this place and I have not tasted one drop of Arden Spirits sence I arrived here nor never expect to while I live nothing stronger than cider I trust that god will give me fortitude in my undertaking I have never made a pretention to religion in my life before I have run a long race tho I trust that I was called in good time for my wickedness by my dear wife who I am—certain will be no little astonished when she gets information of my determination.

Although her brother and cousins were literate, it appears that Elizabeth could read little or not at all and so received news of her husband through his oldest son, John Wesley, a rising young lawyer, or verbal reports through her family. Learning of her husband's decision, she probably offered thanks to Thomas

Chilton, the rigid Baptist who had become David's friend and confidant. Bits and pieces of evidence suggest that, although Crockett did not always stay sober, he did not return to the heavy consumption that had marred his past.

Feeling better than he had for a decade, Crockett left Washington immediately after Andrew Jackson's inauguration on March 4, the Congress having adjourned a day earlier.[27] By the fifteenth of the month, he was home and feeling confident about his chances for reelection.

CHAPTER EIGHT

CONGRESSIONAL REPRISE

Aweek after arriving home, Crockett left on a three-week trip through his and adjoining districts to see what if any damage he had suffered from the fiasco over the land bill. The Jacksonian campaign against him had failed to gain much support beyond carping in newspapers and at militia meetings and taverns. A pseudonymous piece had appeared mocking his campaign style as a cross between flattery, drunkenness, venality, and dishonesty. He kissed ugly children and called them beautiful, "Dennis Brulgrudery" told the *Jackson Gazette* on March 7, 1829. He changed his beliefs to match his audience, greeted every man as a friend, attended every social function he could find, and never missed a chance to treat for whiskey. Without exception, he took the side of the poor against the rich.

The charges grew more outrageous as the campaign progressed, and began to receive notice beyond the state. That they were dredged up from the election two years before did not matter to Crockett's detractors. The *Missouri Republican* printed a purported Crockett campaign speech from 1827: " 'Friends, fellow-citizens, brothers & sisters: [Governor] Carroll's a statesman—Jackson's a hero and Crockett's a *horse*!!! . . . they accuse me of adultery, its a lie. I never ran away with any man's wife that wasn't willing in my life. They accuse me of gambling; it's a lie—for I always plank the cash. Fi-

nally . . . , they accuse me of being a drunkard; it's a d——d
lie, for whisky can't make me drunk.' "[1]

On his journey in early April, Crockett discovered that his
demand that occupants receive a grant of their land from the
General Government was so popular that a candidate could
scarcely be found to oppose him. Pleasant M. Miller, an upright
Jacksonian who had moved west from Knoxville, was desig-
nated by the party in late March to bear its standard. On April
4, he had printed in the *Jackson Gazette* a circular letter to voters
in which he declined to run against Crockett. Miller said that
he no longer supported Jackson because he had betrayed his
principles by appointing to his cabinet men who were serving
in the Congress, thereby obscuring the line between the two
branches of government and depriving the states of their
elected representatives. The Jacksonians turned to Adam
Huntsman, a prominent lawyer who had lost his leg in the War
of 1812, and William Fitzgerald, another rising attorney and
neighbor of Crockett in Weakley County. Believing Crockett
unbeatable, both found convenient excuses to avoid the race.
General John Cooke, who had found himself too good for the
rabble two years earlier, similarly refused to try again.

At last, Adam R. Alexander agreed to run for his former
seat. Heeding the results of straw polls conducted at militia
musters around the district, Crockett predicted that he would
beat his opponent by 5,000 votes. Confident of victory, he traveled to the adjacent Eighth District to campaign successfully for
Cave Johnson, an independent like himself, against the incumbent, John H. Marable, and to the Sixth, where he sought
through faint praise to maintain the appearance of polite relations with James K. Polk while working behind the scenes to
thwart the reelection of the man who had become his foe.
Crockett's cynical political act fooled no one.

In Memphis he visited the Pinch, a poor section of the city
overlooking Catfish Bay, where he made a speech from the
deck of a flatboat, reminiscing on his nautical misadventure.
Having earlier addressed the town's solid citizens, he was in the
mood for tales and games. After amusing his audience with

anecdotes, he bet a gallon of whiskey that "he could jump further into the bay, make a bigger splash and wet himself less than any other man in the crowd."[2] After three-hundred-pound Eppy White agreed to the terms, Crockett surrendered without getting wet, and the bet was quickly consumed. Although his reputation was built on such appearances, they were so quickly embellished that it is no longer possible to separate definitively the real from the apocryphal, to say, for example, whether there was a bet or a mass drunk following the event.

Passing through Nashville during his travels, he encountered his friend Sam Houston, who had just thrown the state into a turmoil by sending his young wife, Eliza Allen, home and resigning the governorship. He told Crockett, as he had announced to others, that he planned to cross the Mississippi to the Arkansas Territory and live among the Cherokee, his "adopted brothers," who had removed there from East Tennessee. The separation, which came about, Houston later explained, because eighteen-year-old Eliza Allen was "cold" to him—perhaps the short-lived marriage was never consummated—ruined his political career in Tennessee and set him on a twisted, sometimes drunken course for Texas.[3]

In August, Crockett nearly doubled Alexander's vote, polling 6,773 (64 percent) to 3,641 (34 percent), with two lesser candidates drawing 156 and 12 respectively. Crockett was at the height of his popularity in West Tennessee.

Within a month, he sent to the *Jackson Gazette* (September 26, 1829) a long letter, probably worked over by his friend Thomas Chilton, addressing the slanders leveled against him during the election. It also cast light on his feelings about politics. "[F]or the last eight years of my life," he said, "and it has so happened that once every two years of that period, just before August, I have been charged upon with all the artillery which malice hatred and envy could bring into the field to bear against me, for the purpose of laying me out, and establishing my character and standing in society, in the obvious position of a scoundrel, without having even once in the course of my life, so far as has come to my own knowledge or belief, either directly or indirectly, deserved the imputation."

But he could not let pass the accusations of dishonesty emanating from a Gibson County neighbor named David Gordon, a Baptist preacher, who first approached Crockett in the fall of 1824, saying he held a 236-acre warrant and asking whether he knew of that amount of "good quality" vacant land nearby. Crockett showed the "old man" a parcel, which he claimed, and collected neither a finder's fee nor a reward for his assistance. Not long after moving to the new farm, Gordon's wife died, he married a younger woman, and then his entire family fell ill. Crockett carried water to the ailing family every morning for several weeks and twice rode forty miles to fetch a doctor.

Crockett became associated with Gordon again in the summer of 1827 when he hired David C. Phillips to build a horse-turned mill on his farm, paying him a fifty-dollar advance. Phillips owed Gordon twenty-five dollars and was being pressured by him to repay it while falling behind schedule in his work. Crockett finally offered to pay off his debt to Gordon if he finished the mill on time. Phillips constructed "in place of a horse mill, a mere rattle-box unfit for any other use than to scare the crows with, for which purpose it unfortunately stood in the wrong place, so that it answered no purpose at all," and so Crockett paid no one. The matter lay dormant until 1829, when Gordon, inspired by Crockett's opponents, accused him of reneging on his word.

"It has been usual with me," Crockett wrote, "to treat most of the fabricated malicious electioneering stories about me with silent contempt, but when we consider that the author of the present one is a preacher of the Gospel, whose very calling is calculated to cloak his falsehoods, and inspire confidence in the truth of his statement, it is presumed this fact would of itself be sufficient apology for troubling the public with the present communication." After paying respect to the Baptist Church, he congratulated himself for exposing one of its black sheep.

On October 16, David Phillips filed suit against Crockett in the Weakley County Court for the money owed on the mill he had miscreated. On the same day, a Francis Long also sued Crockett for debt. Phillips lost. Long's case was continued repeatedly until April 1832, when the court declared it lacked jurisdiction. These disputes clearly marked the beginning of a two-year-long drive by the Tennessee Jacksonians to discredit and unseat the gentleman from the cane. By consorting with their political enemies, primarily William Seaton and followers of Henry Clay, and by criticizing the Tennessee legislature for failing to deal honestly and responsibly with land issues, he had offended the Jacksonians, who already viewed him with distrust because of his opposition to the general in the 1823 senatorial vote.

There were abundant precedents for turning personal matters into political issues, especially when it was inexpedient to attack someone over policy. The two most notable examples were Houston's disastrous marriage and the Eaton Affair, which convulsed the Jackson administration in its first year and led ultimately to the election of Martin Van Buren as vice president and president. On July 18, 1816, Margaret (Peggy) O'Neale, the sixteen-year-old daughter of a popular tavern owner, had married John B. Timberlake, a tall, handsome purser on leave from the navy because of a discrepancy in his accounts. Peggy's father loaned the young rake $15,000 to open a business, at which he was decidedly unsuccessful. In the 1820s, John Eaton, a senator from Tennessee staying at O'Neale's tavern, Franklin House, took a liking to Peggy and arranged for Timberlake to return to sea. Known as a lovely, loose woman who had affairs with politicians, including Martin Van Buren, Peggy became John Eaton's mistress, and he set out to keep her. When Franklin House failed, Eaton, a wealthy planter, set O'Neale up in a new tavern, which became headquarters for the Tennessee delegation, and continued his affair with Peggy. Eaton also posted bond for Timberlake, when his accounts came up $10,000 short after a long tour of duty, and arranged for him to go to sea for four years on the USS *Constitution,* during which time he committed suicide.[4]

On another occasion, Richard Call, one of the wild Tennesseans, who later became territorial governor of Florida, tried to rape Peggy Timberlake in her father's tavern. She fought him off and reported the assault to Jackson, who confronted his colleague. Call argued that, because Peggy was a fallen woman, he could not have raped her. Refusing to accept that lame defense, Jackson ordered him to apologize, and he did, reluctantly. After being elected president, Jackson told Eaton, who was to become secretary of war, to marry Peggy and make an honest woman of her. Eaton obliged, but the other administration wives treated her like a pariah, bringing the Washington social scene, around which so much of political life revolved, to a painful halt.

Rumor had it that Vice President Calhoun was behind the intrigue as part of an elaborate plot to undermine Van Buren in the race for what both thought would be an open presidency in 1832, the argument being that because Van Buren, as secretary of state, had to host dinners and other events, a boycott of Peggy Eaton would both undercut his effectiveness and strain the political alliances on which he depended for advancement. Van Buren could support his president and Peggy Eaton, while losing everyone else in the executive branch, or he could join in ostracizing her and offend Jackson. Quite possibly, Van Buren originated the report that Calhoun was behind the social conflict. Then too the wives needed no added incentive to shun the wild Peggy. Whatever the origin of the snub, Jackson, remembering the charges of bigamy and adultery made against Rachel and still mourning her death, tried to force Peggy Eaton on the wives, to no avail.

Accurately reading the situation, Van Buren, as secretary of state, sought to bring Peggy Eaton social acceptance. Although he failed, he gained the gratitude of Jackson. The creator of the Albany Regency, the New York political machine, Van Buren was already known as the "Little Magician" for his political prestidigitations. Beginning with the Eaton Affair and continuing over the next six years, his feats would confirm his reputation as one of the shrewdest operators of his day, a man without scruple or principle, save that of acquiring power through intrigue. A short, stout man, fastidious in his appearance, he had served New York as governor and senator while acting as a major power broker in presidential politics through the 1820s. After supporting Crawford for the presidency in 1824, he switched to the Jackson camp, bringing with him a number of New York intellectuals and artists, including James Kirke Paulding and Washington Irving, as well as his political followers, many of whom were radical supporters of workingmen's rights and an expanded franchise. He steadily wormed his way into Jackson's confidence, serving not only as secretary of state but also as the administration's patronage boss.

The Twenty-first Congress convened on December 7, 1829, in an atmosphere of political uncertainty. The Eaton Affair preoccupied the president and his cabinet, while the Congress was a place where sectional and party loyalties frequently collided. With their leaders out of office, the Adamsites and Clayites—National Republicans—hunted for battles with the Jacksonians—Democratic Republicans—and found them on questions ranging from public lands to Indian removal and internal improvements. Often people changed long-held positions as they chose sides. Home in Kentucky but still active in directing strategy, Henry Clay, for example, cynically transformed himself from an implacable foe of Indians into an equally outspoken opponent of Jackson's plan to move the eastern tribes west of the Mississippi. To the surprise of many of his supporters, Jackson took a strong stand against government funding of internal improvements, stating that the money was better used in paying off the national debt.

A week after the session opened, Crockett acted to remove the issue of Tennessee lands from James Polk's standing Committee on Public Lands and place it with a select committee, which he would chair. This seemingly simple procedural motion was intended not only as a slap at the rest of the Tennessee delegation but also as a way of keeping Tennessee separate from the looming general debate over cession of public lands to the states. With an assist from the Clayites, he won approval for his committee over Polk's protest. The following week, December 22, he again bested Polk on a procedural matter, having all material relating to Tennessee's claims and petitions for disposal of its public lands turned over to his select committee. Despite their earlier protestations, Polk and several other Tennesseans served with him.

Procedural victories were all he would ever gain. On January 29, 1830, the select committee introduced its bill, basically the one defeated the previous year revised to accommodate everyone's criticism. The bill would have ceded to Tennessee 444,000 acres in the Western District, equal to the total of the 640 acres that should have been set aside in each of the state's townships for the common schools. The state could sell the land and apply the proceeds to education, but it would also have to grant the right of preemption to occupants, allowing them to purchase at least 200 acres they had either improved or intended to improve for $0.125 an acre, payable, cash in full, within a year.

North Carolina again protested vigorously that its interests were being ignored and on May 3 the bill was tabled 90 to 69. When Crockett pleaded for consideration of a revised bill, which would simply grant the occupants preemption rights they could exercise by purchasing their 200 acres directly from the General Government within two years, all the Tennesseans but Cave Johnson deserted him, and he lost again. The defeat was especially bitter because at the same time the Congress passed and Jackson signed the General Preemption Act of 1830, which applied to current occupants of public lands, excepting Tennessee.

Previously, only squatters who occupied their land before it came under the domain of the federal government were technically granted the right to purchase it, without competitive bids, at the minimum price. Because squatters not meeting that criterion were subject to imprisonment of up to six months and a hundred-dollar fine, both of which were difficult to enforce universally for political reasons, the government had applied a rather loose if inconsistent procedure for determining whether their occupancy preceded government acquisition. By 1820, individual preemption petitions were almost automatically granted, but no systematic procedure existed, and it was still possible for a settler to run afoul of local officials and speculators and be dispossessed. While not a substitute for coherent policy, the General Preemption Act did clarify the situation by declaring every current squatter on public lands a legitimate occupant eligible to purchase his farm.[5]

Crockett moved in the second session, the winter of 1830–31, for reconsideration of his tabled bill, but he again failed. By then, he had openly broken with the Jacksonians, and his pet measure had become relevant only as the defining issue in what promised to be a tough campaign in the Western District.

In tandem with Chilton, Crockett had earned a reputation for being contrary long before the vote on the land bill. He delighted in goading his opponents on the floor of the House and in the salons of Washington where he was becoming increasingly well known because of his tales and defense of the poor. On January 22, 1830, he demanded a full report on the military academy at West Point, saying: "I want to know if it has been managed for the benefit of the noble and wealthy of the country, or of the poor and orphan."[6] Introducing, in February, a resolution to abolish the academy, he said: "It was not proper that the money of the Government should be expended in educating the children of the noble and wealthy; that money was raised from the poor man's pocket as well as the rich."[7] He complained that it was impossible for all but the graduates of West Point to receive commissions, and those gentlemen were not up to the task of commanding soldiers. They were "too delicate, and could not rough it in the army like men differently raised. When they left the school, they were too nice for hard service." The resolution was tabled, printed, and allowed to die.

In March, he joined a solid coalition from the South and West in demanding that an appropriation for Revolutionary War pensioners cover militiamen. "I came here to do justice to every man," he declared, "and under all circumstances, and if I cannot do this, I will not vote for a partial law." The volunteer deserved the money more than anyone, he argued. "The regular sold himself to the Government for bounty of land and money," he said, "which he received long since; and the others went and fought for the love of their country; they left their homes and their wives and children, and fought bravely through the war and received the little pittance of common wages."[8] The defenders of the militiamen, including the Jacksonians, lost resoundingly, 122 to 56.

At the end of March 1830, he became embroiled in the debate over a road from Buffalo to New Orleans when he offered an amendment specifying that a leg of it should run from Washington to Memphis. For the first time, the *Register of Debates* reported parts of Crockett's speech in something approximating his natural, convoluted style. He proposed that it was silly to build a road from Buffalo to Washington to New Orleans when going to Memphis by land and then New Orleans by river would be quicker and more efficient. Examining why the congressmen from the East were so eager for this internal improvement, he said,

[T]heir present kindness is merely a bait to cover the hook which is intended to haul in the western and southern people; and when we are hooked over the barb we will have to yield. Their policy reminds me of a certain man in the State of Ohio, who, having caught a racoon [*sic*], placed it in a bag, and, as he was on his way home he met a neighbor, who was anxious to know what he had in his bag. He was told to put his hand in and feel, and in doing so he was bit through the fingers; he then asked what it was, and was told that it was only a bite.[9]

The East offered the West and South "a hook and a bite" that carried with them servitude and economic dependence. For that reason, Crockett concluded, "I cannot consent to 'go the whole hog.' But I will go as far as Memphis." Chilton followed suit less colorfully. After the amendment lost, the original bill came up for action, and to the consternation of all who had

170

listened to his pronouncements, Crockett voted for the entire route—Buffalo to New Orleans, saying "he had always been in favor of the road, and had exerted himself to have it carried through his district, if the western route should be selected."[10] Failing that, "he would vote to go through any gentleman's state with a road or a canal that was for the good of the Union." Again, his side lost, 105 to 88, a significant defeat. The performance itself was vintage Crockett: strenuously object to something, offer an absurd amendment, lose, and then vote for the original measure, providing no coherent explanation for the shift.

He continued his string of defeats when he joined the call for an override of Jackson's April veto of the Maysville-to-Lexington Turnpike bill, which appropriated funds for the federal government to buy stock in a company building the Kentucky segment of the national road from the Ohio River to the Gulf of Mexico. Jackson had vetoed the measure because he wanted to take a stand against intrastate internal improvements and, doubtless, as an act of vengeance against Clay. Van Buren—whose state had completed the Erie Canal on its own initiative—and a number of eastern and southern Jacksonians, who had long argued that the involvement of the federal government in internal improvements was unconstitutional because nowhere specifically allowed, supported the president. The westerners, on the other hand, even many of his allies, opposed him. Roads, bridges, canals, navigation, and public buildings were essential for economic development in the West, and only the federal government had the money to support them. Crockett stood by his region and his friends in Kentucky.

When the House sustained the veto, it effectively served notice that a majority supported, at least provisionally, Jackson's attack on one of the more egregious inequities of Clay's American system—approving public works on the basis of political influence, not national need. The public reasons Jackson gave for his action were that it was not legitimate to fund purely local projects from the general budget and that, in any event, the money was best applied to retiring off the national debt, his top priority. He pulled up short of endorsing Van Buren's position that a constitutional amendment was required to make any support of internal improvements or private corporations legitimate.

Politically, the veto was part of a concerted effort on the part of Jackson to destroy the sectional alliance of West and East, personified in the coalition of Henry Clay and John Quincy Adams, which had deprived him of the presidency in 1824 and had provided the votes to install the American system. Internal improvements provided money for public works and development in the West, while the high tariff that funded them protected industries in the East. The working-class leaders who supported Jackson and Van Buren wanted to break the power of those "monopolists" by dealing a death blow to the American system, while at the same time southerners wished to abolish the tariff, which hindered their ability to gain top dollar for their cotton or to purchase goods from abroad at reasonable rates. The system had worked because Henry Clay and his allies had crafted compromises that allowed representatives from every region to vote for the entire package while opposing, in principle, various of its components. Jackson brought down that fragile house of cards.

Crockett's battles with the Jacksonians ruined his ability to provide constituent services. In March 1830 when the *Jackson Gazette* was stricken, without warning or explanation, from the list of printers of the laws of the United States, its editor, Charles D. McLean, asked his congressman to investigate. McLean believed that he was being punished for treating Crockett seriously and for criticizing Jackson for not abiding by his campaign pledge of "rotation and reform," designed to throw corrupt officials out of office, cut waste in government, and regularly change personnel. Crockett wrote to patronage boss Van Buren that the switch should not have been made without his advice and consent. He also observed that the *Gazette* had never endorsed him for office, while the *Memphis Advocate*, the new public printer in the Western District, had always supported him.

Van Buren never answered, but Crockett sent his side of the correspondence to the *Gazette,* which printed it. He also began to mail it copies of all speeches and bills, clearly indicating to McLean and his constituents that he was breaking with the Jacksonians. Among other items, he included the message that Chilton, whom insiders knew to be his close friend, had deserted the ranks of those seeking "reform and retrenchment."[11]

Crockett's declaration of independence came in the middle of May 1830 when he openly opposed Jackson's Indian-removal bill in a long speech written for him by Chilton.[12] Inexplicably held out of the *Register of Debates,* the speech appeared in a thin volume, published in Boston on the heels of the May 24 vote narrowly approving the measure, 102 to 97, and soon reached western voters. Removal of the remnant southeastern tribes to territory west of the Mississippi was a central plank in Jackson's platform, a continuation of his lifelong campaign against the Indians. He had announced his plan in his 1829 inaugural and a year later presented to Congress a request for $500,000 to begin relocating Cherokee, Choctaw, and Chickasaw Indians. The plan also called for moving farther west those Indians who had previously resettled in Arkansas Territory at the government's behest.

Indian agents were attempting to coerce the tribes to move, telling them that their federal protection was going to be withdrawn and, if they decided to remain on their often prosperous farms, they would be subjected to state law. The Indians well enough understood that state governments would find means to expropriate their property without compensation—or allow individuals to steal it with impunity.

Jackson was pursuing with typical vigor and crudeness a policy in effect since Jefferson's administration, but in 1830, the National Republicans and some of his nominal allies, like Crockett, took a strong stand against him, not only because they believed the Indians were being done a grave injustice but also because they saw an opportunity to weaken him politically. These opponents argued that Indian removal involved abrogation of sacred treaties and an unacceptable surrender of federal jurisdiction over Indian lands to the states. Nearly two years later, Jackson proved their point when he refused to abide by a Supreme Court ruling against a Georgia statute requiring whites on the Cherokee reservation to swear allegiance to the state. Chief Justice John Marshall, in throwing out the statute, had ordered the release of two New England missionaries, who had been sentenced to four years' hard labor for their refusal to obey. Jackson's comment, which has echoed through the years, was, "John Marshall has made his decision, now let him enforce it."[13]

No mechanism existed for Marshall to do so, and although Clay and a number of other anti-Jacksonians found the president's disobedience an appalling breach of his oath of office, they could not muster support for any action against him. (The state of Georgia posthumously pardoned the two missionaries in 1992.) Few leaders supported Indian rights in any absolute way, and other events soon drew the nation's attention from Georgia, primary among them the presidential election of 1832, the fight over the Second Bank of the United States, and an attempt by South Carolina to repudiate the tariff. A man who simply did what he wanted and let others justify or condemn it, Jackson negated the argument that he bowed to states' rights and betrayed his constitutional responsibility in the Georgia case by forcing the nullifiers in South Carolina to back down and obey the law.

Many people felt, and still feel, that Crockett would have sided automatically with the Jacksonians on removal of the Indians because his grandparents had been killed by Cherokee raiders, he had fought the Creek, and he was living on land gained through a treaty with the Chickasaw. But Indians had saved his life when he was a militiaman starving on the march back from Florida and again when he lay sick on an Alabama trail, and he genuinely believed that Jackson's policy was a betrayal of the trust they had placed in the United States. In his speech and a circular letter to his constituents on February 28, 1831, he argued that the General Government was mistreating the Indians and stealing their land. The Indians had been urged

174

to become farmers, like the white man, he said, only to be told after doing so that they should move across the Mississippi and become hunters again. After agreeing to move, some had skipped their planting in the spring and then learned at the hour of departure that, if all did not agree to relocate, none would go. They were left to starve, because the General Government turned a deaf ear to their pleas. Crockett opposed the coercive nature of the policy, and he objected to appropriating $500,000—the amount sought for the removal—for the president to use without congressional oversight.[14]

Defending his vote as one of conscience, Crockett admitted that many of his constituents would excoriate him for it. He did not care. He said:

> The moment he should exchange his conscience for mere party views, he hoped his maker would no longer suffer him to exist. . . . If he should be the only member of that House who voted against the bill, and the only man in the United States who disapproved it, he would still vote against it; and it would be a matter of rejoicing to him till the day he died, that he had given the vote.[15]

The *Jackson Gazette*, which had been defending his work on the land bill—or at least his diligence in pursuing it—published on June 26 the text of his speech against Indian removal, along with an editorial "regretting" his stance.

The *Gazette's* response was mild. The Jacksonians rapidly spread the message through the Western District that Crockett had betrayed them. His "extreme intimacy" with "the notorious Chilton" and other Western apostates was blamed, and bits and pieces of speeches were circulated among the district's newspapers to prove it. In August, the *Gazette* ran a notice from the *Memphis Advocate*, which cited a report from the *Louisville Focus* about a Crockett appearance in that city. He had gone, apparently during the congressional recess, to visit Chilton. When Crockett was asked, while there, to comment on the difference between Missouri's two senators—David Barton, a Clayite, and

Thomas Hart Benton, a Jacksonian—he "replied in his own homely style, 'Why, Sir, I'll tell you the difference between them: when the *first* speaks, he empties the *upper* house; when the *other* speaks, he empties the *lower.*' "[16]

By August, it was common knowledge that Crockett had "bolted" the ranks of Jacksonians, and the reaction was decidedly mixed. Voters in the Western District were evenly divided over Jackson's course, with the bulk of the objections focusing on his opposition to internal improvements and—surprisingly—his Indian removal program, which was deemed a violation of the nation's solemn treaties. (The opposition on legal grounds did not translate into a desire to protect the rights of Indians to their ancestral lands; rather, it concerned itself with the fairest way to gain those lands.) Those were Crockett's positions, and, in fact, the Jacksonians condemned him more for breaching party loyalty and consorting with the enemy than for any particular vote. To confuse the issue thoroughly, in the fall, Crockett and his backers adopted the argument that Jackson, not Crockett, had "bolted" by changing his position with regard to internal improvements and the tariff, both of which the president had previously favored.

By then, Crockett was in trouble. In November, the *Gazette* thundered against him, his ghostwriter, and his supporters for attacking Jackson: "With such of our citizens who best know him [Jackson], he stands upon too firm a basis for their confidence in him to be weakened by the puerile and disingenuous lacubrations of an anonymous scribbler."[17] Jackson—rather, Van Buren—had just successfully negotiated with England a reopening of the West Indian trade, which Adams and Clay had lost, and the country was celebrating what was expected to be an economic windfall. Crockett, on the other hand, in backing the "monstrous hydra" known as the American system, had deceived and betrayed his constituents.[18] Worse for his future than the *Gazette's* outrage was the caucus of Jacksonians, which had chosen the Weakley County lawyer William Fitzgerald as Crockett's opponent the following summer. Because the Jacksonians intended to begin the campaign early and pour considerable resources into it, they did not want other candidates crowding the field. Jackson himself had made clear that he wanted "that profligate man Crockett," whom he considered a disgrace to the state, out of office.[19]

Crockett's growing celebrity also became fair game for his critics, many of whom had once cheered the eccentricities they now found disgraceful. An anonymous "Farmer of Madison" endorsed Fitzgerald in a letter to the *Gazette,* December 4, 1830:

It is true, he cant 'whip his weight in wild cats,' nor 'leap the Mississippi,' nor 'mount a rainbow and slide off into eternity and back at pleasure,' nor do we believe he can *compete* at all with the Col. [Crockett] in any *such* feats. But this we believe, that Mr. Fitzgerald will make a better legislator, that he will as far excel Col. Crockett upon the floor of Congress, as the Col. does him in the character of a *mountebank. . . .*

When the second session of the Twenty-first Congress convened in December, Crockett tried three times to have his land bill reconsidered, the last being an "ineffectual attempt" on January 6, 1831. Without the legislation, his election chances were close to nil, and he became increasingly bitter and disruptive, more of a gadfly on the House floor than a functional politician. Usually, his targets were Jackson and the Tennessee delegation, and he used every issue to annoy them. On January 31, 1831, he started a fight over which committee should review the petition of three Cherokee for 640 acres of land each, which he had introduced. Alabama's Clement Clay wanted it sent to Polk's Committee on Public Lands, but Crockett protested that, having been dispossessed, they had appealed to the State of Tennessee for legal representation under its pauper law and been refused. Therefore, he felt that the case belonged in the Committee of Claims. He carried the day, although the Cherokee did not regain their land.

When he pushed for an appropriation to improve navigation

on the Ohio and Mississippi rivers, he lost resoundingly. "I would rather be politically dead than hypocritically immortalized," he announced during the debate, in a typical digression about how Jackson had abandoned his principles with regard to internal improvements while Crockett had remained true to his.[20] "I am yet a Jackson man in principles, but not in name," he said. "The name is nothing. I support those principles, but not men. I shall insist upon it that I am still a Jackson man, but General Jackson is not; he has become a Van Buren man."

Jackson's administration faced a crisis graver than Crockett's defection. By the summer of 1830, with the Eaton Affair continuing to gnaw at the government, it had become clear that Vice President John C. Calhoun was interested only in his own prospects for becoming president in 1832—Jackson having led everyone to believe that he wanted only one term. Because Duff Green, printer for the Senate and publisher of the administrator's newspaper, the *United States Telegraph,* was the mouthpiece for Calhoun, the Jacksonians felt compelled to protect their interests by creating their own publication. They feared that, without a paper for communicating with their supporters around the country, they risked allowing their foes to dictate the terms of debate.

Early in the fall, they selected as their editor Francis Blair, a Kentuckian who had supported Henry Clay and then contended with him over economic policies following the Panic of 1819. Like Amos Kendall, Jackson's ghostwriter and chief behind-the-scenes operative in his kitchen cabinet, who had once tutored the Clay children, Blair had become disaffected when, in 1822, Clay became counsel for the Second Bank of the United States in Kentucky and Ohio and began foreclosing on farmers for lucrative commissions, although the two men remained cordial for some years after Blair joined the Jacksonians. Blair came to Washington and brought out the first issue of the *Washington Globe* on December 7, 1830. Sold by subscription and carrying advertisements in a conscious attempt to make it self-supporting rather than dependent on party largess, the *Globe* quickly established its position.

Although at first Blair was personally sympathetic to Calhoun, his *Globe* was seen as such a threat that the vice president ordered Duff Green to print, in mid-February 1831, letters he had written in 1818, while secretary of war in James Monroe's cabinet, condemning Jackson's military acquisition of Florida. (John Quincy Adams, Monroe's secretary of state, had strongly defended the invasion.) In order to win the vice presidency, Calhoun had lied about his position on the Florida adventure and presented himself as an unwavering Jackson partisan. Although Sam Houston had presented Jackson with evidence of Calhoun's conniving in 1828, the general had chosen, out of political expediency—he wanted to guarantee victory in the South, where Calhoun, a South Carolinian, enjoyed strong support—to ignore it.

Acting because he was intensely jealous of Van Buren, Calhoun believed publication of the letters would strengthen him at his rival's expense. Instead, he committed political suicide. His betrayal of Jackson became knotted with the Eaton Affair, which he was accused of precipitating, and at Van Buren's suggestion, Jackson unraveled the mess by accepting the resignation of his cabinet—Van Buren and Eaton included. Eaton became territorial governor of Florida and then ambassador to Spain before joining the opposition and so alienating Jackson that the general turned his friend's portrait to the wall at the Hermitage. Van Buren's appointment as ambassador to the Court of St. James's was rejected by the Senate in a calculated insult to Jackson by supporters of Clay and Calhoun, which backfired. Cut from any role in the Administration, Calhoun served out his term, then watched as Van Buren became Jackson's running mate and heir apparent in 1832.

Forewarned of Green and Calhoun's broadside against the administration, Crockett had gleefully written a constituent on February 13, "Thare will be an explosion take place this week that will Tare their party into sunder Mr Calhoun is coming out with a circular or a publication of the correspondence between him & the President that will blow their little Red Fox or aleaus Martin van buren into atoms."[21] Crockett's boast was grounded in bitterness and outrage, the firm belief that he had been betrayed, that what he thought should matter to the president no longer did. He said the Jacksonians reminded him of "some large dogs I have seen here with their collers on with letters engraved on the coller *my dog*—or the man's name on the Coller & I have not got a coller round my neck marked my dog with the name of Andrew Jackson on it—because I would not take the coller round my neck I was herld from their party."[22]

At the end of February, Crockett mailed to his constituents a circular letter justifying his newfound opposition to the man whose coattails he had ridden to office four years earlier. With the aid of his ghostwriter, Thomas Chilton, he argued that by favoring Van Buren over Calhoun, the president had betrayed the West and his own principles.[23] Van Buren opposed internal improvements because he wanted the East, with its established network of roads and canals, to remain economically dominant, Crockett said, reflecting the party line of the Clayites. The New Yorker had stacked the administration with his political allies and forced Jackson to violate a promise that he would appoint no sitting representative or senator to an executive office. As secretary of state, the man called the Little Red Fox had forced an increase in public expenditures, demanding such extravagances as an $80,000 budget for the ambassador to the Ottoman Empire. Further, as a friend of Senator William Crawford of Georgia, he had persuaded Jackson to force removal of the Indians purely as a way to exact vengeance against Calhoun— a scenario that conveniently ignored the fact that Crawford, as secretary of the treasury, had sided with Calhoun in condemning Jackson's invasion of Florida. Finally, Jackson had come to office stating that a president should serve only four years, then reversed himself and decided to run for a second term because of Van Buren.[24]

The analysis was simpleminded and self-serving, but the western Jacksonians who felt betrayed by the president's shifting position on issues vital to their interests had few choices. A decisive and bold war leader, Jackson was a political enigma, acting more from personal allegiance and emotion than ideological principle. He had a strong drive to preserve the union, balance the budget, break the power of the eastern industrial interests and others who had opposed him, preserve plantation slavery, remove Indians, and annex territory. How he accomplished these goals was a question of strategy. He made a decision, and others reacted; thus, when he came out against internal improvements or failed strongly to back reform of the government land program, congressmen like Crockett shuddered, realizing they were going to lose votes whatever they did. Blaming the enormously popular Jackson was guaranteed to fail, so they anointed as scapegoat the Magician, the Little Red Fox, Martin Van Buren, for insinuating his way into the president's good graces and undercutting their man, John C. Calhoun.

That strategy worked to a point. Van Buren and Calhoun, the New Yorker and the South Carolinian, had for years strongly supported states' rights, and in the first half of the Jackson administration, they were openly fighting not only for leadership of that faction but also for succession.[25] Calhoun tripped when he challenged Jackson directly and exposed his own betrayal of him in 1818. Later he made matters worse by repudiating his former moderation and elucidating the extreme position that states had the right to nullify federal laws they disapproved and even to secede from the Union.

Crockett had staked his career on gaining passage of his land bill, and when he failed to do so, he could realistically expect nothing more than defeat. Attempting to explain himself to his constituents, he was left to fulminate against his colleagues in the Tennessee delegation and Van Buren's manipulations. None of it mattered. His opponent William Fitzgerald printed a circular letter to the Ninth Congressional District in the March 19, 1831, *Jackson Southern Statesman* (successor to the *Gazette*, which had finally folded after losing its government contract) announcing that as a Jacksonian he would win approval of a land bill without representing the "occupants as a set of sturdy beggars, asking scraps and crumbs at the federal table."

The campaign was in full swing, and it got nasty. Crockett

was declared missing in political action after consorting with "certain uncircumcised politicians"—Daniel Webster, David Barton, and Thomas Chilton. "Whether they have succeeded in the *felony* [of kidnapping him] or whether Davy has strayed away of his own accord is yet unknown," wrote an anonymous "Occupant" to the *Southern Statesman* on March 26. "The last that has been heard of him, he was riding towards Yankee land, upon a broken down pony, which he called *OCCUPANT*. . . . [T]his darling animal has been fed upon hopes and promises, until he is getting lean and gaunt, for the want of more substantial food, for it seems he can get nothing out of Uncle Sam's crib."

The old charges of drunkenness and gambling were trotted out, along with a new one of corruption—that Crockett had committed fraud by missing more than eighty-eight votes, for which he had been paid, at $8 a day, $704. He was said to be not famous but infamous, a laughingstock, a joke, taken seriously by no one except his tavern companions. The Reverend Gordon was brought into print again to accuse Crockett of reneging on his debts. Around the district, slurs and innuendos were spread. Bogus notices were put out announcing Crockett appearances, but when people showed up, only Jacksonians were present with their pamphlets.

On June 26, the *Southern Statesman* began running a series by the pseudonymous Black Hawk, called "Book of Chronicles, West of Tennessee, and East of the Mississippi," which in mock biblical language recounted Crockett's rise and fall: "And it came to pass in those days when Andrew was chief Ruler over the Children of Columbia, that there arose a mighty man in the river country, whose name was David; he belonged to the tribe of Tennessee, which lay upon the border of the Mississippi and over against Kentucky."[26] David turned from Jackson, however, seduced by promises of the cohorts of Henry Clay, who would be chief himself, and so the people of the river country, Black Hawk concluded, should retire Crockett from office for his own good and send to Washington his once loyal supporter, William Fitzgerald.

Continuing into July, the parody was the work of West Tennessee lawyer Adam Huntsman who, in a pointed reminder of Crockett's vote on Indian removal, adopted as his nom de plume the name of the leader of the Sauk and Fox Indians, then agitating to return east across the Mississippi to their ancestral homes in Illinois. Whites along the frontier panicked at the thought of the starving, ragged Indians living in their midst and called for the troops. The year after the election, 1832, a brief and tragic war erupted, with American forces, including young Abraham Lincoln and mercenary Sioux, pursuing the Sauk and Fox back across the Mississippi and slaughtering them when, flying the white flag of truce, they requested a parley. Captured, Black Hawk was hauled to Washington for a meeting with Jackson, and a year later he was touring the East as a "noble savage" improperly suppressed by the whites, not as a vicious war leader. But when Huntsman penned his parody, Black Hawk embodied every reason many whites wanted the Indians removed.

The attacks on Crockett were so varied and frequent that he often did not even bother to respond. From "Talladega" came a report that Crockett, who in 1829 had vehemently denounced the Second Bank of the United States, now supported it. Jackson had announced at his inaugural that he intended to fight against renewal of the bank's charter, scheduled for 1836, but no one knew when the fight would come. Crockett was also charged with abusing his congressional frank by sending only partisan literature back to his district.

On the defensive for the first time in his career, Crockett fought back, with biting humor and undisguised vitriol. Calling his opponent "Little Fitz," Crockett wrote on July 2, 1831, in the *Southern Statesman,* one of the few papers that would run communications from him and his partisans, "I have heard that a mountain was once in labour and when a great multitude had assembled to witness the birth of some wonderful offspring; strange to relate, a little mouse crept out." At other times, he contented himself with calling Fitzgerald the "basest and most unprincipled of men" and having his surrogates accuse him of gambling.

The campaign reached a nadir of sorts in Paris, Tennessee,

where Crockett had announced he was going to thrash Fitzgerald if he continued to accuse him of improperly missing votes and abusing the frank. The candidates had been traveling the circuit, with Crockett delivering uncharacteristic three-hour diatribes and Fitzgerald briefly underscoring the record, when David issued his challenge. In the rotating order of appearance, it was Fitzgerald's turn to speak first. According to the *Nashville Whig*, after laying a handkerchief before him on the table, "he commenced his speech by an allusion to the reports that had been made, and when he said that he was here to re-assert and prove the charges, Crockett arose and stated that he was present to give them the lie, and whip the little lawyer that would repeat it." Fitzgerald restated his case and Crockett charged the table. Fitzgerald waited for him to get within a yard and then drew a pistol from the handkerchief, warning Crockett that if he came closer he would shoot him. After pausing a moment, a chastened Crockett returned to his seat.[27] The retreat from fire, however sane, by a man who was reputed able to "whip his weight in wildcats," in a country where duels—although illegal—were still fought over lesser matters, proved to all who witnessed the event that he was, as Fitzgerald charged, "old" and ready for retirement.

Crockett delivered anti-Jackson speeches in Memphis, where he also attacked the press for its bias against him, but even in his favorite city he was losing support. The straw polls of the militia companies proved that the charges of fraud, however minor they seem today, were hurting his image of rectitude. Combined with his failure on the land bill, they brought him down. He lost the August election by a vote of 7,948 to 8,543—close, considering the forces arrayed against him.

Crockett contested the results, but when the House Committee on Elections tabled his petition on February 6, 1832, Fitzgerald was already seated. His challenge, filed through his friend and fellow boarder at Mrs. Ball's, Nathaniel Claiborne of Virginia, involved charges of intimidation, ballot tampering, and improper electioneering by poll watchers. It was a feeble piece of work, not accounting for enough votes, even if all charges were true, to change the outcome. Crockett could not believe he had lost to Little Fitz.

The long campaign eroded Crockett's finances, which remained tenuous for the remainder of his life despite constant attempts to improve them through property deals, loans, and finally, trading on his celebrity. In May, he sold twenty-five acres around his Weakley County home—probably not including his cabin—to his brother-in-law George Patton for $100.[28] In December, Patton, who continued to live in North Carolina, purchased from David a slave girl named Adeline for $300. Still reeling from his defeat and trying to comfort himself, Crockett added a postscript to the bill of sale: "Be always sure you are right, then go ahead," which became his defining contribution to public life. Here, in retrospect, the adage serves as an ironic commentary on chattel slavery, an institution he never questioned.

In late December and early January, Crockett wrote his backers in Washington informing them of his plans to run for Congress again in 1833 and requesting that they not only continue to cover his outstanding debt with the Second Bank of the United States, which he had apparently assumed to pay his expenses during his four years in Washington, but also that they guarantee additional sums. In a letter of January 7, 1832, he asked Richard Smith, cashier of the Washington branch of the bank, to work with his securities—guarantors—in determining the amount of cash he could withdraw. Groveling ever so slightly, he told Smith that he had come out in favor of the bank in his just-completed campaign and that he expected to be back in Congress before a vote on the charter was taken.[29] He need not have been so unsubtle. As a matter of business and a way of keeping friends, the bank regularly loaned money to politicians and printers of both parties in amounts far exceeding Crockett's request and without requiring sureties.

While struggling to raise cash, he continued his land speculations. Hedging against his defeat and the possibility that Fitzgerald would succeed in guiding a land bill through Congress,

Crockett had his surrogate Yarnell Reece enter 200 acres in his name in the Weakley County occupant entry book. Abner Burgin, his favorite brother-in-law, did the same for himself. On August 22, with the votes not counted but suspecting he had lost, Crockett wrote to a Doctor Jones in Madison County, telling him that he had just had to sell some land to pay off his debts and asking whether he could have a lease, at a favorable rate, on a 20-acre section of a 2,560-acre tract near his existing property. He planned to build cabins, a smokehouse, corncribs, and stables, dig a well, and plant fruit trees. If they proved satisfactory, he might wish to buy the land and move his family there.[30]

During his two-year hiatus, Crockett traveled extensively throughout his district and to Kentucky and even to Washington, visiting friends and political backers. He also involved himself in family affairs. He had missed the marriage of his daughter Margaret, by Polly, on March 22, 1830, having given his consent by mail, and there were other absences for which he could make no amends to the children. The bulk of his effort, as was customary, went into the affairs of the Patton family.

When the ninety-year-old patriarch, Robert Patton, died on November 11, 1832, David was named coexecutor of his estate, along with Patton's only surviving son, George. After moving to West Tennessee in 1829, the elder Patton had stayed under the care of his daughters, most prominently Elizabeth, who nursed him in his final years. He willed the bulk of his estate to Elizabeth and David, Abner and Margaret Burgin, Matilda and James Trospern, Rebecca and James Edmundson, the three children of his deceased son James, and George. He gave $10 each to his daughters and sons-in-law, Sarah and William Edmundson, to whom he had previously loaned $3,000, which they never paid back, and Hance and Ann McWhorter, who, because of an error in the initial survey of the tract he had divided years before among his children, had received an additional 300 acres of land. Patton sought in his will to equalize the distribution.

In October 1833, Crockett supervised the liquidation of the estate's assets—a log cabin, farm implements, and eight slaves, who were Robert's most valuable property. They were Sophia, an eighteen-year-old, who was sold to a neighbor, Lindsey K. Tinkle, for $550; two boys, Adolphus and Samuel, for whom George Patton paid $480 and $372, respectively; and a husband and wife, Daniel and Delila, sold together for $660 to an unnamed buyer.[31] The remaining two boys, William and Alfred brought $400 and $410 respectively, and a girl, Alray, sold for $311. Together, the slaves were worth $3,183, more than three-quarters of the $4,128 realized from the auction.

But the money, which would have helped the cash-starved Crocketts, was still not distributed four years later. Sarah and William Edmundson joined the McWhorters in challenging the will on May 8, 1834, in the Gibson County Chancery Court, whose clerk and master was John Wesley Crockett, whose self-evident conflict of interest went unchallenged. The plaintiffs swore that old Robert Patton had been ninety-six when he died, enfeebled by alcohol, and improperly influenced by the nefarious David and Elizabeth, who in sworn depositions said the charges were nonsense. Alone among the more privileged heirs, George Patton refused to bother with answering the complaint until two years later, after David's death, when John Wesley ordered him to do so. If Patton did not respond, John Wesley promised to sue him so that Elizabeth, whom he called Mother, could receive the money due her.[32]

CHAPTER NINE

THE FAMOUS
BACKWOODSMAN

On August 25, 1831, the comedian James Hackett took the stage in New York to present *The Lion of the West,* in which he played an eccentric, boastful congressman from Kentucky, Nimrod Wildfire. The first American comedy to place a crude backwoodsman in the lead role, the play, written by James Kirke Paulding, was wildly successful, running for two years in New York, then traveling to England, where it was adapted and renamed *The Kentuckian, or a Trip to New York.* It returned to America, where it enjoyed a twenty-year run. The simple farce is a showcase for the "human cataract from Kentucky," who on a visit to New York saves his cousin from marrying a British fortune hunter posing as a lord.

He was a congressman, a militia colonel, a man with little education, a knack for tall tales, and twisted grammar. Introducing himself in a letter to the uncle he is about to visit in New York, Wildfire proclaims, "I'm half horse, half alligator, a touch of the airth-quake, with a sprinkling of the steamboat!"[1] Later, while speaking on the tariff, he says: "[O]f all the fellers on this side the Allegheny mountains, I can jump higher—squat lower—dive deeper—stay longer under and come out drier! I've got the prettiest sister, fastest horse, and ugliest dog in the deestrict—in short, to sum up all in one word on these here Tariff duties, Mr. Chairman—I'm a horse."[2]

David Crockett was a horse too, and those familiar with his misadventures in high society recognized the just-defeated Congressman as Nimrod Wildfire, the odd colonel who stalked New York wearing a wildcat on his head and offering to fight a duel with a long rifle. It was not the garb that led Hackett's audiences to that conclusion—the skin cap having been erroneously associated with Daniel Boone and, therefore, all frontiersmen for decades. Rather, Paulding had lifted whole cloth, and then adapted for the stage, Crockett locutions and printed descriptions of him already in circulation. Early in 1830, preparing to enter a contest, which Hackett was sponsoring for "an original comedy whereof an American should be the leading character," Paulding had written to a friend, John Wesley Jarvis, a widely traveled painter and raconteur, asking him to provide "a few sketches, short stories & incidents, of Kentucky or Tennessee manners, and especially some of their peculiar phrases & comparisons. If you can add, or *invent* a few ludicrous scenes of Col. Crockett at Washington, You will be sure of my everlasting gratitude."[3]

A close friend of Martin Van Buren and ardent supporter of Andrew Jackson, Paulding knew that Crockett had left the party ranks but nonetheless selected him as the hero of his farce, mocking him while trading on his notoriety. In November 1830, Hackett awarded his prize to Paulding, and although the comedy would not debut for nearly a year, the two men made its substance public immediately. After the accounts began to appear, Paulding sent a note on December 15 to Crockett through an intermediary, Richard Henry Wilde, a congressman from Georgia, telling him that he had not used him as the character for comedy and had no intention of holding him up to ridicule.[4] In an accompanying letter, Paulding told Wilde, he had "taken measures to have the whole story contradicted in the newspapers," and three days later the *New York Mirror* ran a disclaimer, which had the effect of reinforcing the identification, as Paulding knew it would. Literary games and hoaxes were common, and the constantly expanding penny press guaranteed that they would gain wide currency.

Crockett sent Paulding a formal, flowery acceptance of his apology—written by Chilton or another of his more grammatical friends—on December 22, there being little else he could do to respond to an unseen script. But the reports would come back to haunt him in his 1831 campaign, when he was accused of being more of a mountebank than a legislator. The Jackson press portrayed him as an illiterate clown and drunken bear hunter while the opposition dailies largely ignored him until his successful comeback in August 1833. Then they began to promote him heavily—albeit with more than a little irony—running excerpts from an irreverent, unauthorized biography published the previous January, which borrowed liberally from Paulding's farce. The most popular Crockettisms were any of several versions of his self-introduction as a devoted Jacksonian and first-term congressman, circa 1827, in which he described his taxonomy as half horse, half alligator, and a touch of the snapping turtle. Riding lightning, wading the Mississippi, fighting bears and the ubiquitous wildcats, he would eat any man opposing Jackson.

Crockett finally saw Paulding's play one evening in December 1833, shortly after his return to Congress. Hackett, back from his tour of England, announced he would perform the renamed comedy at the request of the colonel, who, as the man who had bested Jackson's Tennessee machine, was at the height of his fame. On the appointed night, the theater manager escorted Crockett to his front-row seat. Recognizing him, the standing-room-only audience began applauding and cheering, yelling various Crockettisms from the play and biography—"Go ahead! I wish I may be shot!" When the curtain finally rose, Hackett in the guise of Nimrod Wildfire bowed to the audience and then to Crockett, who returned the compliment, setting off another demonstration.[5]

Dismayed and angered by his defeat, Crockett had decided that to win again he had to trade on his independence and notoriety, which although turned against him in 1831 because of his political failures, remained his strong suit. The victory he needed to convert mockery into praise was handed him, ironically, by the Jacksonians. The Tennessee delegation under Polk's guidance had failed to provide Fitzgerald with the land bill he needed to make himself invincible in West Tennessee, and President Jackson in vetoing the renewal of the charter of the Second Bank of the United States had thrown the national political scene into chaos. The land bill was a victim of the Jacksonians' desire to thwart Henry Clay, who had returned to Washington as a senator from Kentucky and seized upon disposal of public lands as an issue for his presidential campaign in 1832 against Jackson. The Jacksonians favored ceding the federal lands to the states, while Clay proposed a plan, which the Senate approved and the House rejected, to split the proceeds from sales with the states. On the other issues—the tariff and the bank—Clay more successfully forced public confrontations, although the results were hardly what he intended.

Founded in 1816 to repair the nation's finances, which were in a shambles following the War of 1812, the Second Bank of the United States was an immediate anathema to many farmers in the South and West, as well as working men in the East, who viewed it as a dangerous monopoly out to promote the interests of the rich at the expense of everyone else. State banks steadfastly opposed its power to make or break them through its control of the money supply and its unique relationship with the federal government, whose deposits it held. Many of their fears were realized when the policies of the Second Bank of the United States triggered the Panic of 1819. In January 1823, a thirty-seven-year-old Princeton alumnus, lawyer, scholar, and megalomaniac, Nicholas Biddle of Philadelphia, became president of the bank and over the next five years successfully suppressed the multitude of nearly worthless state currencies in the South and West while establishing the United States dollar on a firm economic footing. Although the program initially caused additional economic hardship, it helped the nation move out of the depression.[6]

By 1831, the bank and the nation were riding the crest of a long economic expansion that had seen the opening of the Erie

Canal, the beginning of the B&O Railroad, the birth and growth of steamboat traffic on all large rivers, and an explosive rise in the demand for cotton. The slave trade—the legal domestic and illegal foreign—flourished to supply the plantation system, despite the beginning of a strong abolitionist movement in the North and a dramatic increase in slave rebellions in the South. The most famous and shocking uprising was Nat Turner's insurrection in Virginia in August 1831, during which some fifty-seven whites were killed. Stunned slaveholders and their allies passed increasingly oppressive laws to bolster their peculiar institution. In the East, industry boomed, and with it, demand for workers and capital. Along the southwestern and western frontiers, the thirst for land and money was insatiable—up to 50 percent of the bank's outstanding loans were in those areas.

From the day he entered office, Jackson had planned to abolish the Second Bank of the United States or, at least, to curb its power, although with its charter good through 1836, the end of his second term, should he be reelected, and its considerable resources, it seemed invulnerable. But in 1831, faced with a demand from the U.S. Treasury for specie to pay down the national debt, the bank found itself overextended and short of the necessary money. Scrambling, Biddle ordered a cutoff of all new loans in the West and Southwest, which, combined with poor cotton crops in 1831 and '32, threw the region into economic turmoil.

Jackson and his handful of antibank advisers—primarily Amos Kendall, who had the unlikely official title of fourth secretary of the treasury; Francis Blair, editor of the *Washington Globe;* and Thomas Hart Benton, senator from Missouri—saw the situation as confirmation of their position: that the bank represented an unconstitutional alliance of business and government, monopolistic and elitist. It also was a major supporter of journalists and politicians, loaning partisans of both parties large sums of money, regularly advancing congressmen and other government officials their pay and travel allowances. Prominent Jacksonians, including Kendall, Blair, and John Eaton, owed thousands of dollars at various times, as did opposition printers and politicians, among them Gales and Seaton, Webb and Noah of the *New York Courier and Enquirer*. (The habit of publishers taking money caused far more alarm than the gratuities and advances to politicians—people presumably having higher standards for the journalists.) Biddle generously forgave the debts of his friends, while providing several of them, including Clay, who received a $5,000 loan in 1832 alone, and Daniel Webster, with lucrative retainers as legal counsels to the bank.

In December 1831, the National Republican nomination in hand, after the first national convention called for that purpose, Clay told Biddle to apply for recharter, although the current one had four years to run.[7] Publicly, Clay said that Jackson would not dare to veto the bill. Privately, he calculated that a "negative" would cause such a backlash against the president that it would sweep him (Clay) into the White House, and he could then have the prize he so lusted after. Biddle agreed and sent his request to Congress.

Hoping to forestall a vote on the recharter, Benton persuaded his allies in the House to undertake an investigation of the bank. The committee wrote a majority report, authored by Augustin S. Clayton of Georgia, critical of the bank's operations, while two minority reports supporting it were filed. Because the bank had refused to cooperate, none of the documents proved anything. Virtually all members of the committee, except John Quincy Adams, who wrote one of the minority reports, owed money to the bank, and Clayton received an even larger amount in 1833, just before he reversed his position.

The debate over the bank raged throughout the session, with Benton and Webster delivering long harangues in the Senate, and little being accomplished. In June, on the eve of adjournment, when the Congress was awash with liquor and hurrying to complete its business, Clay engineered a bill to recharter the bank. On July 10, 1832, Jackson vetoed the renewal invoking the interests of the common man and the principle of hard money over debt, which he said caused depressions and advanced the establishment of an aristocracy. The Congress failed to override. Jackson's veto and ringing denunciation of the bank and all it stood for made him more popular than ever among the masses, who provided him with a mandate for continuing the fight. Carrying the West in the autumn presidential election, except Clay's Kentucky, and enjoying wide support around the nation, he nonetheless lost a number of his earliest supporters.

Leading opposition figures and newspapers suspended their attacks only long enough to support Jackson in his confrontation with South Carolina early in 1833. The state had passed an act nullifying the 1832 tariff and provoking a constitutional crisis. Declaring the Union sacred, Jackson pushed through Congress two bills: one authorizing him to use force to execute the nation's laws, and the other reducing the tariff. In typical fashion, Clay, the chief proponent of protectionism, and Calhoun, a native South Carolinian and leading states' rights advocate, authored a bill containing higher tariffs than those Jackson proposed in an effort to damage Vice President Van Buren's chances for the presidency in 1836. Their effort and Jackson's threat to send troops persuaded the South Carolina legislature to rescind the nullification act on March 15. With the crisis eased, Jackson's opponents fell upon him again when he began removing the government's deposits from the bank in the spring of 1833, a process that actually involved drawing down existing accounts and placing new funds in select state banks.

Convinced that he was poised for victory, Biddle began to act as if he were the true power in the nation. He forced an economic contraction that ruined thousands of farmers and businessmen as credit vanished, and by its end in December 1834—eighteen months later—might have reached $50 million.[8] Biddle assumed that suffering people would blame Jackson and call for the bank's restoration to a position of dominance, and briefly the strategy appeared to succeed. In the West, people dependent on debt to run their farms and fuel their speculative ventures broke ranks with the president, claiming his obsession with hard money and destroying the bank was ruining them. Around the country, pensioners were caught in the sudden economic chaos. In the Congress, Biddle's allies, attempting to force a constitutional crisis, argued that Jackson's removal of the deposits was illegal and dictatorial. That is where the situation stood on the eve of the congressional campaign of 1833.

Crockett used the crisis as another weapon against Fitzgerald, whom he called Jackson's "puppy." Intent on vengeance, he accused Fitzgerald of fraud in overstating the miles he traveled between Weakley County and Washington, only to have to withdraw the charge when it was proved false. More correctly, he complained that the legislature in reapportioning the state had divided the Western District in such a way as to cut out Crockett's strongholds in southwest Tennessee: Memphis and the surrounding counties were not in the new Twelfth District he would represent. But he won, drawing 3,985 votes to 3,812 for Fitzgerald, a majority of 173. The people of the district, Crockett said, "determined that I shouldn't be broke down, though I had to carry Jackson, and the enemies of the bank, and the legislative works all at once."[9] Thomas Chilton in Kentucky was among a number of other anti-Jacksonians who were sent back to Washington for the Twenty-third Congress.

Despite their setbacks at the polls, the Jacksonians managed to cling to control of the House, although on a number of issues the majorities were slim, and in some cases they actually lost. In the Senate, the situation was more dire. From the opening of the session, Jackson's opponents, led by Clay, Webster, and Calhoun, pilloried him, calling him King Andrew, a tyrant, a usurper, Napoleon, Cromwell, George III, a superannuated old man.[10] His aides, especially Amos Kendall, were "imps of famine"; Van Buren, as ever, the Little Red Fox or the Magician. That was in polite society. Even many of Jackson's closest allies, like John Eaton and William Lewis, both of whom were heavily in debt to the bank, eventually abandoned him.

The opposition made a martyr of William Duane, who had been dismissed as secretary of the treasury in September 1833 after refusing a direct order to remove the deposits from the bank without informing Congress. His successor, Roger Taney, proceeded immediately to carry out the president's wishes. Clay and his allies demanded that the Senate censure Jackson for his actions, a step they deemed necessary because the House would not impeach him. Finally, on March 28, 1834, the Senate passed its censure resolution and sent it to the House, where it died. But the battle continued, with the lines more clearly and bitterly drawn. In April, Clay referred to his allies as Whigs and a party was born, standing for the American system and being distinctly wary of the common man's judgment.

Jackson's followers, emerging clearly as Democrats, maligned the bank as a "monster," a "hydra of corruption," a dark demonic power seeking to overthrow the Constitution and rob people of their freedom. Biddle was called Emperor Nicholas, Czar Nick, or Old Nick—the devil incarnate. Responding to the Senate's censure, Jackson declared that all property belonging to the nation came under control of the president and his officers because he alone was elected by all the people. His claims fueled the charges that he was out to negate the Constitution. He certainly wanted to expand the democracy, favoring direct election of the president, senators, and even judges, as well as limits on the terms for top government officials.[11]

Crockett had returned to Washington in November 1833 well ahead of the start of the session and taken up familiar quarters in Mrs. Ball's Boarding House, along with his old friends Nathaniel Claiborne and Thomas Chilton. While closely following the bank debate, he set out to settle political scores and seize some of the profits others were gaining from his name. But first he practiced some traditional politics. He wrote to Secretary of War Lewis Cass on behalf of James Rogers, a leader among the Coosa Cherokee in Arkansas, who was seeking appointment as subagent to the Seminole in Florida, now being pressed to move west. Rogers, who was a half-brother of Tiana Rogers, Houston's Cherokee wife, had written Crockett two years earlier, praising him for his opposition to Indian removal, and David returned the compliment. He called in the House for creation of another select committee to consider disposal of land in the Western District and soon introduced a slightly revised version of his favorite bill. It proposed selling upward of 700,000 acres of land at $0.125 an acre to the occupants and applying the proceeds to the support of common schools. A total of 3,500 settlers would be eligible to purchase the 200-acre plots, with about half of them living in Crockett's new district.

Immediately after introducing his resolution, he turned to the matter of his public image. He had dropped forever the posture of the poor, supplicant farmer, which he had employed in his first term and which had earned him scorn in his district. Now he was the unschooled, eccentric backwoodsman, the independent who had taken on Jackson in the name of democracy and won. But to present himself in that fashion, he had to transform existing portraits, which treated him more as a caricature than a serious man. Paulding's farce had held him up to ridicule while containing enough good humor that even Crockett could treat it with equanimity. A slim volume called *The Life and Adventures of Colonel David Crockett of West Tennessee,* which was published in Cincinnati early in 1833 and rapidly ran through several printings, was another matter altogether. Known after its debut as *Sketches and Eccentricities of Colonel David Crockett of West Tennessee,* the book was the work of James Strange French, a young Virginian, who drew anecdotes from Mathew St. Clair Clarke, clerk of the House of Representatives, and other Crockett acquaintances.[12] At least indirectly, through Clarke, Crockett also contributed material on his childhood and hunting adventures.

French began by proclaiming Daniel Boone "of the wilderness," which he described in elegiac terms, and Crockett of the frontier, "a less attractive state."[13] From there, he wobbled into more difficulty as he portrayed an illiterate farmer and hunter at home in his snug little cabin—rustic but neat. The famous man worked outside with the hunting dogs, where he felt most comfortable, while his wife and their daughters placidly knitted inside. No slaves marred this scene of domestic bliss, which stood as a monument to the powers of industry and progress. At the same time, *Sketches* presented criticism of Crockett that, well founded or not, has haunted his name as much as have the charges of gambling, womanizing, and drinking. Crockett was said to be unkind to his second wife, Elizabeth, who is unnamed, because he left the farm work to her while he politicked and hunted. Elizabeth's competence as a farmer and businesswoman never entered the equation.

Damning Crockett with faint praise—even his most amusing lines were said to leap from his mouth without thought and then be forgotten unless someone wrote them down—French argued that he was better off as a bear hunter and backwoods carouser than as a politician, in which capacity he was a confused and ungrammatical speaker, an incompetent who asked for too much in his land bill. By implication, no simple man should dare to enter the corridors of power. Further diminishing Crockett's stature, French reprinted in full Adam Huntsman's 1831 satire "Book of Chronicles, West of Tennessee, and East of the Mississippi."

According to French, Crockett's most outstanding attributes were his humor and originality, which certainly were all that redeemed *Sketches and Eccentricities*. French pirated many of those from Paulding's farce, justifying the theft by claiming they originated with Crockett, thereby further reinforcing the popular identification of Nimrod Wildfire and David Crockett. David was the "yaller flower of the forest," the man who could "whip [his] weight in wild cats" and perform other outstanding feats suitable to a "half-horse, half-alligator."

French's comic hero could be original, to be sure. Comparing his prowess ironically to that of a political opponent, Crockett told how, after spending hours grinning at a raccoon that would not drop, he cut down the tree only to find

that what I had taken for [a raccoon], was a large knot upon the branch of the tree—and, upon looking at it closely, I saw that *I had grinned all the bark off and left the knot perfectly smooth*. Now, fellow citizens, you must be convinced that, in the *grinning* line, I myself am not slow—yet, when I look upon my opponent's countenance, I must admit that he is superior. You must all admit it. Therefore, be wide awake—look sharp—and do not let him grin you out of your votes.[14]

French also reported that Jackson had declared a truce with Crockett long enough to commission him to mount the Alleghenies and wring the tail off Halley's comet, then nearing the earth. Like many other episodes in *Sketches,* especially those relating to hunting and Crockett's verbal pyrotechnics, the tale entered the culture and has endured to the present through dime novels, a series of almanacs that began publication a year later, newspaper accounts, more serious biographies, and finally film and television.

Sometimes fawning, often unflattering, French's portrait and subsequent reprints had increased Crockett's notoriety. He was the talk of the socialites summering at Saratoga Springs, who considered him a cross between a clown and a wild man.[15] He was becoming a vernacular hero, a southwestern version of the popular Yankee, Major Jack Downing, who had a taste for politics, humor, and social satire. But Crockett fumed that the work was unauthorized and untrue, an imposition on the American people.[16] It brought him neither respectability nor profit.

Only he could write his life, Crockett told his family and friends, and he enlisted Thomas Chilton to help him. In December 1833 and January 1834, Chilton, writing in Crockett's name, negotiated a contract with the Philadelphia publishing house of Carey and Hart. Chilton so thoroughly became Crockett that David felt he had to explain the situation. In strict confidence, he wrote Carey and Hart on February 23, 1834:

I wish you to understand that the Hon Thos Chilton of Kentucky is intitled to one equl half of the sixty two and a half percent of the entire profites of the work as by the agreement between you and myself—and also to half the

200

copyright in any subsequent use or disposition. . . . The manuscript of the Book is in his hand writing though the entire substance of it is truly my own The aid which I needed was to clarify the matter but the style was not altered

The letters which you have heretofor received from me were also in his hand writing as I was unwell and not able to write at their dates I deem it necessary to give you this information that you may hereafter know my hand writing and his, as it may be necessary that each of ous should correspond with you when absent from each other. . . . [17]

Other letters from the same period clearly show that Crockett was in fine health, working steadily at his narrative, sitting for a formal portrait by S. S. Osgood, whom he had hired after seeing his work for Henry Clay, and making a large number of social appearances around Washington. He lied to his publishers to explain his and Chilton's initial deception—undertaken to conceal Crockett's limitations—but their arrangement remained unchanged. Content with anonymity, Chilton continued to correspond about the book with Carey and Hart and others as Crockett. For this part, Crockett worried that if the truth of the collaboration became public, people would accuse him of literary fraud. Lacking any concept of what a book was—he had probably read no more than a handful in his life—Crockett firmly believed that the clarity Chilton brought to his words was simply a matter of imposing grammar, punctuation, form, and organization, not of substance. The work was his because he had conceived it and laid out the raw material.

Published around the beginning of March 1834, *A Narrative of the Life of David Crockett of the State of Tennessee* ranks as a classic American autobiography, in company with that of Benjamin Franklin, which, along with the biographies of Daniel Boone, served as a model for the collaborators. Crockett himself owned a copy of Franklin's work, and both men were raised in the shadow of Boone. As described in *Narrative,* for example,

Crockett's misadventures in school parallel those from Boone's youth, and Crockett claims to have named his second homestead "Kentuck," in homage to the master trailblazer. The identifications served to enhance Crockett's reputation as a man who had raised himself from humble origins through hard work and skillful hunting. He was the essential hero of the frontier. Showing Chilton's hand, *Narrative* also contains a number of extended allusions to biblical stories, among them that of the prodigal son.

Narrative captures the full range of Crockett's voice—satirical, self-mocking, comical, bombastic, moralistic to the point of self-righteousness. The stridency and pettiness one finds in his political letters is tempered by Chilton. A number of the Crockettisms he retained have since become deeply entrenched in the language—the classic example being "root hog or die." Still, *Narrative*'s most famous contribution to the culture remains its epigraph:

> I have this rule for others when I'm dead,
> Be always sure you're right—Then Go Ahead!

Like many other sayings and incidents, the second line of this verse, which Crockett had begun using several years earlier as his motto, appears in the bogus *Sketches,* as do a number of anecdotes. *Narrative* also presents biographical details found in the *Sketches* in a more realistic and believable fashion, which has the paradoxical effect of simultaneously affirming and undercutting the veracity of the earlier work.

Chilton organized the convoluted but amusing Crockett fragments into a picaresque tale of a young vagabond, a morality play of the apprentice becoming a man while engaged in a struggle for freedom and dignity, and a frontier-adventure story of Indian fighting and exploration. He interspersed running political commentary and satire, writing of the Jackson administration, the rise of Van Buren, Crockett's stubborn independence, and the raging debate over the Second Bank of the United States. The result is a lean, realistic, amusing campaign narrative, which, for all its virtue, fails to divulge such basic information as the names of Crockett's siblings, wives, and children, and remains reticent about many circumstances of his life.

To Crockett's great joy, *Narrative* was an immediate best seller, which solidified his celebrity. Promoted by the Whig press, he became one of the best-known politicians in the country, although his fame had less to do with his abilities than with his public persona. Swept up in the excitement and the apocalyptic rhetoric of the bank battle, he began to take at least half-seriously the ironic suggestion, which he had alluded to laughingly in his book, that he should run for president to save the nation from Jackson.

His behavior on the House floor grew ever more disruptive. He turned nearly every discussion into a diatribe against Jackson's removal of the deposits, usually couched in country idioms spiced with biblical allusions, all borrowed from Chilton. Gales and Seaton and other publishers no longer tried to disguise Crockett's antics or dress up his talk, which often came out garbled. In discussing the appropriations bill on April 8, for example, Crockett went off on a rant about the corruption attendant to Jackson's program of reform and retrenchment in government, concluding that "he had lived now in the civilized part of the country long enough to find that when he was only a backwoodsman he knew little about matters. . . . [W]hat he had seen in this civilized part of the country had pretty much satisfied him that the whole of it was like the cry of the fellow who undertook to shave a hog—'great cry and little wool!' "[18]

He paused long enough to secure a postal route for the small hamlet of Troy, Tennessee, which had been awarded one during Fitzgerald's reelection bid only to have it vanish when he was defeated. But with that exception, Crockett largely ignored the interests of his constituents as he focused early in the New Year on keeping his name in the news. Unpopular in the House, his antics played well with a public disgusted with the bombastic posturing of many politicians and those who reveled in seeing Jackson taunted. The more attention he gained, the more he lost sight of the fact that in the corridors of power he was useful for annoying the Jacksonians but ultimately insignificant.

In casting the battle over the bank as a constitutional showdown between a dictatorial president and a democratic Congress, he followed the arguments of Calhoun, Clay, and Webster—the Great Triumvirate. Like many westerners and southerners he saw the bank as the source of loans for his various ventures, and he suffered when Biddle started his contraction of the money supply. But rather than blame him, Crockett turned his pain and ire against Jackson, with whom he already had major disagreements. Fearful that his country was going to ruin but unable to look past his intense personal antipathies or to grasp the broader economic implications of the bank war, he made common cause with the capitalists, monopolists, planters, and large speculators against the long-term interests of his constituents—the poor, the small farmer, the artisan. (Of course, self-deception affected the Democrats as well. Destruction of the bank did not improve the lives of the working class or institute the reign of Jefferson's celebrated yeomen farmers, many of whom were wiped out in the panic.)

As early as January, the lion of Washington was planning a tour of the East to promote his book. He told his son John Wesley in a January 10 letter discussing the proposed journey, which he thought would follow the congressional recess in July, that he intended never "to go home again until I am able to pay my debts," made more burdensome than usual by the depression and the cost of his last campaign.[19] Because he saw the book as the means to that end and because its sales started so strongly, he agreed to move up his timetable to April, in response to a request from eastern Whigs, who hoped to use him to rally popular sentiment. Believing that his land bill would pass upon his return, Crockett felt he could safely leave while Congress was in session, despite having suffered defeat in 1831 partly because of absenteeism. To cover himself, he told people in his district that he was traveling for his health, announcing the same thing on his return to the House, so it would enter the widely circulated *Register of Debates*.

Despite his open alliance with the Whigs and his rabid anti-Jackson rants, Crockett was not alienated personally from all of his old Tennessee friends. On April 23, two days before his scheduled departure, he visited the parlor of Octavia Claudia Walton Le Vert, reportedly the most sought-after young woman in Washington, with Sam Houston, who, in town from Texas where he was speculating in land and politics, was courting her.[20] (Tiana Rogers had been Houston's common-law wife while he lived with the Cherokee. When he moved to Texas, they "split the blanket.") Octavia Claudia's mother, a writer of some renown, was considered one of the most accomplished women in the capital, and her home was a gathering place for gentlemen of position and pretension. Houston and Crockett were as odd a pair as she could hope to entertain—the huge, alcoholic renegade who seemed to prefer life among the Indians and was recognized as Jackson's agent in Texas; and the celebrity from the backwoods who listened attentively to the promise of land in that Mexican province.

Crockett left Washington on April 25 and for the next two weeks was paraded through Baltimore, Philadelphia, New York, Boston, and other eastern cities as an American original. Feted, rewarded with gifts—a rifle in Philadelphia, an India-rubber slicker in Roxbury, Massachusetts, wool in Lowell, pocket money everywhere—he was expected to condemn Jackson and Van Buren, savage the advisers who comprised the kitchen cabinet, defend the bank, and talk nicely about the protective tariff, which he had consistently opposed. Balking only occasionally at the hectic schedule, he portrayed himself as an upholder of Jacksonian principles, which the president had abandoned, and a modest hunter who had answered the call to duty but would just as happily be in the woods with his dogs, chasing a bear. Initially, he retained enough of his self-deprecating humor and modesty to recognize that many people who came to hear the fire-breathing, whiskey-snorting "wild man from the West" would be disappointed to find him anything less than picturesque.

From Baltimore, where he spoke in the wealthy suburb of Mt. Vernon Place under a statue of George Washington, he traveled by steamboat and train to Philadelphia, home of Nicholas Biddle. The city's young Whigs presented him with a watch, chain, and seal bearing part of his famous slogan—"Go Ahead"—and fitted him for a custom rifle. The man who had received his greatest boost in life from an advantageous marriage then delivered a speech alluding to Benjamin Franklin: "Andrew Jackson, both cabinets and Congress to boot, can't enact poor men into rich. Hard knocks and plenty of them can only build up a fellow's self."[21] His outspoken defense of the poor vanished, not to return for the remainder of the tour. Vitriol and venom replaced humor in his speeches.

On April 29, Crockett started a whirlwind visit to New York, following an itinerary that would befit a contemporary politician. The first night, he attended a burlesque. The following day, he spoke at the Stock Exchange on Wall Street, where he was more incongruous than ever, and then lunched with Seba Smith, the creator of Major Jack Downing, who had first endorsed and then split with Jackson over the bank. The two agreed that their fictional personae would exchange letters. The irreality surrounding Crockett increased as he then visited Peale's Museum of Curiosities and Freaks before attending a banquet, whose guests included his colleagues and fellow bank supporters Augustin S. Clayton of Georgia and Gulian C. Verplanck of New York. On May Day, he paid a call on newspaper editors, then toured the city's Sixth Ward, where, viewing the Irish immigrants in the tenements—strong supporters of Jackson and Van Buren—he said, "These are worse than savages; they are too mean to swab hell's kitchen."[22]

From there, he went to meet the banker Albert Gallatin and other business leaders, who later that month would force Biddle to end the bank's ruinous contraction of the money supply. Worn out, tired of being led around, Crockett protested against delivering yet another speech—at a theater in the Bowery—before agreeing to a token appearance. After a day trip to Jersey City for a shooting match—at a hunter's forty yards rather than a sportsman's one hundred—he was in a more cooperative mood and set out for Boston by way of Providence.

He was in full cry. In Boston, he announced, "This thing of man-worship I am a stranger to; I don't like it; it taints every action of life; it is like a skunk getting into a house—long after he has cleared out, you smell him in every room and closet, from the cellar to the garret."[23] Accepting his gifts and praise, he complained in Boston about a statue of George Washington dressed in a Roman toga, feeling the classical allusion, which he did not understand, inappropriate and imperial. Mocking a visit Jackson had made the previous year to Harvard for an honorary law degree, Crockett said he had also been invited to the university but declined, fearing it would declare him an LL.D., which stood for "lazy lounging dunce."[24]

Exposed to the marvels of American industry, he experienced a political conversion that has befuddled and upset his supporters since. Textile magnate Amos Lawrence, who liked to argue that his mills were models of cleanliness and light compared with those in England, led Crockett on a tour of his operations and presented him with a suit of fine domestic wool from a Mississippi tailor. That night, Crockett dined with a hundred Lowell Whigs and delivered a speech praising the health and happiness of the five thousand women toiling in the mills.[25]

Compared with the tenements he had just seen in New York and the rural poverty he had experienced all around him in Tennessee, the factory workers did appear well cared for; and Crockett, not given to analysis, unaware of issues surrounding workers' conditions and industrialization, responded positively to what he saw and what his hosts told him. Unabashedly, he said he had realized that the protective tariff was essential to American manufacturing, which in turn was vital to the well-being of the nation and its citizens. He felt that if southerners would visit the North, as he had, they too would see the light and no longer press for nullification of the tariff. Peace and unity would reign in the land.[26]

Coming from a man who had first won election to Congress attacking the tariff and had voted consistently against it, the statement so astounded his supporters and opponents that

many assumed the Whigs had bought him, with money or promises of glory and passage of his land bill. They could not believe
that he had simply been seduced by kindness, attentiveness,
and a sight not as bad as the gruesome images he had conjured
based on hearsay. Always erratic, firm only in his defense of
the occupants of his native district, he had altered course because he had been swayed by the presentation of his hosts and
his rage at Jackson. Those who knew him also understood that
Crockett on the campaign trail changed his beliefs to match his
audience.

From Boston, the celebrity retraced his steps, his triumphant
tour broken only by the theft of his wallet and $168 on the
Jersey Shore. Chances are good that his admirers gave him at
least that much money as gifts on his way through Baltimore
to Washington, where he arrived around May 13, still more
interested in his fame than in politics, which he found as frus-
trating as ever.

On May 16, Crockett introduced an amendment to appropriate $60,000 for improving navigation on the Forked Deer,
Hatchie, and Obion rivers, a bit of government largess he had
first requested from the state of Tennessee ten years earlier.
He lost without a vote being taken. The House was generally
throwing out requests for funds for shipping channels, but the
summary dismissal of Crockett's proposal gave a warning that
his land bill was in trouble.[27] The Jacksonians arranged that the
measure was not even brought up for consideration during that
session, which adjourned on June 30.

Crockett opposed them at every turn—from extending the
date of adjournment to naming a new committee to investigate
the bank and demanding a vote on the Senate resolution challenging the removal of government deposits. On Polk's motion,
the resolution was tabled and effectively killed, although Crockett had taken the extreme step—given that the House was debating a procedural matter—of demanding that the sergeant-
at-arms bring to the floor absent members.[28] On June 17, in a
debate on a fortification bill, he ranted against Jackson's advis-

ers, "a set of imps of famine, that are as hungry as the flies that we have read of in Aesop's Fables, that came after the fox and sucked his blood. . . . [T]hey are a hungry swarm, and will lick up every dollar of the public money."[29] Two days later, he rose again, "[W]e have no Government at all, and God only knows what is to become of the country in these days of miserable misrule."[30] Shattering all rules of collegiality, he brought an end to his effectiveness as a legislator. He would accomplish nothing for the remainder of his term.

Polk suffered a stinging defeat himself when, near the end of the session, the House elected his Tennessee colleague John Bell as speaker. Jackson had backed Polk, who had been heavily favored for the post, but clever maneuvering by Whigs, who threw their support to Bell at the last moment, upset them both. Jackson was outraged because Bell was a man of questionable loyalty. In 1835, he worked against Van Buren; and five years later, he became governor of Tennessee as a Whig.

While subverting himself in Congress, Crockett maintained an active correspondence and social life. Immediately upon returning from his tour, he had agreed to sit for another portrait, this one by John Gadsby Chapman, which proved so mutually pleasurable that he posed for a full-length painting in hunting garb, with a rifle, and three dogs found on the street. He preferred the mutts to Chapman's pedigreed hounds because they looked more authentic. There was no coonskin or wildcat cap, only the sort of broad-brimmed hat the somewhat overweight, middle-aged hunter with a kind and cheerful expression favored. Chapman, who found his subject to be a man who skillfully manipulated his celebrity—even with casual visitors—and took care with all his gear, worked with Crockett almost daily from May 15 to June 29, when the portraits were done.[31]

He discovered Crockett one morning stripped of his customary buoyancy. David had just received a letter from home, and he told Chapman: "[A] son of mine out west has been and got converted. Thinks he's off to Paradise on a streak of lightning.

209

Pitches into *me*, pretty considerable."[32] The unnamed son was John Wesley, who, after being the offspring who communicated most regularly with his father, had become swept up in the temperance drive of the Second Great Awakening. He must have taken his father to task for sins of omission and commission, especially since David had in January accused him of neglect for not writing often enough.[33]

Caught up in his sense of self-importance, looking beyond Congress to some greater glory as a famous man—as president or author—David Crockett was the one not taking care of political or domestic business.

CHAPTER TEN

THE LONG FALL

The paint on his portrait drying, Crockett left for Baltimore on June 29, not even waiting for the adjournment party the next day. He had a date in Philadelphia on the thirtieth to pick up the ball-and-cap rifle the Whigs had ordered custom-made for him, attend festivities on the Fourth of July with Daniel Webster, and visit the offices of his publisher, Carey and Hart, to discuss sales of his book. Learning that the high-quality gunpowder and caps needed for his new gun were not available in West Tennessee, his hosts secured a donation from the Du Pont company, as well as an introduction to one of its officials on July 5. Crockett was moving in the top circles of American industry, and he was impressed.

With books, gunpowder, a rifle, and a few additional gifts— a butcher knife, a tomahawk, and a pitcher for Elizabeth— Crockett left Philadelphia for Pittsburgh, where he boarded a steamboat for home. Cheering crowds greeted him at each stop along the Ohio River, and in Cincinnati he tarried long enough to deliver a speech. After three days of politicking in Louisville, he boarded another steamboat and arrived on July 22 at Mill's Point, where his second son, William, met him for the thirty-five-mile ride to Weakley County.[1]

Restless to be back East in the limelight, Crockett was home barely three months, with most of them spent traveling around

211

the district. His father died in September, and he became executor for his minimal estate on the fifteenth. But nowhere is there a recorded thought about the event. On October 27, David and Elizabeth filed their answer in the Gibson County Chancery Court to the suit the McWhorters and Edmundsons had filed in May, demanding that Robert Patton's will be set aside. Three weeks later, Crockett was visiting Chilton in Elizabethtown, Kentucky, where on November 22, he gave his stock speech condemning Jackson and Van Buren. He added a toast to his friend, "a zealous, talented, and vigilant representative of the people."[2] They left for Washington, with Crockett paying a visit to Nicholas Biddle and his publisher in Philadelphia.

The economic crisis Biddle was just beginning to reverse had combined with several bad harvests and lingering campaign debts to bring Crockett to his most precarious financial state since the Shoal Creek flood a decade earlier. Even with his best-selling autobiography, he could not generate enough income to cover his expenses. No evidence exists that he was gambling heavily, as he had in his first years in office, although he may have joined a few games and lost. Rather, his difficulties appear to have been rooted in his profligacy, his generosity—he helped everyone who asked—and the cost of supporting his family, farm, and political career.

The state of his finances forced him on October 7, 1834, to appeal directly to Biddle for assistance. Writing from John Wesley's house, he was disturbed and plaintive:

I am on my way home from Nashville my Business was to arrange my Bill which I had drawn on my friend Boyd McCleary and got Mr Poindexter to indorse

But when I got to Nashville I found that he had not accepted it and I was so compleatly cowed that I could not ask any person to indorse another I was distressed to find my disappointment

I then concluded to draw a draft on my friends Mrrs Cary & Hart with a hope that they have been successful in the sale of my books—

If this arrangement should not answer I know of no other way that I can do but to pay you when I get to Washington I am more distressed in having a friend protested in Bank then any thing in the world I will—leave home the last of the first week in Novimber and I expect to come through Philadelphia at which time I will see you and I will try and have matters arranged.[3]

He added that, although two men were said to be preparing to run against him in the next election, he expected no opposition, an assertion he, as a great vote counter who knew the Jacksonians were desperate to beat him, must have made in an effort to prove his creditworthiness to Biddle.

By law, the Second Bank of the United States could offer bills or notes, signed by its president and chief cashier, which circulated as currency. In 1827, to expand the bank's money-producing ability, Biddle had created the "branch drafts," which, signed by the branch president in any particular location, circulated as if they were bills, for which they could eventually be exchanged. As he prepared to return to Washington in the fall of 1834, Crockett had prepared a draft for $500 at the Nashville branch, offering as a guarantor, or security, long-time supporter Boyd McCleary. But because he was either pressed for funds or alienated from his friend, McCleary refused to back the draft, and branch president George Poindexter, who apparently had already provided the funds, was forced to list Crockett in the Protest Book, as a bad credit risk. Occurring in Nashville, a Jackson hotbed, and involving the institution he was so avidly supporting, the event provided Crockett's opponents with abundant opportunity to mock him, especially since Biddle's largess toward his political allies was widely known. Crockett was chagrined, but rather than turn on the bank, he followed Poindexter's advice and appealed directly to Biddle for assistance.

By the time Crockett reached Philadelphia, his predicament had worsened. He had sought to draw the money from Carey and Hart, only to have them also refuse to honor the draft

213

because by November his book's sales were not strong enough to warrant $500 more. Accustomed to paying out thousands of dollars to politicians and publishers, Biddle did not hesitate to fill what he considered Crockett's modest request. He would, he said, loan Crockett $500 directly from bank funds to square his account at the Nashville branch and allow him to repay it when he could. He also would remove his name from the Protest Book.

Crockett conveyed the information to Poindexter and confirmed it with Biddle in a letter from Washington dated December 8, 1834. He asked in a postscript that Biddle inform Poindexter himself that the bank loan originating in Philadelphia was intended to cover the draft protested in Nashville and not an attempt to secure an additional $500.[4] The same day, Crockett wrote Carey—whose name he always misspelled—and Hart, requesting a full accounting of his book sales and offering to sell them his copyright because he was in desperate need of cash. He added that he had discussed with William Clark, a congressman from Pennsylvania, the new book he had outlined on his visit with the publishers. They had conceived the account of Crockett's tour as a way to renew interest in his autobiography and probably recommended Clark.[5] Eager to proceed with a collaborator who demanded less of the profit than Chilton, Crockett accepted their suggestion.

He thought his prospects were improving. On December 13, Biddle sent Crockett a statement of his account, a promissory note, and a check, which he and then Poindexter had to endorse.[6] The same day he wrote to Poindexter:

> Mr. Crockett's draft for $500 endorsed by you and discounted by the Bank came back protested for want of acceptance; I told Mr. Crockett that it was better for you both to have it removed from the Protest Book and that a new note would probably be discounted to take up the old one. He has accordingly requested me to prepare one for him, & to let you know that it was merely to reinstate the former note and was not a new engagement.[7]

Crockett thanked Biddle three days later, when he returned the signed note and check for $500, saying they would "give me much relief and I hope will not be any disadvantage to the Bank I hope never again to be so hard pressed as I have said poverty is no crime but it is attended with many inconviniences."[8] There is no record that he repaid the loan in the fifteen months left in his life. Certainly, after his death, as the bank itself prepared to close out its official business, it was taken care of—paid or made to vanish from the books by the kindness of Nicholas Biddle. A century after Crockett's death, a number of historians have looked at part of the surviving material and deduced that he had been bought by Biddle, but the record belies that. Scrupulous to a fault, abhorrent of debt, Crockett insisted on a clear statement of the money's source and purpose. He was too proud and independent to accept any other arrangement. Had he been on the bank's list of special friends, he would have received what he needed without asking, and the amount would have been far greater than that of the loan.

As he began to alleviate his financial burdens, he turned to his equally pressing political crisis. His reelection bid the following August was totally dependent on passage of his land bill, which he told his constituents was guaranteed because "every member from Tennessee that I have talked to says it will pass."[9] Simultaneously, he also was pressing for money to improve navigation on the Western District's rivers, in an effort to please the growing number of people who were not occupants but who wanted improvements for marketing and travel. He was not being naïve about the importance of the land bill, which remained the measuring rod for congressional candidates in West Tennessee, only about its chances.

"I have been in all the counties," attorney Adam Huntsman—the Black Hawk of the "Chronicles"—told James K. Polk, as he prepared to run against his former client, "and Crockett is evidently loosing ground or otherwise he never was as strong as I supposed him to be perhaps it is both. . . . [But] if he carries his land Bill I will give him strength. Otherwise the conflict will not be a difficult one."[10]

Crockett failed even to bring his land bill to the floor for discussion, much less a vote, despite increasingly desperate efforts to do so between December and March, when the Twenty-third Congress adjourned. His bill to improve navigation on his district's rivers similarly died, the Jacksonians in the House being in no mood to assist him in any way. Although the Second Bank of the United States would remain in existence for another half-dozen years, it had surrendered to the Jacksonians and embarked on a policy of expansion that set off a frenzy of inflation and land speculation. More battles would ensue before the bank finally closed its doors, but by late in 1834 Biddle had heeded the elders of American banking and industry who said they would stop supporting him unless he ended the contraction, and he had realized that the voters were backing the Democrats on the recharter issue, not the Whigs. In January 1835, Jackson gained more glory, when on the twentieth anniversary of his victory at New Orleans he announced that the national debt, incurred during that war, was retired. Few doubted that Jackson was in control in Washington. As the rhetoric and resolutions were damped, Crockett was eased out of the limelight—not dropped, just shifted off center stage.

He was left to snipe at his colleagues and complain about the slow pace and endless speeches that marked the business of the House. Claiming that he was tired of depending for information on "hireling newspapers," he joined a partisan battle over the number of copies of a critical report on the Post Office to be printed, before the House had even received it.[11] The Whigs prevailed in ordering 3,000 full copies of three volumes each, and 20,000 single-volume copies, compared with a normal run of 2,000. The postmaster general, William T. Barry, a Kentuckian who had served since the beginning of Jackson's first term, was notoriously inept and was believed to be actively corrupt, feeding business and contracts to his friends. His tenure gave the lie to Jackson's emphasis on reform of government corruption, and so the Whigs were eager to publicize and condemn the sordid operations of the vital service. Barry finally resigned on May 1, and Amos Kendall replaced him. As post-

master general, Kendall acceded to the censorship of abolitionist material by southern postmasters in mid-1835, a decision
that underscored the commitment of the Democrats, despite
their liberality in other economic areas, to chattel slavery.[12] But
he cleaned up the most egregious forms of corruption in the
Post Office.

The Whigs' victory over the Post Office in February was costly
and trivial, especially for Crockett, who could show little more
in terms of accomplishment. Underscoring his failure was the
debate over a bill that would provide 160-acre parcels to squatters in Arkansas who had been ousted by force from Choctaw
lands they had illegally occupied. There was less justice in
awarding land to the Arkansans than to the occupants in Tennessee, but the bill came from Jackson and passed. Speaking
in support of the measure, Crockett told the House on February
13, "He would give every citizen a portion of the public lands
who would settle upon it. No act of the President's life pleased
him so much as the avowal of this sentiment. He was in favor
of the bill; but speaking had become so fashionable on that
floor, in this pressing stage of the business of the session, that
he began to believe in the doctrine that silence was a virtue."[13]

Crockett's increasing marginality and obstructionism in the
House reflected his waning interest in the process of legislation
as much as his failures in securing passage of his bills. He had
grown to prefer the more public forum of the traveling author
and celebrity backwoodsman who by temperament was to be a
straight-talking democrat, a man of common sense and direct,
moral action—a poor man's Andrew Jackson, as it were, un-
corrupted by power. Despite his disaffection, he worked to hold
on to his seat, flooding the district with anti-Jackson publications
and working with the majority of the Tennessee delegation—
only Senator Felix Grundy and Representatives Cave Johnson
and Polk were not involved—in drafting Senator Hugh Lawson
White for a presidential campaign against Van Buren in 1836.
White, a former judge and colleague of Jackson, was alienated
from his friend for political reasons and agreed to the propo-

sition, according to many reports, because his new wife, a Washington boardinghouse owner, was ambitious on his behalf. Since June, when he first received intimations of an uprising in his home state, Jackson had raged against "Bell, Crockett & Co.," whom he felt had betrayed him and Tennessee, while duping White. Jackson wanted them run from office.[14]

The Whigs encouraged that schism while failing to decide on a single nominee. Following old, discredited habits, they ultimately ran multiple candidates, hoping each one would carry enough states in his native region to throw the election into the House of Representatives. By that plan, White was to carry the Southwest and share the South with Willie P. Mangum of North Carolina, while Daniel Webster and William Henry Harrison, the acclaimed hero of the War of 1812 who had settled into retirement as an obscure clerk in Ohio, would capture the North. The Whigs did not realize that the democratic movement Jackson had brought to power was too entrenched to permit a return to the situation in 1824, when Henry Clay and John Quincy Adams struck their corrupt bargain. Further confusing the situation was the position of White and his Tennessee supporters. Although nominated as a Whig, he ran as a "true Jacksonian" and upholder of the democratic ideal.

To White's supporters within the Democratic party, Van Buren was an unworthy heir; to the Whigs, he was the devil incarnate, a mock-Jackson who would perpetuate the worst of a bad administration. He was the mastermind of the spoils system, the manipulator of the growing government. More profoundly, he was blamed for the restiveness of the working man and his continuing migration west in search of land, as well as a general increase in lawlessness and violence that bred fear and anger around the country. Crockett's ambitions and his unbridled hatred for the vice president dovetailed with Whig political schemes. "I have sworn over the last four years," he said in December, "that if Van buren is our next President I will leave the united States will not live under his kingdom and I see no chance to beat him at present."[15]

Early in January 1835, Carey and Hart had sent him a much-needed two-hundred-dollar advance against his second book, which was running late because his ghostwriter was unable to keep up with the notes and press clippings Crockett was providing. He also worried that people might get the wrong impression from its title page, which he first saw on January 11. "You have stated," he told Carey and Hart in a letter the following day, "that it is written by my self I would rather if you think it could sell as well that you had stated that it was written from notes furnished by my self—But as to this I am not particular more than it will purhaps give some people a chance to cast reflections on me or to the correctness of it."[16] The publishers addressed his query by incorporating so many avowals of Crockett's sole authorship into the text that they become unbelievable.

Sometime in February, Crockett and Clark finished, and in March *An Account of Col. Crockett's Tour to the North and Down East, in the Year of Our Lord One Thousand Eight Hundred and Thirty-four* left the press. It is an amusing if unliterary tract, part travelogue, part political propaganda, and part satire. Bits and pieces of the language, many of the sentiments and descriptions are Crockett's. The news accounts of speeches and visits, which are summarized or reprinted, are authentic. But vast sections of facts and figures and a number of letters—an exchange with Major Jack Downing, for example—are fabrications, and the whole lacks the literary touch of Thomas Chilton.

"I am no man's man," Crockett had announced in Louisville. "I bark at no man's bid. I will never come and go, and fetch and carry, at the whistle of the great man in the white house no matter who he is."[17] The tour over, with pages to fill, he and his ghostwriter, who did not share the copyright or title page, turned to an ad hominem attack on Van Buren, reprinting an elaborate and not very successful parody of a letter Thomas Hart Benton had written in December to a group of disaffected Mississippi Jacksonians.

The Mississippi Democratic Convention had asked Benton, the lead opponent of the bank in the Senate and an outspoken proponent of cheap public lands, to accept the vice presidential slot on an anti–Van Buren ticket. Benton had declined in a long-winded letter explaining why Van Buren should receive their full support and praising him as a true Democrat. Claiming to have been asked by the same convention to run for president, Crockett—conveniently forgetting that the supposed request had come in 1833—sent to the *National Intelligencer* in mid-January 1835 his long refusal couched as an ironic endorsement of Van Buren. He wrote:

> My friends said to me, your name stands, big, and if you come out and make believe that you don't want to be president, and talk about democracy, aristocracy, Jefferson, Madison, Crawford, persecution, the war, the bank, gold currency, hard money, but, above all, Jackson and the battle of New Orleans, and then hurra for union, harmony, concession, Van Buren, and the great state of New York; the seceders will tack and run back into the democratic republican fold, which means the Van Buren fold.[18]

He added that if Van Buren, a northerner, were elected in 1836, then the way would be open for him, Crockett, eight years later to become president. Although featured in *Tour,* the newspaper exchange did little to improve the book's quality or sales.

While working on *Tour,* Crockett decided to lend his name to a more lengthy biography of Van Buren. In January he announced his intent to Carey and Hart, and he continued to press the point after they balked, fearing charges of libel.[19] At the end of *Tour,* he announced the volume, which the publishers, bowing to political pressure from the Whigs, brought out early in the summer of 1835 under a false imprint, Robert Wright. *The Life of Martin Van Buren: Hair-Apparent to the "Government" and the Appointed Successor of General Andrew Jackson, Containing Every Authentic Particular by Which His Extraordinary Character Has Been Formed* is the work of Augustin S. Clayton of Georgia, the one-time opponent of the Second Bank of the

United States who was converted into a supporter after receiving a loan of $3,000.

The Whigs considered the outrageous rant, which thoroughly trashed its subject, amusing, and although much of the humor is now dated, the negative image of Van Buren has persisted. The vitriol and venom echo Crockett at his most abusive. The words and images are also unquestionably his, worked into the overall style of the book, which is closely argued and grammatical. The political indictment of Van Buren comes from Clayton, a former judge, who sought, as did so many of the New Yorker's foes, to portray him as the polar opposite of Jackson by praising the popular president to the heavens and damning his vice president. They hoped, of course, to persuade voters to support the best man, not the chosen Democrat. "Van Buren is opposite to General Jackson as dung is to a diamond," says the *Life*. "Jackson is open, bold, warm-hearted, confiding, and passionate to a fault. Van Buren is secret, sly, selfish, cold, calculating, distrustful, treacherous...."[20] Elsewhere, Van Buren is accused of a false gentility and the worst sort of dandyism: "he is laced up in corsets such as women in town wear, and, if possible, tighter than the best of them. It would be difficult to say, from his personal appearance, whether he was a man or woman, but for his large *red* and *grey* whiskers."[21]

A common argument holds that Crockett was hijacked by Whig propagandists who used his fame for their own nefarious political ends—and that he never knew the difference. But Crockett the politician proposed and helped compile both the *Tour* and *The Life of Martin Van Buren*, which, although in language beyond his measure, reflect his attitudes. Wanting sales and increased credibility, he lost on both counts. As an author of a best-selling memoir, he misunderstood the source of his popularity, believing that it derived from his outspoken opposition to Jackson and his independence. He realized that people were more interested in a bear hunter than a farmer, but he resolutely failed to grasp that they wanted more stories of life in the backwoods, more tales of guns, dogs, and bears.

221

In 1834 and 1835, two indifferent novels were published featuring Crockettesque characters—*The Kentuckian in New York; or, The Adventures of Three Southerns* by William Alexander Caruthers and *Elkswatawa; or, The Prophet of the West* by James Strange French, author of the bogus Crockett biography. The works blatantly exploited the rising national interest in vernacular characters, and today are little remembered and harder to find. *Elkswatawa* was so roundly condemned in the magazine *Southern Passenger* that French stopped writing.[22] Following Crockett's tour of the East, a "Crockett Victory March" was written and soon widely performed. But the most popular Crockett tract of 1835 was one that pulled most of its material from *Sketches and Eccentricities* and presented him as a Jacksonian, tried and true, a hunter, a rough-and-tumble, hard-drinking backwoodsman.

Published by Snag and Sawyer of Nashville, *Davy Crockett's Almanack of Wild Sports of the West, and Life in the Backwoods* was the work of Charles Ellms, a Boston illustrator and editor, who had already created the *American Comic Almanac* and the *People's Almanac*.[23] Ellms had been looking as early as 1833 for a narrator for a new almanac, one who had supported Jackson in 1828 and backed Van Buren as his successor. It was an easy leap to Crockett and a decision to mention only his Jacksonian heritage while concentrating on humor and backwoods scenes. He announced himself with the boasting speech that was already synonymous with his name—that he could "run faster,—jump higher,—squat lower,—dive deeper,—stay under longer,—and come out drier, than any man in the whole country."[24]

With useful information about crops and weather, tides, and eclipses sandwiched between the tales and woodcuts, the Crockett *Almanack* proved an immediate success and continued until 1856, with forty-five numbers being produced in Nashville, New York, Boston, Philadelphia, Baltimore, and Albany. Neither Crockett nor his heirs ever had anything to do with them—editorially or financially—copyright laws being lax and most of the material coming from other people's work or the illustrators themselves. He could curse their portrayal of him but neither block their publication nor gain royalties. Ephemera, they were the most popular reading matter on the frontier, save, perhaps, for the Bible.

Throughout the spring and summer of 1835, Charles A. Davis, assuming the voice of Seba Smith's down-east hero, Major Jack Downing, kept up a running correspondence between their character and Crockett in a broadside called the *Downing Gazette*.[25] Davis was director of the New York branch of the Second Bank of the United States and a personal friend of Nicholas Biddle. Smith, of Portland, Maine, had long supported Jackson before breaking ranks during the fight over the bank's charter. Following the split, Smith agreed to let Davis pen anti-Jackson diatribes under Major Jack Downing's name, a decision which, years later, after deciding that the battle had been unnecessary and destructive, Smith regretted.[26] Crockett, who had met them in New York the year before, brought humor and name recognition to the *Downing Gazette*, while providing anti-Jackson and anti–Van Buren broadsides from his district. Following form, he would mail reports or newspaper clips to the editor, Davis, with a postscript telling him to clean up the material and print it. Crockett gained nothing beyond a little additional notoriety from his exchanges with Major Jack Downing. As soon as Crockett lost his reelection bid, the letters stopped, there being nothing less useful to the Whigs than a loser.

Crockett could not convince the majority of his constituents that he was their champion, their best voice in Washington. The Jacksonians devoted considerable resources to Adam Huntsman's campaign, sending into the Twelfth District Senator Felix Grundy and Governor William Carroll. They also flooded it with proadministration material and negative articles on Crockett, including, just four days before the vote, a report that he had misstated his travel mileage to and from Washington, claiming 1,000 miles each way when he should have taken 750. Recognizing the tactic as the one he had used against William Fitzgerald two years earlier, Crockett protested, to no avail.[27]

Huntsman claimed the campaign turned on national issues—the bank, the protective tariff, federal money for internal improvements, all of which he was against.[28] He recognized as well that Crockett had neglected those in his district who honestly disagreed with him by refusing to send them publications they requested or even to answer their letters. Because it was axiomatic that a congressman was to represent even those people who opposed him, Crockett's action was viewed as a serious breach of etiquette. The old charges of buying votes with liquor also weighed, although by 1835 they were hardly worth repeating.

Lacking a record of accomplishment, Crockett fell back on the humor that had carried him to prominence. After the election, he related an episode to his ardent admirers in Memphis, who had been stuck in a different district. Traveling the circuit together, Crockett and Huntsman, known as Timber Toe because of his peg leg, had spent a night at the home of a stalwart Jacksonian with a beautiful daughter. That night, after the household had fallen asleep, Crockett took up a chair and crossed to the daughter's room, where he rattled the door as if trying to enter. When she began to scream, he placed his foot on the lower rung of the chair, so that its leg would tap the floor, and hobbled back to his room. Jumping into bed, he feigned sleep, while the irate farmer, convinced he had heard Huntsman's peg leg, confronted his guest, a notorious rake. Finally, Crockett intervened to save his opponent from being thrown out of the house in the middle of the night and won the farmer's vote. Later, he so enjoyed his joke that he told friends about it, and Huntsman was finally exonerated.[29]

But his humor was not enough. He lost by 252 votes, 4,652 to 4,400. Crockett accused the Union Bank of Jackson of buying votes for $25 each, but offered no proof. "I have always believed since Jackson removed the deposits that his whole object was to place the Treasury whare he could use it to influance elections and I do believe he is determened to sacrafise every dollar of the treasury or make the little flying doutchman his successor."[30] He felt he was a martyr to integrity, he told Carey and Hart:

Francis Ford played Crockett in the 1911 film *The Immortal Alamo*, produced by George Milies and directed by William F. Haddock. Only a handful of stills, including this one of Crockett killing a Mexican soldier with his sword, survive. There are no prints of the entire film.

By 1932, Crockett's original cabin in West Tennessee was abandoned and in disrepair. Two years later it was dismantled and moved to a high school in Rutherford, where its restoration was delayed for twenty years by the Depression and World War II.

Edward Everett sketched the ruins of the church at the Alamo mission, San Antonio de Bexar, in 1847, the year before U.S. Army engineers undertook a restoration, which resulted in the now familiar facade.

This view of the Alamo ruins clearly shows the church and convent (*left*), which became known as the long barracks. Between them lies the hospital. In the foreground would have been the plaza.

The cover from the *1847 Almanac* shows Crockett locked in deadly combat with a wildcat and reprints his favorite adage: "I leave this rule for others when I'm dead, be always sure you're right, then go ahead!"

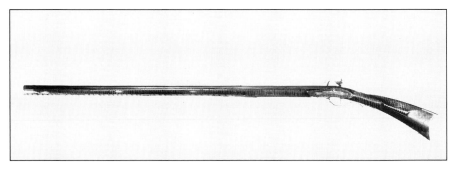

A .58-caliber long rifle, like the one favored by Crockett, found in the rubble of the Alamo. Several guns owned by Crockett still exist, including Pretty Betsy at the Smithsonian Institution.

James Bowie, the notorious knife fighter, slave smuggler, and land speculator, was co-commander at the Alamo until illness forced him from the field.

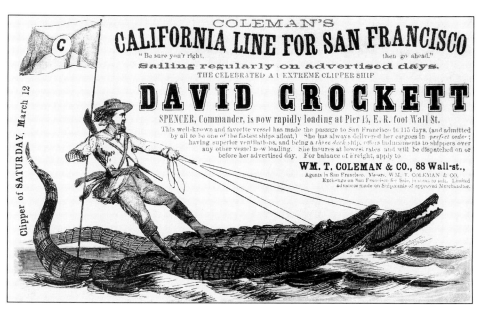

A sailing card for the clipper ship *David Crockett,* ca. 1865. The card boasts that the ship had made the passage from San Francisco to New York in 115 days and never delivered spoiled cargo.

Crockett achieved his greatest fame in Washington City, as it was then known, as a congressman from the backwoods of western Tennessee. This view from beyond the Navy Yard, across the Potomac, clearly shows the dominant role the Capitol played in the life of the small city and the nation. The aquatint by W. J. Bennett was published by Lewis P. Clover of New York, ca. 1834.

Mrs. Ball's Boarding House, where Crockett stayed during his years in Congress, would have resembled the homes shown in this watercolor by August Kollner in 1839, three years after the frontiersman's death at the Alamo.

CROCKETT MAKING A CHARACTERISTIC CANVASS. (245)

This illustration from Buffalo Bill Cody's *Story of the Wild West and Camp-fire Chats* (1902) shows a Pan-like Crockett speaking in front of a backwoods saloon.

BORN TO COMMAND.

OF VETO MEMORY.

HAD I BEEN CONSULTED.

KING ANDREW THE FIRST.

By 1832, the anti-Jacksonians were launching increasingly hysterical attacks on President Andrew Jackson for what they considered a despotic disregard for the Constitution and judiciary. His foes also savaged him for vetoing a bill to renew the charter of the Second Bank of the United States as well as a number of bills for roads and other internal improvements.

I am grattifyed that I have spoken the truth to the people of my District regardless of Consequences I would not be compeld to bow to the Idol for a Seat in Congress during life I have never knew what it was to sacrafice my own judgment to grattify any party and I have no doubt of the time being close at hand when I will be rewarded for letting my tongue Speake what my hart thinks I have suffered my self to be politically sacrafised to save my country from ruin & disgrace and if I am never again elected I will have the grattification to know that I have done my duty.[31]

He had told his constituents that if they elected him he would "serve them to the best of my ability; but if they did not, they go to hell, and I would go to Texas."[32] Short of cash, weary of the intransigence of Congress, eager for an adventure he might turn into a book, wanting more land than he could ever acquire in West Tennessee and, despite enjoying good health, feeling the weight of his forty-nine years, he was going where he could make enough to cover all his debts and provide well for his long-suffering family. With her relatives nearby, her children with David just reaching adulthood—Robert, the oldest, was nineteen; Matilda, the youngest, fourteen—Elizabeth opposed the move, arguing that they were too old to start over and that the farms they owned were sufficient. Texas was too far away. But Crockett was driven to do something to match his public image, and he assumed the entire Patton-Crockett clan would follow, as they had in the move to West Tennessee.

The family remained divided over the will of Robert Patton. In June, David and Elizabeth had again filed an affidavit responding to charges from William and Sarah Edmundson and Hance and Ann McWhorter that they had used nefarious means to persuade the dying man to leave them only $10 each. In October, William Patton and George W. Harper, the son and son-in-law of Robert's dead son James, who had lived in Mississippi, appeared at Crockett's farm to claim their part of the estate. They filed court papers challenging the Edmundsons and McWhorters to produce their evidence or drop their suit, but because George Patton had still sent no answer from North Carolina, the case lingered. Crockett and Abner Burgin paid Harper $125 in cash toward his wife's inheritance. Having persuaded William Patton to join them on their trip to Texas, they equipped him with horse, gear, and rifle for $200, which they deducted from his share.[33] Until George acted, they could do no more.

On November 1, 1835, David, Abner Burgin, William Patton, and Lindsey K. Tinkle, a close neighbor, left Weakley County for an exploration of Texas. They stopped for several days in Memphis, where Crockett visited with his longtime backers, and then went on a tour of the town's taverns. A participant, James Davis, recalled that Crockett at one point "advocated going home, on the ground that it was a bad night for a frolic, unless we wanted a fight, and although he was in hunt of a fight, he did not want it on this side of the Mississippi River; that we had been virtually ordered out of one, and actually out of the other, of the only two decent drinkeries in the place."[34] They found a third and continued drinking and listening to Crockett's tales until quite late. The next day, he and his party left for Arkansas.

Whether they traveled overland to Little Rock or took the longer route by steamship down the Mississippi and then up the Arkansas River to that town is uncertain. In the decades following Crockett's death, people came forth with recollections of his journey, which they believed but which often conflict with other accounts. Few can be verified, although chances are good that they traveled by horse, picking up companions along the way and reaching Little Rock by November 12. The local newsmen came out to see the colonel and cover his remarks at a banquet in his honor at the City Hotel. They found him amusing and well behaved, a far cry from the vulgar buffoon the Jacksonian *Arkansas Times* had expected. (The Whiggish *Arkansas Advocate*, of course, was not surprised.) Wherever he went on the frontier, the people came to see the man who had been commissioned to wrestle with Halley's comet, then swinging past the earth, and even if they did not find a wild giant, they enjoyed his humorous and rough charm.

The party moved deliberately southwest to the Red River, stopping long enough at the now nonexistent town of Lost Prairie, Arkansas, for Crockett to trade his engraved watch, given him by the Whigs of Philadelphia, to Isaac N. Jones for another watch and thirty dollars, because his funds were running low. Months later, Jones heard of Crockett's death at the Alamo and mailed the watch to Elizabeth, with a note of explanation. She shared the letter with the Jackson *Truth Teller,* from which *Niles' Weekly Register* picked it up on August 27, 1836, and presented it to the nation. Hezekial Niles, editor of the widely read Baltimore publication, had run occasional brief notices of Crockett's westward progress, but few of the East's other Whig papers had bothered.

After crossing the Red River, Crockett and his friends passed through Clarksville, then turned east and south along the river's course. His former colleague from North Carolina, Sam Carson, had recently moved to that region, and David thought he too would settle eventually somewhere along the Red River, perhaps near Choctaw Bayou.[35] He thought Texas "the garden spot of the world. . . ."[36] There was, he said, "good land and plenty of timber and the best springs and . . . mill streams, good range, clear water and every appearance of good health and game aplenty. It is the pass where the buffalo passes from north to south and back twice a year, and bees and honey plenty."[37]

Pursuing his plan, he went to Nacogdoches, where, when last he had heard, Sam Houston was practicing law and selling land. The newly named commander in chief of the forces of the provisional government of Texas, Houston was the man to see about the "agency" to a tract of the Red River country. But he was in the field attempting to organize the army and thwart a move in the General Council of the provisional government to depose him and Governor Henry Smith. On January 17, he ordered his friend Jim Bowie to San Antonio de Béxar to blow up the Alamo, a mission turned fortress, which was held by troops under Lieutenant Colonel James C. Neill and which nearly everyone in Texas believed to be indefensible. Houston did not want the Mexicans to be able to use the Alamo for launching attacks deep into Texas, nor did he want to leave troops in such an exposed position, far from support. Soon thereafter, Smith was impeached, and Houston was without a command, on his way to negotiate with the Comanche—at least to ensure their noninterference in the American colonists' struggle with Mexico.

Finding Houston absent from Nacogdoches, hearing more loudly than ever the rumors of war and the promise of a league and a labor (about 4,605 acres) for any man who would enlist to fight for Texas freedom, Crockett and William Patton took the pledge, while Abner Burgin and Lindsey Tinkle started back for Tennessee. Officially on January 14, 1836, before Nacogdoches judge John Forbes, Crockett and his nephew, along with sixty-five other men, affixed their names to an oath of allegiance to "the Provisional Government of Texas or any future republican Government that may be hereafter declared," Crockett having refused to sign until the word "republican" was added to the standard text. He would tolerate no "man worship."[38]

In Nacogdoches, where the ladies invited him to dine, and nearby San Augustine, where a cannon was fired to welcome him, Crockett was a hero. On January 8, in San Augustine, he delivered "one of his corner speeches" and so stirred the crowd that a number of observers wished he would represent them in the coming convention.[39] He repeated to all audiences his refrain about telling his constituents that if they did not reelect him they could go to hell, and he would go to Texas. It never failed to draw cheers.[40]

CHAPTER ELEVEN

A TIME TO DIE

In joining the Texas Revolution, Crockett proved that for all his flirtations with eastern Whiggery, he was a man of the frontier, a Jacksonian at his core, a man who had broken ranks over politics only to return to fight for an ideal—freedom. The key to liberty and opportunity was land; and as a border captain, army general, and president, Jackson had embodied the expansionist drive of the young Republic, making real its Manifest Destiny. Passionately, he and many other Americans, Crockett among them, believed that Texas, the vast expanse from the Sabine River to the Rio Grande, belonged to the United States. They viewed it as a part of the Louisiana Purchase that President James Monroe had wrongly ceded to Spain in 1819 as compensation for Jackson's invasion and annexation of Florida. The question for these Anglo-Americans was not whether but when and how the United States would reclaim its territory.

For several years, it appeared that the Americans would gain Texas through the weight of sheer numbers. In 1821, Spain granted Moses Austin and his son Stephen a patent to establish the first official Anglo colony in Texas, which they called San Felipe de Austin, and they continued their effort after Mexico declared its independence that same year. To encourage Anglo-American immigration, Mexico in 1824 and '25 passed laws providing up to a league (4,428.4 acres) of land to anyone who took an oath of allegiance and converted to Catholicism. Because married men were eligible for the maximum and single men for a lesser amount, more than a few colonists staked claims in two jurisdictions—as family men in one, bachelors in the other. At $0.125 an acre, the price of this land was one-tenth that of public land in the United States, and the amount available nearly sixty times greater.

Stephen Austin was the most prosperous and influential of the *empresarios,* or agents, managing the Mexican colonization program in exchange for land and profits. The *empresarios* advertised throughout the States in newspapers, fliers, and sales offices, describing Texas as a veritable Eden abounding in game, blessed with the most fertile soils, greatest trees, and sweetest water to be found, a place where a man could become anything he dreamed. People responded—lawyers, physicians, merchants, farmers, ranchers, planters, adventurers, and speculators. They crossed the Sabine and Red rivers or sailed from New Orleans to Galveston Bay in a rising tide. A thousand new settlers arrived each month in the early 1830s, often having left little more than the letters *GTT*—Gone to Texas—painted on the doors of their abandoned homes. The border became rife with intrigue and scams.

Despite their oaths, the immigrants recognized no authority but their own, there being little reason to do otherwise. The majority of the province's 3,500 Mexicans were centered around San Antonio de Béxar, the major market town; La Bahía del Espíritu Santo, renamed Goliad in 1829, an old mission; and Nacogdoches, the border town known for gambling and prostitution where, more than any other, the cultures mixed. Mexican garrisons were small, civil authority minimal. Outside the old colonial centers, the territory resembled nothing so much as the American frontier with its clusters of ramshackle, often rough and rude towns where men vastly outnumbered women and cash and dry goods, not to mention luxury items, were scarce.

Soon after assuming office in 1825, President John Quincy Adams offered through Joel R. Poinsett, a Jackson ally and the nation's first ambassador to Mexico, to purchase the territory for $1 million, but his offer was flatly rejected. Again through Poinsett, a skilled diplomat and well-regarded politician, Andrew Jackson upped the ante to $5 million. The Mexicans refused to consider it, and finally demanded the ambassador's recall when he began meddling overtly in their affairs. Poinsett's successor, Anthony Butler, a corrupt and dissolute South Carolinian, hopelessly soured relations when, on his way to Mexico City through Texas, he announced that he planned not only to offer $5 million for the province but also to bribe selected officials, including General Antonio López de Santa Anna, the most compelling political leader in the nation, to see that the transaction occurred.

The majority of the immigrants settled into their lives, little concerned with whether they were on Mexican or American territory, as long as they were left in peace. Among those embracing the culture and people they found was an adventurer, slave runner, and notorious knife fighter named James Bowie. Louisianans, the brothers James—called Jim—John, and Rezin Jr., designer of the famous Bowie knife, had smuggled slaves with the New Orleans pirate Jean Lafitte, engaged in land scams along the southwestern border, and filibustered in Texas in the early 1820s. In 1828, thirty-two-year-old Jim Bowie, who liked to tell stories of alligator wrestling in his youth, drifted down to San Antonio—known then as Béxar—and became, to all appearances, Mexican. He took out citizenship, converted, courted and in 1831 married the nineteen-year-old daughter of the town's richest family—María Ursula de Veramendi. Bowie's Mexican citizenship entitled him to purchase 11 leagues of land at $0.05 an acre, and he used his new family connections to gain some 700,000 acres more.[1] His fortune collapsed in 1833 when Ursula and her father and mother died in a cholera epidemic. Broke and depressed, Bowie fell into alcoholism.

A man who dreamed of Texas was Sam Houston, the disgraced former congressman and governor of Tennessee, who was living in Arkansas among the Cherokee in 1830, drinking so heavily—although never with the Indians—that he had

231

earned for himself the name Oo-tse-tee Ar-dee-tah-skee, or Big Drunk. In his alcohol haze, he fancied himself as the Roman warrior Marius at Carthage and schemed of empires in the Rockies or Texas, a land that was drawing his fancy. Affecting costumes from Roman togas to Cherokee turbans and Mexican blankets, Houston appeared to many of his friends, including Andrew Jackson, to be dangerously out of control. When Jackson heard that the man who had once played a major role in his "literary bureau"—a group including John Eaton and Jacob Isacks that wrote speeches and pamphlets—dreamed of using the Cherokee to conquer Texas, he placed him under surveillance. Houston kept scheming.

Anglo-Americans represented 75 percent of the population in Texas, and they were increasingly assertive. Concerned at what they saw as an American takeover, Mexican officials outlawed immigration from the United States and banned slavery in the province. They also sought to break the settlers' monopoly on shipping and levied taxes, in an attempt to pressure people into leaving. The colonists ignored the new laws, and the Mexicans strengthened their garrisons to enforce them.

A minority of strong-willed men, many of whom had benefited from the years of lawlessness, demanded separation from Mexico. They wanted either Houston or Governor William (Billy) Carroll of Tennessee to lead them.[2] Houston desired the glory for himself, not his enemy Carroll, but early in 1832 his plans were delayed when the House of Representatives placed him on trial for caning William Stanbery, a representative from Ohio. Stanbery had proclaimed in a speech that John Eaton had been forced to resign as secretary of war because he had fraudulently tried to award Houston a contract for supplying government rations to the Cherokee. When Houston, in town negotiating on behalf of himself and the Indians for that contract, heard the charge, he challenged Stanbery to a duel. After Stanbery declined, Houston severely caned him. As a former member of Congress, he was tried in the House for assault, the trial running from mid-April to mid-May. Francis Scott Key represented Houston, who had been ordered by Jackson to exchange his buckskins for a gentleman's suit for the occasion. After a month of empty rhetoric, Houston was found "guilty of contempt in violation of the privileges of the House" and ordered to be reprimanded by the speaker, his drinking companion Andrew Stevenson.[3]

Stanbery pressed civil charges of assault against Houston, who was convicted and fined $500. He then continued his vendetta by launching an investigation of fraud in the awarding of an 1830 Indian supply contract to Houston, which failed to find any evidence of wrongdoing. Stanbery did not return to Congress in 1833.

Jackson, who had kept some distance from his protégé until his legal affairs were settled, welcomed him back under his aegis and gave him a confidential mission, the nature of which has never been fully revealed.[4] It is certain that Houston was determined to capture Texas as redemption for himself and a gift to Jackson, who loaned him $500 toward his adventure. As Houston prepared to leave Washington, the situation in Texas had already taken a turn toward full revolution in the small coastal town of Anahuac, the sole port of entry left open by the Mexicans.

At the center of the dispute was a romantic young lawyer, William Barret Travis, who had arrived in Nacogdoches a year earlier from southern Alabama. His poor family had migrated there from South Carolina when Travis was a child, and he had struggled to educate himself and study law in the small town of Claiborne, where he also taught school. After marrying one of his students, Rosanna Cato, daughter of a wealthy farmer, he had established a small-town legal practice and started a family. Early in 1831, he abruptly left his son and pregnant wife to go to Texas, settling in Anahuac before finally moving to San Felipe, where he usually introduced himself as a bachelor or widower. Reports following him said that he had caught Rosanna having an affair, killed her lover, and blamed the deed on a slave before fleeing, or, more prosaically, simply left. In Texas, he conducted a thriving legal practice, gambled heavily, and bedded as many women as he could, making notes in Spanish in his diary of each conquest. An avid fan of Sir Walter Scott, a man much taken with his image of himself as a dashing palladin, he became involved in the radical politics of the so-called War Party.[5]

The garrison commander at Anahuac, Colonel Juan Davis Bradburn, had angered the Anglo settlers by his very presence, which cast a pall on their activities, and by his attempts to enforce Mexican law. By the spring of 1832, spurred by Travis and a friend of his, Patrick Jack, the local War Dogs had begun compiling a list of grievances against Bradburn and actively provoking him. In May, they forced a confrontation over two fugitive slaves from Louisiana, whom he sheltered and refused to return. Playing a practical joke, Travis appeared incognito at the garrison late one night with a bogus letter reporting on a planned invasion from Louisiana to reclaim the slaves. Not amused, Bradburn had Travis taken into custody after guessing the messenger's identity, and the arrest rapidly disintegrated into an armed confrontation between Bradburn's troops and local settlers. Over the next month, there were more arrests and mobilizations in East Texas. A brief fight between an Anglo-Texas schooner and troops at Velasco on the mouth of the Brazos River produced 42 casualties.

Colonel José de las Piedras from Nacogdoches negotiated a truce. Travis and other Anahuac prisoners were released, and Bradburn was relieved of his command. The garrison withdrew to Mexico, leaving the region again bereft of civil authority. The rebels exulted that they had struck a blow for freedom. Ironically, in issuing a proclamation calling for adherence to the Mexican Constitution of 1824, which they interpreted as guaranteeing self-rule for Texas, the rebels had pledged their support to Santa Anna, the young officer Anthony Butler had said he intended to bribe and the new strong man of Mexico.

The most outspoken revolutionaries were often those with little or nothing to lose, with the young romantic, Travis, being one of the most troublesome and unpredictable of all.[6] Following his escapades at Anahuac, he had concentrated more on women than politics, contracting syphilis and falling in love with

Rebecca Cummings, an inn manager in Mill Creek. His relationship with her became temporarily tangled when, early in 1835, his wife Rosanna tracked him to Texas and demanded her freedom or a marriage. He divorced her and kept his son, whom he then left with friends while pursuing the revolution.

On December 1, 1832, six months after the Anahuac uprising, Sam Houston was on his way to San Antonio de Béxar for a visit, his secret commission from President Jackson in hand. He crossed back into Louisiana early in 1833, then traveled to San Felipe de Austin, where he met Jim Bowie and Stephen Austin, who considered him an adventurer. Later that year, Houston was elected to the Texas Convention, which wrote a state constitution and dispatched Austin to Mexico City to present it to the authorities. He was thrown in jail. The War Dogs wanted blood, but Houston, at the risk of falling behind events, urged caution.

Converting to Catholicism so he could qualify for land grants, Houston settled in Nacogdoches, where he opened a law office and also worked for the former mountain man Phil Sublette and the Galveston Bay and Texas Land Company of New York, a disreputable organization run by Anthony Day, a banker who supported Jackson. He also represented Samuel Swartwout, the corrupt customs collector of the Port of New York and a major Jackson supporter, in his Texas land speculations. A hotbed of intrigue with easy access to the border, Nacogdoches was an ideal place for Houston's political maneuvering, which took him to Washington, Baltimore, Philadelphia, and New York to rally support and solicit money for a war.

In 1835, Santa Anna betrayed the confidence the Anglo community had placed in him and ordered a tightening of Mexican rule in the province. The customs house at Anahuac was reopened and fresh troops were sent north to stamp out smuggling and tax resistance. To underscore their seriousness, Mexican authorities seized a schooner, the *Martha*, outside Galveston.

Travis and his fellow War Dogs gathered shortly thereafter

and marched on the Anahuac garrison, demanding that its commander surrender in fifteen minutes or die. Captain Antonio Tenorio stalled for an hour, as a point of honor, then went under Travis's armed escort to San Felipe, where the Anglo colonists treated him as the toast of the ball and shunned his captor as an irresponsible troublemaker. Travis might have faded into oblivion had Santa Anna not sent his brother-in-law Martín Perfecto de Cos with reinforcements into Texas. Cos ordered the arrest of Travis and his collaborators, and the rumor spread that they were to be killed.

Along with the arrest, the specter of a large-scale invasion roused the Anglo Texans to organize a Committee on Vigilance and Safety, with branches in every town. On September 1, Austin, released from a Mexican prison, returned to San Felipe and declared himself in favor of independence. On October 2, Anglo militia routed Mexicans from Gonzales after a brief battle. On October 9, Goliad fell to the rebels, and four days later Austin led a force of 500 toward Béxar to drive Cos back into Mexico. But after Cos took refuge in the Alamo, the ragtag band of rebels was forced to settle into a siege, which quickly began to wear at its patience and morale.

On November 1, a General Consultation of the various vigilance committees convened at San Felipe—now called Austin—and established a provisional government, selecting as governor, Henry Smith; lieutenant governor, James W. Robinson, who would preside over a General Council; and commander in chief, Sam Houston. Smith and Houston wanted an immediate declaration of independence, but the council opted for a vague resolution calling for the overthrow of President Santa Anna and restoration of the Mexican Constitution of 1824 and self-rule for the province of Texas. The factions seemed able to do little more than agree on appeals to the United States for money, matériel, and men.

Austin relinquished his command at Béxar in order to go to the United States to rally support. Bored and disgusted, Travis followed. The 300 attackers, titularly under the command of General Edward Burleson, obeyed his more aggressive subalterns—Ben Milam, Francis W. Johnson, and Dr. James Grant—who on December 5 started a house-to-house fight through the town toward the Alamo. Milam died in the battle; but on December 10, the Texans accepted Cos's surrender, forcing him to pledge to retreat across the Rio Grande with the last Mexican troops in the province and not to take up arms against them again.

The Anglo Texans began drifting home, leaving the field to volunteers arriving from the United States, who elected Johnson their commander in chief and swore that they would not take orders from anyone in the regular army, especially not Houston. Johnson and Grant pressed a plan they had developed as early as November for a raid across the Rio Grande to Matamoros, saying it would inspire liberal Mexicans to rebel. But they cared less for independence than booty. Grant wanted to reclaim land and mines the Mexicans had confiscated from him; Johnson and the volunteers, among them a former slave trader and West Point dropout from Georgia named James W. Fannin, Jr., wanted to plunder. At the end of December, Johnson traveled to San Felipe to appeal to the General Council for backing. Swept up in the excitement, the council agreed, bypassing Smith and Houston, who had their own plans. Grant and Johnson pressed their attack, taking 500 men and the bulk of the supplies in the Alamo, which was left under the command of Lieutenant Colonel James C. Neill.

By mid-January, Neill's garrison was down to eighty unpaid, nearly naked men. At Laredo, there were, Neill told Houston, 3,000 Mexicans, one-third of whom were headed for Béxar, the remainder for Matamoros to intercept Grant and Johnson. "We are in a torpid, defenseless condition," Neill said, "and have not and cannot get from all the citizens here horses enough to send out a patrol or spy company. . . . I hope we will be reinforced in eight days, or we will be over-run by the enemy, but, if I have only 100 men, I will fight 1,000 as long as I can and then not surrender."[7]

Houston, who had wanted the siege of Béxar lifted in November so he could organize his army, appeared at Goliad and attempted to dissuade Grant, Johnson, and Fannin from proceeding to Matamoros. He failed and, disgusted, left them to their fate. But in Goliad he also met Bowie, who had not received orders in early January to intercept that same expedition of pirates. Houston sent him to Béxar with thirty men—including a dashing young South Carolinian named James Bonham—and orders to blow up the Alamo and bring its remaining defenders and supplies to Gonzales, where he planned to concentrate what loyal forces remained. From there, he could retreat or fight, as necessary. He definitely did not want his army shut up in forts—anywhere.[8] He took no further action for more than a month, as the General Council voted to depose him and name Fannin commander in chief on the basis of his incomplete and undistinguished record at West Point. The council also impeached Smith, who had dissolved it, leaving the provisional government in paralysis until the scheduled convention met on March 1. Negotiating with the Comanche, Houston remained incommunicado during the upheaval.

No sooner had he removed himself from the scene than the Matamoros excursion began to break apart. In the presidio at Goliad, which he named Fort Defiance, Fannin sat with some 420 volunteers, the majority of whom had decided against an adventure into Mexico. With 150 men, Grant and Johnson rode across the Rio Grande to a destination they were too incompetent and poorly provisioned to reach.

The Texas Revolution had disintegrated. Houston, who wanted an organized, disciplined army, considered the majority of the troops in the field drunkards out for rapine and plunder who served no one but themselves and, because of their depredations, the enemy. Underestimating the Mexicans, they acted as if they were on a lark, after which they would collect the land promised in payment for their service. Meanwhile, to finance the conflict, the provisional government offered an acre for every $0.50 donated, and speculators rushed to make pledges, calculating that they could sell their reward for at least the $1.25 an acre being charged for federal land. Contributing to the confusion were the good intentions and excitement of people around the country, especially through the South and Southwest, who had rallied to the cause of Texas liberty.

Yet the actions of the band of rebels neither dominated the nation's attention nor met with universal approval. The government and national press were focused on the war in Florida, where U.S. Army troops and territorial militia were engaged in a bloody campaign against the Seminole and the fugitive slaves living among them. Many Whigs and even some Democrats viewed the Texas uprising as a land grab to extend slavery and upset the delicate balance struck fifteen years earlier in the Missouri Compromise, Texas believed to be large enough to produce as many as four new slave states. These opponents declared any involvement by the United States as a violation of international treaties.

Officially, to appease Mexico and his domestic opponents, Jackson ordered federal district attorneys around the country to observe the movement of volunteers—filibusters—to make sure they did not violate the nation's neutrality laws. But he made clear in all his actions that he approved the battle. Late in January, he ordered troops under General Edmund Pendleton Gaines to take up a position along the Sabine River, which formed the Texas-Louisiana border, ostensibly to protect the United States from attack by Indians or Mexicans. But many people at the time and since have concluded that Gaines was sent to the border from Florida to make certain that Texas gained independence. If necessary, he would have launched an invasion to counter the Mexican forces moving up from the south.

Santa Anna, the ambitious and ruthless president of Mexico, had left his capital in November to suppress the miscreants in Texas who were pledging allegiance to the Constitution he had helped write in 1824 when he led a successful revolt against Agustín de Iturbide, who had declared himself emperor of Mexico. The Anglo Texans' protestations of fealty to that document, by which Santa Anna no longer abided, failed to impress the general, who viewed their uprising as a land grab and move toward independence. Intent on punishing them, he organized an army of 4,000 men at San Luis in December. A month later, he moved them to Saltillo; and on February 12, he reached the Rio Grande, where General Joaquin Ramírez y Sesma waited with 1,500 additional men, including the 850 who had been paroled with Cos. With such a force, Santa Anna believed he would sweep the Anglo Texans into oblivion in short order, and he planned to start at Béxar.

Sesma's presence along the Rio Grande had been known since mid-January, and the rumors of Santa Anna's march had reached Texas long before his troops approached the river. But many of the rebels remained either ignorant or contemptuous of the threat closing on them. Having won several easy victories, they considered the Mexicans inferior to them on all counts.

Paradoxically, the siege of the Alamo and the slaughter of its defenders was both avoidable and inevitable—avoidable because Houston had given specific orders to destroy the old mission and withdraw all forces to more defensible ground; inevitable because three different commanders, Neill, Bowie, and Travis, and the Mexicans shared a conviction that Béxar was pivotal to the control of Texas and therefore necessary to have and hold at all cost. Also, the lack of communication and the breakdown of command meant that Bowie and Travis were able to make a decision beyond their strategic abilities. For his part, Crockett moved south from Nacogdoches around January 15 with eighteen men who called themselves the Tennessee Mounted Volunteers and planned to join the rebel force they had heard was in the vicinity of the Rio Grande. Crockett was looking for Houston and a fixed garrison preparing to vote for delegates to the Constitutional Convention, believing that he would win the election. He proceeded at a leisurely pace, requisitioning supplies on chits from the provisional government. Because of his fame, he was feted wherever he went, and he reveled in the attention.

* * *

Bowie arrived in Béxar on January 19. At the same time Houston ordered him to destroy the Alamo and withdraw, he had also verbally given him permission to hold on to the mission should he decide that was the best approach. Bowie had abundant reasons to do so. Relatives of his dead wife still lived in the town, which he considered a gateway to the rest of Texas. "It serves as the frontier picquet guard and if it were in the possession of Santa Anna there is no strong hold from which to repel him in his march towards the Sabine," he said.[9] Despite his orders from Houston and his recognition that the force at hand could not possibly defend the Alamo—it would be "a waste," he said—he felt it was essential to try to hold out if Texas were to be saved. "Colonel Neill and myself have come to the solemn resolution that we will rather die in these ditches than give it up to the enemy," he told Governor Smith.[10]

He was not insubordinate. Like Neill and the garrison, he was committed to Smith, Houston, and total independence for Texas. But he was unaware of Houston's plan to employ hit-and-run tactics to harass the Mexicans and so turned to a more traditional form of engagement, while recognizing its futility. Bowie and the other Alamo defenders escaped the contradiction inherent in their presence by convincing themselves that help was always on the way from Houston or, more likely, Fannin in nearby Goliad. Once it arrived, they would prevail.

Travis arrived on February 3 with thirty mounted men, having protested all the way from San Felipe that the assignment was beneath him. After leaving the siege of Béxar in late November, he had agitated for a commission as lieutenant colonel in command of a nonexistent Legion of Cavalry, which Smith finally provided on Christmas. Charged with raising a hundred men, Travis had enlisted only thirty-nine when Smith ordered him to reinforce Béxar. No sooner had he started than nine men deserted, and he protested to Smith that he did not wish to enter enemy territory and risk his reputation with so few men and such scant resources.[11] But he was not relieved.

The garrison was mired in a political controversy. On January

23, Bowie and Neill had petitioned Smith for permission to elect delegates to the Constitutional Convention from their command because election judges in Béxar were refusing to allow their men to vote, arguing that they were merely occupying troops, citizens of neither Texas nor Mexico. On February 1, ballots were cast around Texas for the fifty-nine delegates, with Houston earning a seat but Crockett, on the trail, not receiving any votes. On February 5, with Travis and his men in camp, Béxar's defenders proceeded with their own election and two days later dispatched Sam Maverick and Jesse Badgett, two of Béxar's Anglo residents, to the convention as their delegates. The following day, Crockett and his dozen or so men—the others having dropped out along the way—received a hearty welcome when they entered the city. He had doubtless heard that troops loyal to Houston were in Béxar, and he must have been disappointed to learn he had missed the election.

The famous bear hunter and the notorious knife hunter, each of whom had a reputation as a hard drinker, doubtless enjoyed meeting each other, and one can imagine Travis preening for the former congressman. Crockett probably gave a speech, as he had along his route, about hell, Texas, and independence.[12] Maybe he threw in Santa Anna, heaping on him the scorn he had previously poured on Martin Van Buren.

The 142 or so men of the garrison threw a fandango in Béxar to celebrate the arrival of Crockett, who in their imaginations loomed as a warrior second to none, except, perhaps, Bowie and the absent Houston. The party continued until well past midnight, when a courier arrived with a report on the advancing Mexicans, which Bowie, Crockett, and Travis, who reluctantly gave up his dancing, considered and laid aside as requiring less attention than the party.[13] That day, Neill turned his command over to Travis and left for a twenty-day furlough to care for a sick member of his family. As the senior officer in terms of service, and post commander, he had been considered superior in the order of command to his fellow colonels. After he departed, a rift developed between Travis and Bowie—Crockett being content to remain a kind of visiting star—that threatened to shatter the defense.

Finding himself in command of a troop that did not recognize his authority, Travis called on the volunteers to elect their commander. Not surprisingly, they chose their companion and natural leader Bowie, who boldly proclaimed himself in charge of the regulars as well.[14] To celebrate his victory, Bowie, who had suffered a relapse of a disease that no one could properly diagnose, threw a two-day drunk during which he harassed the citizens of Béxar and emptied its jails. Travis complained bitterly to the governor about Bowie's behavior while reiterating his belief in the importance of defending Béxar to protect the "Interior." "Without a footing here," he said, "the enemy can do nothing against us in the *colonies*."[15] On the fourteenth, the warring colonels decided that Travis would command the regulars, Bowie the volunteers, and they would make all decisions regarding the defense of Béxar together. They appealed to Smith for reinforcements, saying the Mexicans would shortly be upon them.[16]

The men worked to shore up the Alamo's defenses, erecting gun placements and strengthening the timber palisade that stood between the roofless church and the south wall. Continuing to roam and party through the town, they also received regular intelligence reports about Santa Anna's movements. On the eighteenth, Travis sent Major James Bonham to Goliad with a request that Fannin move immediately to provide men and matériel. But he assumed, based on no knowledge of the countryside or the movement of an army, that the Mexicans would not arrive until the middle of March and so did not hasten his own preparations.

Fannin sat in Goliad paralyzed by fear, self-doubt, and hubris. He told Bonham on the eighteenth that he would not send aid immediately in response to Travis's plea, presumably because he wanted it understood that he was commander in chief. Yet he had repeatedly told his patron, Lieutenant Governor James Robinson, a foe of Smith and Houston, and the dysfunctional General Council that he had taken steps to strengthen Béxar.

At the same time, he complained that he was incompetent and should be relieved.[17] The men at Béxar knew nothing of Fannin's nature. They believed to the end that he would finally send a relief force, since he had under his command more than 400 men, the largest troop of Anglo Texans under arms.

On February 20, Travis received word that Santa Anna had crossed the Rio Grande. On the twenty-first, the dashing young colonel joined the other defenders in a party. Santa Anna ordered Sesma's dragoons, barely twenty-five miles away, to press into the besotted town. Only a cold front blasting across the open countryside with heavy rain prevented them from completing their surprise attack. Sesma's troops entered a nearly deserted town two days later, the residents having evacuated and the defenders, at last realizing their danger, having taken refuge in the Alamo. Travis and Bowie sent another message to Fannin, informing him that they had 146 men with them and expected his immediate reinforcement. They appealed to his sense of duty; he sat in Fort Defiance.

Santa Anna besieged the Alamo not to starve its defenders into surrender but to keep them contained until he could bring the main body of his infantry and artillery up to pulverize them. On entering Béxar the afternoon of the twenty-third and finding that the Anglos had retreated to the old mission, he ordered a blood-red flag, signifying that no quarter would be given, run up the church steeple eight hundred yards away. Matching Santa Anna's theatrics, Travis had the garrison's eighteen-pound cannon fired toward the flag. Bowie sent a note offering to talk, which Santa Anna had a subaltern answer: The troop could surrender unconditionally or die. Travis then sent a messenger and, receiving the same response, fired another cannon shot.

That night Bowie collapsed and, too ill to do more than lie in bed, turned his troops over to Travis. The following day, Travis wrote himself into fame, addressing a florid plea for assistance "To the People of Texas & all Americans in the world." Traveling first to Gonzales, then throughout Texas and the United States, it carried news of the attack:

The enemy has demanded a surrender at discretion, otherwise, the garrison are to be put to the sword, if the fort is taken—I have answered the demand with a cannon shot, & our flag still waves proudly from the walls—*I shall never surrender or retreat.* Then, I call upon you in the name of Liberty, of patriotism & everything dear to the American character, to come to our aid, with all dispatch. . . . If this call is neglected, I am determined to sustain myself as long as possible & die like a soldier who never forgets what is due to his honor & that of his country—*Victory or Death.*[18]

The Mexicans made two probing attacks against the mission the following day, which were easily repulsed. Crockett was everywhere, "animating the men to their duty," an admiring Travis reported.[19] When word reached Goliad of the forays, the garrison speculated that "Davy Crockett 'grinned' them off."[20] With his anecdotes and antics, he boosted morale among men who knew they were locked in a battle to the death. According to some reports, he also played a passable fiddle and would join another defender, bagpiper John McGregor, in duets that more closely resembled the wails and shrieks of the damned.[21]

Travis must have thought he was sending his appeals—to Houston and Fannin again—into a void. On February 27, he dispatched Bonham to Goliad with another message for Fannin, little knowing that the commander in chief had actually led 320 of his men two hundred yards from town before stopping. His wagons had broken down, and he decided to make camp. The next day, he had to send parties to round up oxen they had failed to hobble properly. Fatigued and worried that he might have to fight, he decided then to return to the safe walls of Fort Defiance. No one knows Fannin's reasons, although he suggested that they were strategic, or whether his men could have broken the siege at the Alamo. But his actions and letters bespeak a stupid, cowardly, vain man wrapped in delusion. Back in his fort, he heard that Mexican forces under General José Urrea had slaughtered the remnant of the Matamoros expedition at San Patricio, fifty miles south of Goliad. He wrote

Robinson with the news and added a comment on the volunteers at the Alamo, "[W]ill not *curses* be heaped on the heads of the sluggards who remained at home?"[22]

Santa Anna had maintained a steady bombardment while waiting impatiently for his infantry to arrive. Hearing a report on the twenty-ninth that Fannin was marching from Goliad, he dispatched forces to intercept and annihilate him, not realizing that his quarry had returned to its den. He seems to have half-expected the Alamo garrison to attempt an escape, not wrongly. According to reports, more than a few of them, including Crockett, opined that they were better off fighting in the open than closed up in two acres. On the plains, they could depend on their skill, while inside they had to rely on others, who were not coming.

But Travis's messages had reached people, and around the state bands were mobilizing for Béxar, trying to pick their way through rumor and false reports, especially concerning Fannin's movements. In the predawn hours of March 1, 32 men, calling themselves the Gonzales Ranging Company of Mounted Volunteers, dashed through the Mexican lines and into the Alamo, the first of what its defenders hoped were hundreds of reinforcements, although they were to be the last. After another false start, Fannin on March 2 prepared to send 200 men to Béxar, then stopped again, fearful that Mexicans would over-run him.

In Washington-on-the-Brazos, activity was more directed and frantic. Houston had dramatically reappeared on the eve of the Constitutional Convention, then helped ram through a Declaration of Independence for the Republic of Texas on his forty-third birthday, March 2, 1836.[23] Although not officially elected commander in chief of the army until two days later, he immediately issued an appeal for men to relieve the siege of Béxar and set out for Gonzales to organize the troops. Arriving there on the eleventh, he was too late.

Santa Anna received his reinforcements on the third, bringing his force to 2,400 men and ten cannons. Learning of the arrival of nearly 1,000 fresh troops, Travis penned an urgent appeal to the Constitutional Convention and sent off his last messenger.

The men were growing increasingly restive, low on ammunition and food, worn down by the steady bombardment, despairing of more help. On the fifth, Travis dispatched a final message to Fannin and then sent feelers to Santa Anna through some townspeople who were communicating with the Alamo, to determine whether surrender was possible.[24] He wanted a promise that the lives of all would be spared but was told that any surrender had to be unconditional, with no guarantees. Presumably, he translated that as a death sentence and told the men that the die was cast. All who wanted to leave could try to escape; the rest should prepare for a battle to the death, which might at least delay the Mexican advance by inflicting heavy casualties. Only one man, a fifty-year-old veteran from Europe and friend of Jim Bowie, named Louis Rose, decided to leave the Alamo that night. Rose later recited a flowery speech he said Travis gave, which was eventually transcribed, and reported that the colonel had drawn a line in the sand and instructed all who intended to stay to cross it. The stories added to the romance of the Alamo.

Reading the peace feeler as weakness, Santa Anna ordered his final attack for the morning of March 6. Commencing at 6 A.M., it was over in ninety bloody minutes, as 1,800 men stormed the Alamo and its 183 defenders from the northwest, the northeast, the east, and the south, the weak points. From the north there were two unsuccessful thrusts before the men pushed forward a third time, joining their comrades who had turned from the east in a mass of blood and chaos at the base of the Alamo's thick walls. After fifteen minutes, Santa Anna threw in his reserves, and the attackers began to climb up the walls by hand through the defender's fire. Almost immediately, they were inside the Alamo. To the south, a troop of 100 had been turned from the palisade by Crockett's men, only to gain entry over the southwest wall. A handful of Anglos who tried to flee were cut down by cavalry. The rest withdrew to the long barracks against the west wall, which they had fortified, and there fought to their deaths, the Mexicans granting no mercy.

Piecing together the battle's chronology, historians have determined that Travis died on the north wall during the opening minutes of the assault, impulsive to the end. Jim Bowie was probably killed in his quarters in the low barracks along the south wall, too weak to offer much resistance. Bonham and Dickinson died near the end, when their artillery platform in back of the chapel was blown to pieces.

Crockett survived the carnage, probably in the low barracks near his outpost, and was taken prisoner, along with five or six other men, by troops under General Manuel Fernández Castrillon, an elder statesman among Santa Anna's subordinates.[25] Crockett told his captors that he had been exploring the country around Béxar when he heard of the Mexican advance and, "fearing that his status as a foreigner might not be respected," had sought refuge with the Anglos in the Alamo.[26] There was enough truth to the tale that Crockett could tell it with a straight face and hope it would purchase his life. Castrillon brought his prisoners to Santa Anna, who dismissed him with a gesture of contempt and, in violation of all accepted rules of war, ordered soldiers standing nearby to kill the Anglos. When they balked, reported Lieutenant Colonel José Enrique de la Peña of the elite *Zapadores* battalion (the sappers), officers in Santa Anna's personal entourage drew their swords and "fell upon these unfortunate, defenseless men just as a tiger leaps upon his prey. Though tortured before they were killed, these unfortunates died without complaining and without humiliating themselves before their torturers."[27] Americans would say that, at the end, the unarmed Crockett sprang "like a tiger" for the throat of Santa Anna.

Santa Anna had suffered some 200 dead and 400 wounded, many of them in the crush at the wall, more than a few from friendly fire. Approximately 183 Texans lay dead. Denying them Christian burial, as a final insult, Santa Anna ordered their corpses burned. A Mexican defender, José María (Brigido)

Guerrero, survived by convincing Santa Anna's troops that he had been a captive of the Anglo defenders.[28] A dozen or more noncombatants also survived, including Joe, Travis's slave; Susannah Dickinson and her infant daughter Angelina, both of whom, left to fend for themselves in later years, became prostitutes—so uncelebrated were the survivors; Juana Alsbury, her daughter, and her sister, Gertrudis Navarro, who were Bowie's sisters-in-law; and Señora Candelaria.[29]

Surveying the carnage, Santa Anna called the assault "a small affair."[30] Under the escort of his black cook, Ben, he sent Mrs. Dickinson and her child to Gonzales to spread the word of the massacre. Picking up Joe, freed by the Mexicans, along the way, they arrived on the thirteenth to find Houston and tell him the sad news. He wept at the horror and unnecessary waste.[31] Then, with a force of 374 men and the civilian population of the town, he began a month-long retreat into East Texas that would bring him on April 21 in front of Santa Anna's overextended forces. He also sent orders to the inept Fannin to withdraw immediately from Goliad after destroying the fort.

But Fannin remained in Fort Defiance with his 400 men, still the largest force in Texas, until the nineteenth, when in broad daylight he began a meandering retreat north. General José Urrea's troop immediately surrounded the Texans, who surrendered the next day after token resistance. They were held prisoner for a week in the fort, then on Palm Sunday taken out and shot, with only a few escaping. So, Fannin had managed through his ineptitude, ignorance, and insubordination—abetted by the raucous General Council under Robinson—to allow more than 600 men to be slaughtered in two months.

Cold sober, Houston led his slowly growing army and assorted colonists east toward the border where General Gaines and his American troops were stationed, ready to cross in violation of official orders and international law had it been necessary to save the revolution.[32] As it was, Gaines and his officers simply turned their heads while enlisted men slipped into Texas to join Houston's army. If the U.S. military and Jackson knew what Houston was planning, many people in Texas did not, and they pilloried him for his long retreat, accusing him of cowardice, opium addiction (he did use it for pain, as was common), and worse. But he stuck to his plan, drawing Santa Anna's forces across the territory and fueling the general's megalomania.

Fear and anger spread across Texas in advance of Houston's withdrawal. His army swelled to more than 1,000, then dropped to less than 800 as volunteers returned to their homes to protect their families. The news of the Alamo reached the United States by the end of March and within weeks had spread across the nation, stirring patriotic fervor that translated quickly into volunteers and money. The Texas Revolution evoked memories of the American War of Independence; and Crockett's death especially expanded the conflict beyond Texas, for he was a national celebrity, recognized and admired. Friends and foes "shed tears" when they heard of his death.[33] Whatever oaths they had taken to Texas, his compatriots were American, and their deaths required vengeance.

After a series of twisting marches, Houston had positioned his force of 783 men between the advance troop of Mexicans that was pursuing him and the remainder of its army. On April 18, he learned that the lead force was under the personal command of Santa Anna, and he moved quickly to confront him, taking up a position at the confluence of Buffalo Bayou and San Jacinto Bay, east of present-day Houston, on April 20. There was a brief skirmish, then calm until the next day, with Santa Anna content to bide his time waiting for reinforcements. Late on the afternoon of April 21, while the Mexicans took their siesta, Houston ordered his men to charge, and within eighteen minutes they had overwhelmed the Mexican force of 1,150 at a cost to themselves of 9 dead and 34 wounded, Houston among them. The Mexicans lost more than 400 dead and 200 wounded. Briefly, the Texans ran amuck with cries of "Remember the Alamo!" Nightfall brought an end to their madness, and Santa Anna surrendered the next day.

* * *

It was nine more years before Houston finally delivered his prize to Jackson, retired and near the end of his life. Domestic and international politics prevented annexation before March 1, 1845, when the Senate approved statehood, and even then the pace was rushed because of a fear that Houston on behalf of Texas was negotiating an agreement with the British. It was a tangled web that ironically ended the political career of Crockett's nemesis Van Buren and elevated his Tennessee foe James K. Polk to the presidency. Van Buren had agreed with Henry Clay to keep the question of Texas statehood out of the 1840 presidential election, which the Whig William Henry Harrison won by exploiting the images and issues of Jacksonian democracy while appealing to people's desire for a change. Irate over the loss, Jackson maneuvered to deny Van Buren the Democratic nomination for 1844 in favor of Polk. Although statehood came two days before Polk's inauguration, he led the nation during the bloody war of aggression against Mexico.

David's eldest son, John Wesley, rode his father's martyrdom into the House of Representatives for two terms beginning in 1837, when Adam Huntsman opted not to run for reelection. In February 1841, the Whig congressman secured passage of a land bill granting the occupants of the Western District the right to buy their farms at $0.125 an acre, the land having first been turned over to the state. It was a bill remarkably similar to the one Polk had proposed in 1829.[34] John Wesley Crockett refused to run again in 1843.

Neither Crockett nor his heirs was ever granted the league and labor of land he had imagined he would claim, but his widow, Elizabeth, was awarded his full soldier's share and finally made the move she had once opposed. In 1838, Robert Patton Crockett, his eldest son by Elizabeth, went to Texas as administrator of his father's estate and a volunteer in the war the republic was waging against the Comanche. He served with distinction and in 1854 brought his mother, his sister Rebeckah, his stepbrother George, and George's wife Rhoda to Hood

251

County, southwest of Dallas, in the more or less peaceful state of Texas. Elizabeth, who learned of her husband's enlistment and death on the same day—two weeks after the fall of the Alamo—had received 1,280 acres from David's estate, and Robert another 1,280 for his military service.[35] Loyal to the legend as much as to the man, she wore widow's black until her death in 1860. She remained a private, quiet person, the antithesis of the gregarious David.[36]

CHAPTER TWELVE

THE LEGENDARY HERO

Among the heroes of Texas independence, two stood above the rest—Sam Houston and David Crockett, one a giant among men, a military chieftain of classical proportions; the other a yarn spinner of renown and martyr to liberty. With his usual hyperbole, Thomas Hart Benton called Houston another Mark Antony, a self-created military genius.[1] Yet in the immediate aftermath of the battle, when he was suffering from a serious leg wound, Houston was refused passage on the official boat of David G. Burnet, the president of the new Republic of Texas and the latest in a long line of incompetents to hold office there, a man moved by fear and jealousy. Although many other politicians shared Burnet's emotions, the people adored Houston, twice electing him president of the republic and governor of the state. He also served terms as commander in chief of the Texas army and as U.S. senator. Now married, a father and teetotaler, he had thoroughly redeemed himself from his disgraceful term as governor of Tennessee and the drunken binge that had followed his resignation. In 1860, he was the best-known and most popular man in America, but neither party would nominate him for the presidency because of his independence.[2] When Texas seceded, he refused to take the oath of allegiance to the Confederacy; and although he was abused in speech and print, such was his stature that he was not bothered by Regulators, the mounted vigilantes who had banded together in every southern state to intimidate and punish slaves and free blacks who were outspoken or rebellious and whites who opposed slavery, discrimination, or secession. Whippings, beatings, lynchings, and burnings were the preferred tactics of the Regulators.

Crockett's martyrdom completed his elevation to myth, which had begun in his lifetime but had become bogged down in partisan politics—largely through his miscalculations. He became at once the immortal voice of the backwoods and a symbol of the union between the frontier and the "civilized" east, with all the contradictions and ambiguities inherent therein. Writers and politicians freely manipulated this legendary Crockett to suit their own ends and in so doing nearly obliterated the man himself.

The mythic Crockett took a variety of forms. In the almanacs, he was a comic Hercules—a superb hunter and marksman; a ferocious and sly warrior, as distinct from a strategist or general; a crude practical joker; a womanizer and prodigious drunk. He hated blacks, Indians, Yankees, squatters, and all others different from himself. In a variety of melodramas, popular novels, and later films, he was a noble ignoramus, an unschooled poet of the soul, a skilled woodsman and courageous fighter for justice and liberty.

In the guise of the superman of almanacs and romances, he joined Daniel Boone at the head of a pantheon of western heroes, including Mike Fink, Ben Harding, and Colonel Plug of the rivers; John Colter, Hugh Glass, Jim Bridger, Jed Smith, Kit Carson, and Jim Beckwourth of the mountains. As a mythic hero—but not as a historical figure—he was a match for Andrew Jackson, Sam Houston, and, later, Honest Abe Lincoln, who never quite achieved the transcendence of the others because of the Civil War.[3] (Southern whites, for example, would never embrace him.) Too often, the legends associated with these men, especially Fink, Harding, and the mountain men, have usurped their lives. They have become little more than their fictional counterparts from other regions and vernacular traditions—Major Jack Downing, the downe'ster; Horse Shoe Robinson, a yeoman farmer who fought in the Revolution; Mose, an urban free black, and Pompey Smash, a black "screamer" (or outrageously comic wild man), both of whom were stars of blackface minstrelsy; and the later heroes, Paul Bunyan, John Henry, Johnny Appleseed, and Pecos Bill.

Crockett's publishers, Edward Carey and Abraham Hart, were the first to recognize the commercial and literary value of his death. Soon after word reached Philadelphia of the fall of the Alamo, Carey approached one of the house's authors, Richard Penn Smith, about writing a pseudonymous account of Crockett's Texas adventures. Carey and Hart felt that such an "autobiography" would help them sell their remaining stock of Crockett's *Tour,* which had not done well commercially. Smith, a local playwright and novelist, agreed to the proposition and, collecting a couple of letters Crockett had sent Carey and Hart about his plans, every book on Texas he could find, and, apparently, Augustus Baldwin Longstreet's *Georgia Scenes,* he immediately began writing. Plagiarizing freely, he turned in the first part of the book the next day, as promised, and continued to keep ahead of the typesetter, allowing Carey and Hart to produce the book, *Col. Crockett's Exploits and Adventures in Texas, Written by Himself,* under the dummy imprint T.K. & P.G. Collins, almost overnight.[4]

Exploits was presented as Crockett's diary, kept up to the final moment of the Alamo, then found in the ruins by a gentleman identified only as Charles T. Beale, who sent it on May 3, 1836, to Alex J. Dumas (a blatant invocation of the celebrated French novelist, which should have alerted people to the spurious nature of the text) for publication. A popular and critical success, *Exploits* sold 10,000 copies in its first year—the equivalent of 168,000 today—and rapidly cleaned out the supply of the *Tour* as well. Failing to discern the clues that the memoir was a hoax, English critics praised its humor, satire, and authenticity, while American readers freely recycled its anecdotes and tall tales into almanacs and other Crockett lore. Smith's most enduring book continues to appear real enough to many editors and publishers that they include it in works by Crockett, and even some biographers and scholars refer to it for information on the thin grounds that small parts—for example, the discussion in August 1835 of his intention to go to Texas, should he lose the election—have their origins in authentic sources. Following extant rumors, the book reported, in an epilogue, that Crockett had been captured and killed after the fall of the Alamo, while trying to throttle the victorious Santa Anna.

Openly anti-Jackson, *Exploits* had no impact on the 1836 election, which brought Martin Van Buren to the White House; but by 1840, the romance of the backwoods had become so entrenched in the culture that symbols central to the Crockett *oeuvre*—hard cider, log cabins, and coonskin caps—were appropriated by candidates of both parties. Henry Clay became closely associated with the raccoon, earning the sobriquet Old 'Coon. But the chief beneficiaries were the Whig presidential candidate, William Henry Harrison, and the Tennessee gubernatorial candidate, John Bell, both of whom campaigned in a coonskin cap. Both won. Although other factors were more pivotal to the election—the financial panic of 1837 and Van Buren's loss of the backing of the radical workingmen's party, the Locofocos, to name two—the cynical manipulation of the image of the democratic, populist backwoodsman by the Whigs clearly had an influence. The election of Zachary Taylor, another war hero, in 1848 was the Whigs' only other presidential victory before they collapsed into the Republican Party, which successfully united westerners, Free Soil advocates, eastern business interests, abolitionists, and the remnants of the Locofocos.

Among Democrats, Van Buren's vice president, Richard Mentor Johnson, the Kentuckian known as the slayer of Tecumseh, having thoroughly alienated all but his most ardent supporters with his eccentricities—his shabby dress and demeanor, his seeming lust for power, his affair with the eighteen-year-old sister of the mulatto mistress he had sold down the river, his ownership of an inn in his native Kentucky, which was considered scandalous—adopted verbatim the language of the Crockett almanacs, claiming he "was born in a canebrake and cradled in a sap trough."[5] He was fighting to retain his post, but he could not overcome the failures of his president or the low esteem in which he was held.

The transformation of Crockett into a backwoods superman, the personification of the frontier spirit, which Boston illustrator Charles Ellms had begun with his *1835 Almanack,* picked up momentum after Crockett's death. For the next six years, the almanacs, although produced in Boston, carried a Nashville imprint, then shifted to New York, Boston, Philadelphia, Baltimore, and Albany. By 1856, when characters like Kit Carson, the mountain man and scout, began to replace Crockett, some forty-five numbers had been produced. A hero more suited to the time of migration across the plains, buffalo hunting, and Indian wars, Carson nonetheless fit into the tradition of Boone and Crockett. Like them, he was featured in *Story of the Wild West and Camp-Fire Chats,* a 1902 book by another famous character, Buffalo Bill Cody, for whom Crockett was "the most singular, and in many respects the most remarkable, man in the history of pioneer settlement in the great west."[6] His bear stories and wit, Cody said, set him head and shoulders above the rest.

Usually carrying subtitles referring to hunting and life in the backwoods, the Crockett almanacs on a practical level contain information on agriculture and meteorology. In their woodcuts and tales—written in a "cracker" vernacular—they are raunchy, fantastic, and violent. Their Colonel Crockett—sometimes a Germanic Kurnel Krockett—performs Herculean feats that are beyond the social pale but necessary to the preservation of proper order, rather like the heroes of contemporary action-adventure films of the Rambo variety. Politicians like Sam Houston regularly recounted Crockett's escapades as a campaigner or as an American "original." Samuel Clemens, born in 1835, converted their base humor and the comic realism of Crockett's autobiography into the art of Mark Twain. The opening pages of *The Adventures of Huckleberry Finn,* for example, echo those of Crockett's *Narrative*—the protest that although the reader has read of him elsewhere he has surely not received the real story in the proper language.

After the first two numbers, attributed to Crockett, the illustrations became increasingly crude, the tales more racist and xenophobic as the authors exhausted existing anecdotes and began inventing their own. In 1837 and '38, the heirs of Crockett were fraudulently credited as publishers. The following year, Ben Harding, a former congressman from Kentucky, was listed as narrator of the Crockett almanacs, and shortly thereafter, when Turner and Fisher of New York began to list themselves as the publisher, Harding was transformed to Hardin, a crusty old sailor. Grotesque and brutish, Harding/Hardin was soon joined as a character in the growing Crockett legend by the Mississippi boatman, Mike Fink, who added yet another dimension of jingoistic violence to the backwoods world.

Present in an understated way even in James Kirke Paulding's play, hostilely racist attitudes began to find fuller expression through the legendary Crockett as early as the *1837 Almanack*. After running through his standard, boastful self-introduction, the woodcut superman added comments that came to represent the only David Crockett people knew for more than fifty years:

Congress allows *lemonade* to the members and has it charged under the head of stationery—I move also that *whiskey* be allowed under the item of *fuel*. For *bitters* I can suck away at a noggin of aquafortis, sweetened with brimstone, stirred with a lightning rod, and skimmed with a hurrican. I've soaked my head and shoulders in Salt River so much that I'm always corned. I can walk like an ox, run like a fox, swim like an eel, yell like an Indian, fight like the devil, spout like an earthquake, make love like a mad bull, and swallow a nigger whole without choking if you butter his head and pin his ears back.[7]

Ellms and his collaborators had pilfered the cannibalism that ends this boast from *Crockett's Exploits,* where an Anglo-Texas hunter and scout who has brought a report to the Alamo says, "I promise to swallow Santa Anna without gagging, if you will only skewer back his ears, and grease his head a little."[8] From Mexicans to blacks to Indians were easy transitions—all being deemed threats, whom Davy, as protector of the common man, would vanquish.

The hateful tenor and ethnic humor of the almanacs were manifestations of dramatic transformations in American society, which involved the expansion of the political franchise to all white men and the concomitant suppression of Indians and tighter restrictions on free men of color as well as slaves. The ruling elite sought to diffuse the potential for upheaval by playing to racial, ethnic, and even geographical jealousy, turning white against black or Indian, Irish against German, southerner against Yankee, immigrant against native-born American. Squatters—poor whites—were pariahs, lower on the social scale than everyone but blacks—slave and free—whose inferiority was considered inherent in their skin color. They were, by definition, childlike, almost subhuman. In the Northeast, terms of derision were applied to immigrants as the preservation of power became a game of uniting against the other, whoever he might be. Even the Civil War represented less a reaction to that divisive racism and jingoism than a struggle to preserve the Union, whatever the cost.

The nation was on the move, growing in population from 13 million to 50 million, filling in the gaps on the map, developing its roads and canals, expanding its factories, farms, and cities. Trains and steamboats extended their network, speeding travel and trade—at considerable profit, the railroads being awarded public land for laying track—while the telegraph did the same for communication. The reaping machine, mass-produced iron plows, and the cotton gin facilitated the broad advance of agriculture, which expanding markets encouraged. The maturing frontiers of the Northwest and Southwest were filling with professionals and storekeepers—representatives of a more stable society.

The independence of Texas gave way to statehood and war

259

between the United States and Mexico in 1846—capping more than a decade of conflict. In the South, the long campaign of Indian removal, begun under Jefferson's administration and accelerated under Jackson and Van Buren, reached its terrible apogee in the winter of 1838–39 when a quarter of the Cherokee herded westward along the "Trail of Tears" died. In Florida, American soldiers prosecuted a war of attrition against the Seminole, who, although battered and driven south on the peninsula, would not be conquered. Henry Clay liked to proclaim during the 1840 election that Van Buren had lost his war with the Florida Indians.[9]

In the Rockies, the mountain men, having trapped the beaver out of the streams, held their last great rendezvous on the Green River in 1835 and ushered in the era of the settler, the rancher and farmer, the buffalo hunter and cowboy. Not a few of those mountain men, including Kit Carson, became wagon-train guides, Indian scouts, and land speculators. From Texas to Oregon and then California, immigrants spread across the continent.

Industrialists and their cohorts in the East, usually identified with the Whigs, continued through the 1840s their long habit of attempting to discourage western migration, fearing a loss of workers, of political power, and of the civilization they believed they were building. Through books and periodicals, they portrayed the frontier as a rough and dangerous place, uncivilized, unfit for temperate people. They were partly correct. The Indians fought back, as did the land itself, unloosing plagues of insects, harsh and sudden storms, and floods. Far from medical care or assistance from neighbors, people often died lonely deaths. Faltering on the difficult journey by wagon across the Oregon and Santa Fe trails, many immigrants turned back or perished. Epidemics, like that of cholera in the mid-1830s, which swept down the Mississippi from Canada, killed thousands, as did endemic diseases like malaria. In the hands of eastern writers, even the heroes of the West were men beyond the pale of civilization, loners adapted to a harsh environment, sometimes noble, other times clownish, always lacking in refinement and education.

The frontier was predominantly male, rough and violent, superstitious, sudden in judgments, awash in liquor and gaming, a place devoid of art and all but the rudiments of education. Thieves abounded: For example, a nest of some five hundred river pirates under a sociopath named John Murrell plagued the settlers around Memphis into the 1830s, hijacking boats, stealing slaves, running gambling dens, and passing counterfeit money. The angry citizenry of Vicksburg finally hanged five of them, inspiring their fellows along the river to drive the rest out, a positive example of people's justice often cited in defense of vigilance committees. (Not until Disney came along did a variant of this event become a showcase for the courage and ingenuity of Davy Crockett.) But urban crime and unrest over immigration, rents, and working conditions, which were often abysmal, were also commonplace, as were slave uprisings, which numbered in the hundreds.

The physical hardships of frontier life reinforced a central piece of the newcomers' baggage—that nature existed to be conquered, like its people and animals. Settlers ripped their profit from the forests, game, and ground, leaving a legacy of destruction. Many people, including Crockett, would hunt all manner of game for pelts and food until it was gone. They would buy and improve a parcel of land, then sell it and move on, acting on a small scale like the speculators they publicly abhorred. Often they sought more distant lands, where, they were convinced, the game was fatter, trees taller, and soil richer. Many sought the Mother Lode.

Inexorably, as the nation expanded economically and geographically, it edged toward a showdown over slavery, the continued existence of which was dictating migration and thwarting southern economic development. Political leaders struggled in vain to retain the outlines of the Missouri Compromise and maintain a balance of political power between slave and free states. With the annexation of Texas and the Mexican War, the issue began to move to the fore of the national debate. Northerners and westerners began to adopt a Free Soil argument—that all new lands should benefit white laborers and artisans, not plantation slavery. The dispute broke asunder the Democratic and Whig parties following the Kansas-Nebraska Act of 1854, which repealed the Missouri Compromise and opened the plains territories to an orgy of bloody conflict. Born from the turmoil was the Republican Party, which embraced Free Soil and finally passed the Homestead Act, opening land to small farmers.

Crockett, the comic demigod of the almanacs, looms over this world. He dominates nature—wringing the tail off Halley's comet; draining the Gulf of Mexico to bring the United States and Texas together; freeing the earth from its frozen axis with bear grease and a swift kick. Animals and people are brutalized in outrageous battles, cannibalized, or turned into pets or slaves. "One day, I war sarved an ungracious trick by a red niggar," says the Davy of *Crockett's 1850 Almanac,* complaining about an Indian's effort to attack him, "and I never will be revenged till I've extinctified the whole race of varmints. . . . No human ever hated an Injun more than Davy Crockett. . . ."[10] This Crockett gouges the eyes from his Indian foes, kills and boils them, "with tender vermints, sitch as toads, lizards, a crocodile's tail, and other spurious vegetables that was calculated to set well on a delicate stomach" for his wife's sick pet bear.[11] He demolishes Haitians with sugarcane stalks and holds blacks—always "niggars"—in total contempt.

Squatters and "Pukes" (Missourians), Yankees and peddlers, also feel his wrath. When a squatter tries to dupe him into lying about the age of the man's homestead, so he can qualify to keep it, Davy Crockett says, "Do you see what that cow has just let drop? It ar not honey or apple sarse, ar it? Now if you don't sit down and eat every atom of it, I'll make daylite shine through you quicker than it would take lightning to run round a potato patch."[12] On another occasion, he beat a squatter who had offended him until the man "war took up for dead. His nose war knocked to one side, and looked as crooked as a pesky Gum Swamp Injun's heart, and one of his eyes stuck out like a lobster."[13] The conquest made Crockett "a military hero" in the eyes of folks who had witnessed it, he says, and they pressed him to run for president. It was an odd fictional fate for a man who had devoted his political career to defending squatters from speculators trying to seize their hardscrabble farms, for a man who had risked the wrath of his president and constituents to vote against Indian removal.

Not surprisingly, women in the distinctly white-male world of the almanacs fare little better than Indians, blacks, or squatters, their chief attributes being enormous physical size, insatiable appetites for food and sex, and bodacious ugliness—"ugly" sometimes meaning its opposite. Although they occasionally rescue their men from trouble, they can never outshine them. In one episode, Crockett's wife, despite losing a thumb and forefinger trying to skin a catfish alive, runs a hickory rail down the throat of a six-hundred-pound black bear that is chasing him toward their cabin. Her assault distracts the animal long enough for Crockett to kill it with his knife after a "desperate contest."[14]

Crockett's daughters are "the tallest and fattest, and sassyest gals in all America. They can out-run, out-jump, out-fight, and out-scream any critter in creation, and for scratchin: thar's not a hungry painter, or a patent horse-rake can hold a claw to 'em."[15] Crockett's wife in this grotesque fantasy world is Sally Ann Thunder Ann Whirlwind, another woman of great ugliness. In one scene, she batters Mike Fink senseless after he, disguised as an alligator, tries to scare her.[16] Fink's wife, Sal, is herself "horrid handsome, that loved him the wickedest that ever you see," despite his keeping her in rags.[17]

Says Crockett of Sal Fergus (yet another of the seemingly endless number of Sals peopling the almanacs): "She could scalp an Injun, skin a bear, grin down hickory nuts, laugh the bark off a pine tree, swim stark up a cataract, gouge out alligator's eyes, dance a rock to pieces, sink a steamboat. . . . But her heart growed too big; and when I left her to go to Texas, it burst like an airthquake, and poor Sal died."[18] Wanting the ladies only on his terms, Crockett, in another episode, cures himself of love by swallowing a thunderbolt.

Davy of the almanacs works his will with women. In the first issue, for example, he is caught *in flagrante* with the mistress of a stagecoach driver and forced to fight the man to escape. Boasts Crockett:

> As quick as the critter saw me, he flew into such a rage that he crooked up his neck and neighed like a stud horse, and dared me down. Says I, stranger! I'm the boy that can double up a dozen of you. I'm a whole team just from the roaring river.—I've rode through a crab apple orchard on a streak of lightning. I've squatted lower than a toad; and jumped higher than a maple tree; I'm all brimstone but my head, and that's aquafortis. At this he fell a cursing and stamping, and vowed he'd make a gridiron of my ribs to roast my heart on—I jumped right down upon the driver, and he tore my trowsers right off of me. I got hold of his whiskers and gave them such a twitch that his eyes stuck out like a lobster's. He fetched me a kick in the bowels that knocked all compassion out of them. I was driv almost distracted, and should have been used up, but luckily there was a poker in the fire which I thrust down his throat, and by that means mastered him. Says he, stranger you are the yellow flower of the forest. If you ever are up for Congress again I'll come all the way to Duck river to vote for you.[19]

The tale, like a score of others in the almanacs, supported the view of his detractors that the man was indeed an adulterer.

Drinking, fighting, gambling, hunting, fornicating, and going to revival meetings, militia musters, corn shuckings, barn raisings, political rallies, and traveling minstrel shows were recreations in the growing frontier settlements. Crockett's name was invoked in music during and after his life—"The Crockett Victory March" in the early 1830s, *Crockett's Free and Easy Song Book* of popular tunes in 1837, and "Colonel Crockett: A Virginia Reel" in 1839—but until the "Ballad of Davy Crockett" blew off the charts in 1955, the most enduring song associated with him was "Pompey Smash: The Everlastin and Ukonkerable Skreamer," a classic of blackface minstrelsy.

White musicians E. P. Christy, Dan Emmett, and Thomas Rice drew from the rhythms and lyrics of slave and frontier songs—some of them performed by singers like George Dixon Washington in blackface in the 1820s—to create blackface minstrelsy in the 1840s, which overnight became one of the most popular forms of mass entertainment. Samuel Clemens once commented that he preferred it to opera, and most Americans knew its tunes far better.

The music had direct ties to Crockett. A Jackson campaign anthem and Washington favorite in the 1820s was "The Hunters of Kentucky," which carried a boast that the men were of the "half horse, half alligator" variety, a description picked up and recycled by writers on Crockett from James Kirke Paulding to the present. Appearing in 1846, "Pompey Smash" detailed the escapades of its hero, a black alter ego to Davy of the almanacs, from which it borrowed liberally. Pompey praises Davy's grinning prowess and recounts a fight between them:

We fought haff a day, an den we greed to stop it,
For I was badly whipt, an so was Davy Crockett,
When we took for our heds, gosh we found 'em boph missen,
For he'd bit off mine, an I'd swallow'd hissen.
Den boph did agree for to leff de oder be,
For I was rather hard for him, an so was he for me.[20]

The song gained such currency that by the end of the century, transformed into "Davy Crockett," it had entered the realm of folk music.[21]

Following the Civil War and Reconstruction, a sensitive, romantic Crockett, a noble child of Nature, walked the stage and rose from the pages of popular books. In his most famous incarnation, Frank Mayo's theatrical adaptation of Frank Murdock's play, *Davy Crockett; Or, Be Sure You're Right, Then Go Ahead,* Crockett becomes the Lochinvar of the canebrake, the knight errant of the backwoods.[22] To win his darling Eleanor, a wealthy neighbor who had left to get an education and then returned, this natural poet of the soul must overcome his sense of inadequacy over his illiteracy—especially compared with her refinement—and rescue her from a marriage arranged by an evil guardian intent on gaining her inheritance to pay his debts. Along the way, Davy proves his steadfastness when a pack of ravenous wolves traps him and Eleanor in a cabin, which he secures from their assault by barring the door all night with his arm—it would not have done for them to duplicate the "courting" that Crockett and his Polly reportedly engaged in under similar circumstances. "This night," Eleanor cries, "has shown me all your noble self—your loyalty, your unselfish devotion."[23]

Through his love, Crockett later saves Eleanor—Nell—from her potentially disastrous marriage, the clutches of her guardian, and the uncle of her fiancé, by carrying her from them on the back of the black stallion Devilskin. The cuckold, guardian, and uncle track them to Dame Crockett's house, where the plot, such as it is, quickly resolves itself into a morality play. The fiancé realizes that Nell loves Davy and releases her from their engagement. Opting for life in the backwoods, Nell signs her fortune over to her guardian to satisfy his debts, and he, after bravely protesting her generosity, accepts. The uncle has money but is forever marked as a manipulative, evil man. Davy and Nell marry and live happily ever after to the strains of "Home, Sweet Home."

This "frontier melodrama" ran through more than two thousand performances in the United States and England from 1874 until June 6, 1896, two days before Mayo's death.[24] Sentimental and devoid of redeeming literary value though it is, the play served as the basis for no less than three silent films and inspired a score of children's books and novels. Unlike the Davy of the almanacs, who was weaned on whiskey, this boy grows among trees and animals, learning honesty and industry from his father. If they mention it at all, these children's tales make a virtue of the poverty that was the family's constant companion. Learning woodcraft early and well, Davy becomes the essential hunter, an identification intensified when Theodore Roosevelt, late in the century, formed his Boone and Crockett Club of

Gentlemen Hunters. The melodramatic Davy is never abused by the men he begins to work for when only twelve; rather, he learns from them the virtue of hard work.

Excluding the number of biographies and "autobiographical" writings, which rely to one degree or another on fictional characters and events, historical novels about Crockett are common and not particularly interesting. They tend to go out of print quickly and are difficult to find: Even *Wave High the Banner* (1942) by Dee Brown, adjudged by academics the best of the lot, is absent from most libraries, despite the author's success with *Bury My Heart at Wounded Knee* and other best sellers on the West. A number of maudlin plays of varying quality and claims to historical accuracy have also entered the *oeuvre* in this century without achieving more than passing notice of Crockettites. Film and television have been the favored Crockett media for the past fifty years, with Disney producing programs on the man and every Alamo movie featuring him prominently, often at the expense of Travis and Bowie.

For many people, Crockett's defining moment is his martyrdom at the Alamo, and the image they have fixed in their minds is from Walt Disney—Davy swinging his rifle like a club while fading into glory. That warrior's death became the Truth, although throughout the nineteenth century most Crockett biographies, following *Exploits,* described how heroic Davy had been captured and struck down while leaping for Santa Anna's throat. An alternate ending, grasped at briefly by David's son, John Wesley, held that he had been enslaved in Mexico. The news came into the United States by way of William E. White, who claimed to have met the imprisoned Crockett in a Salinas salt mine.[25] Congressman John Wesley Crockett formally requested Secretary of State John Forsyth on April 4, 1840, to investigate the persistent, bogus report.

By the 1950s, American filmmakers and writers were fixated on the notion that Crockett had died while killing Mexicans, in no small measure because, fresh from the Second World War and the conflict in Korea, they were obsessed with the hero's death in battle. The growing myth of the Alamo demanded too that all the brave defenders died fighting. Disney, the myth-maker, liked the high drama, and the vast popularity of his television program made it difficult for people to present any other possibility. The 1955 film *The Last Command,* starring Sterling Hayden as Jim Bowie and Arthur Hunnicutt as Crockett, and John Wayne's *The Alamo* (1960), followed Disney's lead, with some variation. Having confessed Communist leanings in his youth to the House Un-American Activities Committee, Hayden wanted to prove his patriotism in *The Last Command,* and so there was no question but that Davy would die fighting—trying to blow up the powder magazine no less.[26] In his portrayal of Crockett, John Wayne, lanced and dying, accomplished the feat and took a score of Mexicans with him into glory.

So firmly planted was the image in the American consciousness that when Texas historian Dan Kilgore resurrected the old reports in 1978 that David Crockett was captured, along with five or six others, at the Alamo and hacked to pieces on Santa Anna's orders, he was pilloried, called a traitor, a Communist dupe, and worse.[27] Compounding Kilgore's sin was the fact that he had cited evidence from Mexico—the diary of Lieutenant Colonel José Enrique de la Peña—that Crockett had tried to pass himself off as a traveling naturalist, a tourist who had nothing to do with the battle. Ironically, the diary was no more news than Kilgore's reprise of the Alamo's final moments—the media just picked up his article and made it appear radical.

Although dissenters accused the Texas historian of being part of a "Communist plan to degrade our heroes," a number of revisionists and journalists seized on the essay to underscore their view of Crockett as an unaccomplished lout.[28] Diametrically opposed in most regards, both sides believed that Crockett was somehow less a hero for being captured and mutilated, a bizarre notion given that the goal in any conflict is survival—if only to die another day. Crockett was more valuable politicking and telling tales than throwing down his life to preserve an indefensible mission.

* * *

At the height of his fame, *Niles' Weekly Register* addressed its readers: "We have been often times asked, 'What sort of man is colonel Crockett?' and the general reply was . . . 'just such a one as you would desire to meet with, if any accident or misfortune had happened to you on the high way.' "[29] He was the "original" common man.

NOTES

INTRODUCTION

1. Alexis de Tocqueville, *Journey to America*, ed. J. P. Mayer, trans. George Lawrence (London: Faber & Faber, 1959), p. 254.

2. Harriet Martineau, *Retrospect of Western Travel* (London: Saunders & Otley, 1838).

CHAPTER ONE
DISNEY MEETS DAVY

1. The Walt Disney company would not grant permission for me to quote the first stanza of "The Ballad of Davy Crockett" because I would not allow its public relations staff to review the manuscript of this book.

2. "The Biggest, Shortest Fad," *Entertainment Weekly*, December 14, 1990.

3. *Ibid.*

4. Peter T. White, "Ex-King of the Wild Frontier," *New York Times Magazine*, December 11, 1955.

5. "The Wild Frontier," *Time*, May 23, 1955.

6. *Ibid.*

7. "Mr. Crockett Is Real Shot as Salesman," *The New York Times*, June 1, 1955.

8. White, "Ex-King."

9. *Ibid.*

10. My request to examine the Disney archives relating to the three Crockett series was summarily denied on the grounds that too much effort

was involved. The National Archives office in Philadelphia contained relevant papers from Disney's suit against the Schwartzes and their company, Davy Crockett Enterprises—Civil Action 8231, filed May 6, 1955 in the United States District Court for Maryland.

11. William E. Giles, "Davy Crockett Sales Soar as Lawyers Feud on Trademark Rights," *The Wall Street Journal,* May 11, 1955.

12. *Ibid.; Time,* May 23, 1955.

13. "Random Notes from Washington: Hero Stands in for Davy Crockett," *The New York Times,* June 20, 1955, which does not identify Whitman.

14. James Reston, "Davy Crockett Can't Do Everything," *The New York Times,* May 22, 1955.

15. "Davy: Row and a Riddle," *Newsweek,* July 4, 1955.

16. John Fischer, "Personal & Otherwise: The Embarrassing Truth About Davy, the Alamo . . . ," *Harper's Magazine,* July 1955.

17. Margaret J. King, "The Recycled Hero: Walt Disney's Davy Crockett," in *Davy Crockett: The Man, the Legend, the Legacy, 1786–1986,* ed. Michael A. Lofaro (Knoxville: University of Tennessee Press, 1986), p. 152.

18. *People,* January 12, 1987.

CHAPTER TWO
HONOR THY FATHER

1. David Crockett, *A Narrative of the Life of David Crockett of the State of Tennessee,* ed. James A. Shackford and Stanley J. Folmsbee (Knoxville: University of Tennessee Press, 1973), pp. 16–20.

2. Albert R. Hogue, "Davy Crockett and Others in Fentress County Who Have Given the County a Prominent Place in History" (Crossville, Tenn.: Chronicle Publishing Co., 1955).

3. Dale Van Every, *Ark of Empire: The American Frontier, 1784–1803* (New York: William Morrow & Co., 1963), p. 86.

4. Stanley J. Folmsbee and Anna Grace Catron, "The Early Career of David Crockett," *East Tennessee Historical Society's Publications* 28 (1956), p. 60.

5. James Atkins Shackford, *David Crockett: The Man and the Legend,* ed. John B. Shackford (Chapel Hill: University of North Carolina Press, 1956; reprinted 1986), p. 5.

6. *Ibid.,* p. 8.

7. *Narrative,* pp. 19–21.

8. There has long been speculation that this parcel, which lay on the Holston Road, contained the site of John Crockett's inn, but a number of local historians and the State of Tennessee concluded that that establishment lay closer to present-day Morristown. (The chance for reflected glory and tourist dollars made for a lovely fight in the late 1950s.)

9. *Narrative,* p. 20n.

10. *Ibid.,* p. 23.

11. *Ibid.,* p. 25.

12. *Ibid.,* pp. 26–37.

13. *Ibid.,* p. 30.

14. *Ibid.,* pp. 38–39.

15. *Ibid.,* p. 40.

16. *Ibid.,* pp. 42–43.

17. *Ibid.,* p. 45.

18. *Ibid.,* p. 45.

19. *Ibid.,* p. 47.

20. Marquis James, *The Life of Andrew Jackson* (Indianapolis: Bobbs-Merrill Co., 1938), pp. 35–36.

21. Marquis James, *The Raven: A Biography of Sam Houston* (New York: Blue Ribbon Books, 1929).

22. Robert V. Remini, *Henry Clay: Statesman for the Union* (New York: W. W. Norton & Co., 1991), p. 12. Remini's excellent book is the basis for this summary.

23. *Narrative,* p. 48.

24. *Ibid.,* p. 49.

25. Shackford in *David Crockett* was the first to focus on the Crockett chronology.

26. *Narrative,* p. 54.

27. *Ibid.,* p. 59.

28. *Ibid.,* p. 59.

29. *Ibid.,* p. 60.

30. *Ibid.,* pp. 62–64. In *Life and Adventures of Colonel David Crockett of West Tennessee* (later known as *Sketches and Eccentricities of Colonel David Crockett of West Tennessee*) and subsequent melodramas, in which even intimations of sex are forbidden, Crockett bars the door with his arm against a pack of ravenous wolves.

31. *Ibid.,* pp. 65–66.

32. *Ibid.,* p. 69.

33. A number of biographers feel that Margaret was born in 1815, with her mother dying in childbirth. I have rejected that date based on the fact that she was married on March 22, 1830, to Wiley Flowers, a wedding that seems more likely to have occurred when she was closer to eighteen than to fifteen years of age.

CHAPTER THREE
SERGEANT CROCKETT

1. Howard Zinn, *A People's History of the United States* (New York: Harper Colophon Books, 1980), p. 126.

2. *Narrative*, p. 105. Crockett is the original printed source for this story, which he said came to him from a survivor.

3. Daniel Feller, *The Public Lands in Jacksonian Politics* (Madison: University of Wisconsin Press, 1984), pp. 18–20.

4. *Narrative*, p. 72.

5. *Ibid.*, p. 75.

6. *Ibid.*, p. 82.

7. *Ibid.*, pp. 88–89.

8. *Ibid.*, p. 89, n. 15.

9. *Ibid.*, p. 90. In this century, some scholars have pointed to Crockett's recollection as proof that his opposition to Indian removal in 1830 was a sham, while others have found in this same description evidence of disapproval of white behavior. The confusion arises from the subtle irony of the written scene. Crockett the politician clearly wished to establish his credentials as a scout and fighter to ward off rabid criticism of his opposition to Indian removal. The grotesque account of the atrocity and the quasi-cannibalism that followed would have amused many among Crockett's readers, as it does today, and offended others, while graphically conveying his view that whites could be as brutal as the "savages" they fought.

10. Shackford, *David Crockett*, p. 28.

11. *Narrative*, p. 101.

12. *Ibid.*, pp. 109–110.

13. *Ibid.*, p. 115.

14. *Ibid.*, p. 118.

15. James S. French in his *Sketches and Eccentricities of Colonel David Crockett of West Tennessee* reported that Polly died while Crockett was away. But because that cannot be confirmed and Crockett says she died after his return, the biographer must equivocate.

16. *Narrative*, p. 125.

17. *Ibid.*, p. 126.

18. *Ibid.*, p. 124.

19. The war records say third; the discharge, fourth, which is doubtlessly a scribe's blunder.

CHAPTER FOUR
AN ADVANTAGEOUS MARRIAGE

1. Shackford, *David Crockett*, pp. 34–35. Shackford serves as the basis for this description of Elizabeth Patton, although my conclusions differ radically.

2. *Narrative*, pp. 126–127.

3. Elizabeth's headstone in Hood County, Texas, says that she and David were married in 1815 in Lawrence County, Tennessee. Led by

James Shackford, who wrote in the middle of this century, most of Crockett's biographers have insisted that their wedding could not have taken place until late spring or early summer 1816, citing the belated second-hand reminiscences of the presiding preacher, Richard Calloway, and the bureaucratic fact that Lawrence County did not exist until 1817, the year the Crocketts moved to the area. Since David and Elizabeth's first son, Robert, was born sometime in 1816, if Shackford's date is correct, he was conceived out of wedlock, a not uncommon event at the time and one in keeping with rumors that Crockett was a womanizer and adulterer but at odds with Elizabeth Patton Crockett's reputation as a sensible, upright woman.

4. Private conversation with Ann Fears Crawford, former director of the Daughters of the Republic of Texas Library, the Alamo (hereafter, DRT Library), and a western historian.

5. Shackford, *David Crockett*, p. 35.

6. Shackford cites a 1921 history of Alabama stating that this valley was first settled in 1816 as evidence that Crockett's remarriage and exploration occurred in that year. Precise settlement dates being notoriously hard to fix and the time being late in 1815, I have decided to stick with Crockett's chronology. In keeping with settlement patterns throughout the country, squatters doubtlessly started dropping along the road as soon as hostilities had ended, although it might have taken them some time to record the claims. Then too Crockett recalled the trip nearly twenty years later and could simply have retroactively applied the name.

7. *Narrative*, p. 132.

8. *Ibid.*

9. Conventional wisdom among biographers who have worked with their old, crabbed chronology is that the Crocketts moved in early autumn of 1817, a date that must make of David, who says they lived there several years before the county government became operational, a prevaricator and the residents of the region superhuman organizers because within two months their justices of the peace had received approval from the state legislature. Some historians also claim that Crockett lived during the winter of 1817 in Fentress County, near the Kentucky border, but I find their arguments more suggestive of the possibility that David B. Crockett, probably a cousin, lived there.

10. Alabama Department of Archives and History, Montgomery, Alabama.

11. In the Tennessee Historical Society, Nashville.

12. From the informational material at the David Crockett State Park Visitors Center.

13. *Narrative*, p. 133.

14. *Ibid.*, p. 134.

15. *Ibid.*, p. 137.

16. *Ibid.*, p. 138.

17. *Ibid.*, p. 138.

18. *Ibid.*, p. 135, n. 25.

19. Typewritten transcript in the DRT Library, marked from E. J. McHenry, Memphis, Tennessee, with no indication of the location of the original.

20. John L. Jacobs to the *Morristown* (Tennessee) *Gazette* on November 22, 1884. The typescript by Annie Bell Bryson, Franklin County, North Carolina, of a clipping in her mother's scrapbook is located in the University of Tennessee Special Collections.

CHAPTER FIVE
THE CAMPAIGNER

1. *Narrative*, pp. 139–140.

2. *Ibid.*, p. 145.

3. *Ibid.*, p. 141. Crockett, of course, was not yet a bear hunter, although his credentials as a backwoodsman were well established.

4. *Ibid.*, pp. 141–142.

5. *Ibid.*, p. 142.

6. The name was sometimes given as Murfreesborough. I have opted for what became the accepted spelling.

7. The story first appeared in *Sketches*. Shackford in his biography identifies the man as Mitchell, pp. 52–53.

8. James, *Jackson*, p. 336.

9. *Narrative*, p. 145.

10. Shackford, *David Crockett*, pp. 55–56.

11. James, *The Raven*, p. 47.

12. James D. Davis, *The History of the City of Memphis* (Memphis: Hite, Crumpton & Kelly, Printers, 1873), p. 198.

13. *Narrative*, p. 147.

14. *Ibid.*, p. 150.

15. *Ibid.*, p. 154.

16. S. H. Stout, "David Crockett," *American Historical Magazine*, vol. VII, no. 1 (January 1902), p. 17.

17. *Narrative*, p. 190.

18. *Ibid.*, p. 191.

19. The Chicago Historical Society, Archives and Manuscript Department. The typescript of this document is incomplete and inaccurate. Clearly written in a hand other than Crockett's—and more illegible, though that is hard to believe—it dates from 1824 when Crockett would have been in Nashville, not from 1827, when he would have been campaigning in West Tennessee. The 4 is open and mistaken for a 7.

20. *Narrative*, p. 167.

21. *Ibid.*, p. 168.

22. *Ibid.*, pp. 168–170.
23. Shackford, *David Crockett,* p. 64.

CHAPTER SIX
MURFREESBORO TO MEMPHIS

1. Circular Letter of 1824 addressed to "Fellow-Citizens of the counties of Humphreys, Perry, Henderson, Carroll, Madison, Gibson, Dyer, Tipton, Haywood, Hardeman, and Fayette" in the Tennessee Historical Society, Nashville.
2. *Journal of the House of Representatives: First Session, Fifteenth General Assembly of the State of Tennessee,* p. 47.
3. *Ibid.*, p. 229.
4. *Ibid.*, p. 213.
5. Stanley J. Folmsbee and Anna Grace Catron, "The Early Career of David Crockett," *East Tennessee Historical Society's Publications* 28 (1956), pp. 83–84.
6. *Nashville Whig,* September 29, 1823.
7. Folmsbee and Catron, p. 78.
8. *Nashville Whig,* October 13, 1823, "Report of the President of the Bank of the State of Tennessee to the Legislature," September 15, 1823.
9. Remini, *Henry Clay,* pp. 234–50.
10. Daniel Walker Howe, *The Political Culture of the American Whigs* (Chicago: University of Chicago Press, 1979), p. 14.
11. *Narrative,* p. 172n.
12. Stanley J. Folmsbee and Anna Grace Catron, "David Crockett: Congressman," *East Tennessee Historical Society's Publications* 29 (1957), pp. 41–42.
13. Shackford, *David Crockett,* p. 69.
14. *Gibson County Circuit Court Minute Book A, 1824–32,* typescript copy in the Tennessee State Archives.
15. Crockett sets this trip in 1826, and I have followed his chronology, although it is possible that it took place early in 1827, the date being in any event less significant than the event and meeting with Winchester.
16. Davis, p. 147.
17. *Narrative,* p. 198.
18. Davis, pp. 149–50.
19. *Ibid.*, p. 71ff.

CHAPTER SEVEN
THE BEAR HUNTER GOES TO CONGRESS

1. W. F. Cooper Letter-Book, June 20, 1848, in the Cooper Family Collection, Tennessee State Archives. Also, Shackford, *David Crockett,* p. 83.

2. The *Jackson Gazette*, April 4, 1829, offers up John Cooke as a possible candidate.

3. *Narrative*, p. 204.

4. *Ibid.*

5. Robert V. Remini, *The Election of Andrew Jackson* (Philadelphia: J. B. Lippincott Co., 1963), p. 85.

6. David Mitchell Saunders to William Alexander Graham, September 15, 1827, in *The Papers of William Alexander Graham*, ed. J. G. de Roulhac Hamilton (Raleigh, N.C., 1957), vol. 1, p. 159.

7. James Erwin to Henry Clay, September 30, 1827, Clay Papers, Tennessee Historical Society; and quoted in Folmsbee and Catron, "David Crockett: Congressman," p. 44.

8. Shackford, *David Crockett*, p. 86, for information on Carson.

9. Letter to James Blackburn, February 5, 1828, in the Tennessee Historical Society.

10. Copy of loan agreement in Barker Texas History Center, University of Texas.

11. The letters were printed in the *Jackson Gazette*, January 31, 1829.

12. Letter to James Blackburn.

13. Daniel Feller, *The Public Lands in Jacksonian Politics* (Madison: University of Wisconsin Press, 1984), provides a fine discussion of this complex issue.

14. *Gales and Seaton's Register of Debates in Congress*, vol. IV, pt. 2, p. 2519. The printer mistakenly records 420,000.

15. *Ibid.*

16. *Ibid.*

17. Letter to James L. Totten, Trenton, Tennessee, February 11, 1828, in the University of Tennessee Special Collections.

18. Josephine Seaton, *William Winston Seaton of the National Intelligencer: A Biographical Sketch* (Boston: James R. Osgood & Company, 1871), p. 184.

19. Shackford, *David Crockett*, draws some curious conclusions about the Clarke-Crockett relationship, which are in line with his ill-founded notion that Crockett was the victim of a Whig conspiracy to promote him as a competitor to Jackson, p. 257ff.

20. *Register of Debates*, vol. V, p. 162.

21. *Ibid.*, p. 197.

22. *Ibid.*, p. 206.

23. *Ibid.*, p. 210.

24. Letter to John H. Bryan, May 26, 1829, in the Elias Carr Papers, East Carolina Manuscript Collection, East Carolina University.

25. Letter to Davison McMillen, January 16, 1829, in Herbert Weaver, ed., *Correspondence of James K. Polk: Volume I, 1817–1832* (Nashville: Vanderbilt University Press, 1969).

26. Letter to George Patton, January 27, 1829, in the Tennessee Historical Society Collection, Tennessee State Library and Archives.

27. Crockett spoke repeatedly of his good health during this period, most specifically to Gales and Seaton in a letter dated April 18, 1829, in the Personal Miscellaneous Papers (David Crockett), Rare Books and Manuscripts Division, The New York Public Library, Astor, Lenox and Tilden Foundations.

CHAPTER EIGHT
CONGRESSIONAL REPRISE

1. *Jackson Gazette,* August 15, 1829. The *Gazette* ran a perfunctory defense of its representative.

2. Davis, pp. 110–11.

3. Crockett letter to Gales and Seaton; and James, *The Raven.*

4. James, *Jackson,* pp. 385–87, 476ff. James provides a thorough account of the affair.

5. Feller, pp. 127–29.

6. *Register of Debates,* vol. VI, p. 554.

7. *Ibid.,* p. 583.

8. *Ibid.,* p. 634.

9. *Ibid.,* p. 717.

10. *Ibid.,* p. 804.

11. *Jackson Gazette,* March 27, 1830, and April 10, 1830.

12. Crockett's ghostwriter is unknown, but the religious references and the nature of the argument, repeated in a circular letter written a year later, indicate that he and Chilton were collaborating.

13. James, *Jackson,* p. 603.

14. *Speeches on the Passage of the Bill for the Removal of the Indians Delivered in the Congress of the United States* (Boston: Perkins & Marvin, 1830); and "David Crockett's Circular to the Citizens and Voters of the Ninth Congressional District of the State of Tennessee," February 28, 1831, in the Library of Congress.

15. *Speeches on the Passage of the Bill for the Removal of the Indians,* p. 253.

16. *Jackson Gazette,* August 14, 1830.

17. *Ibid.,* November 20, 1830.

18. *Ibid.,* November 27, 1830.

19. Andrew Jackson to Samuel Jackson Hays, April 1831, quoted in Folmsbee and Catron, "David Crockett: Congressman," p. 66.

20. *Register of Debates,* vol. VII, p. 789.

21. Letter to A. M. Hughes, February 13, 1831, Tennessee Historical Society.

22. *Ibid.*

23. Shackford, *David Crockett,* correctly identifies Chilton, p. 107.

24. "David Crockett's Circular Letter."

25. Remini, *The Election of Andrew Jackson*, p. 3.

26. Shackford mistakenly dates the "Book of Chronicles" to 1833, and scholars since have automatically followed suit.

27. The undated report is contained in James A. Shackford's papers at the University of Tennessee Special Collection.

28. The deed was not recorded in the Weakley County record books until April 14, 1832.

29. Letter to Richard Smith, January 7, 1832, in the Connaroe Collection, Historical Society of Pennsylvania. Shackford mistakenly records this letter as being sent in 1833.

30. Letter to Doctor Jones, August 22, 1831, in the Southern Historical Collection, Library of the University of North Carolina at Chapel Hill.

31. Crockett Family Papers, Tennessee State Library and Archives.

32. John Wesley Crockett to George Patton, July 9, 1836, Tennessee Historical Society.

CHAPTER NINE
THE FAMOUS BACKWOODSMAN

1. James Kirke Paulding, *The Lion of the West: The Kentuckian, or a Trip to New York*, revised by John Augustus Stone and William Boyle Bernard, ed. James N. Tidwell (Stanford, Calif.: Stanford University Press, 1954), p. 21.

2. *Ibid.*, p. 27.

3. *The Letters of James Kirke Paulding*, ed. Ralph M. Aderman (Madison: University of Wisconsin Press, 1962), p. 113.

4. *Ibid.*, p. 112.

5. Benjamin Perley Poore, *Perley's Reminiscences of Sixty Years in the National Metropolis* (Philadelphia: Hubbard Brothers, Publishers, 1886), pp. 180–81.

6. This section is based on Ralph C. H. Catterall, *The Second Bank of the United States* (Chicago: University of Chicago Press, 1902); and Arthur M. Schlesinger, Jr., *The Age of Jackson* (Boston: Little, Brown & Co., 1945).

7. Remini, *Henry Clay*, p. 380ff.

8. Catterall, p. 325.

9. *Narrative*, p. 210.

10. Catterall, p. 350.

11. Remini, *Henry Clay*, p. 463.

12. The book presents a bibliographical puzzle. It was first published as *The Life and Adventures of Colonel David Crockett of West Tennessee* in 1833 in Cincinnati, with a second and subsequent editions under *Sketches and Eccentricities of Colonel David Crockett of West Tennessee* (New York: J. & J. Harper, 1833). James Strange French was the original author of record.

Crockett's biographer from the 1950s, James Atkins Shackford, attributes the book to Mathew St. Clair Clarke, clerk of the House of Representatives, claiming it was part of the master Whig conspiracy to make David a national figure and alternative to Jackson. But Shackford substitutes supposition for proof. The Whigs were not interested in promoting Crockett for the presidency, while Clarke was not above helping Crockett's opponents as well as Crockett. Surely, given his feelings of betrayal over the publication, he would have named Clarke as the culprit had he believed him responsible. Edgar Allan Poe attributed the work to French, and although Shackford accepts his authority in other cases, he inexplicably denies it here. Shackford's chief evidence is a comment by J. C. Derby, a book editor, in his memoir, *Fifty Years Among Authors, Books, and Publishers* (New York: G. W. Carleton & Co., 1884), that Crockett's publisher, Abraham Hart, had told him that Mathew St. Clair Clarke was author of the autobiography. Shackford thinks Hart confused *Sketches*, which he did not publish, with *Narrative*, but it is more likely that Clarke, a Pennsylvanian, introduced Crockett and Chilton to Carey and Hart, in Philadelphia. Hart could also have confused Clarke with William Clark, ghostwriter for Crockett's *Tour,* which Carey and Hart published. Joseph J. Arpad is one scholar who has followed the copyright and Poe in naming French the author.

13. *Sketches,* p. 19.

14. *Sketches,* pp. 125–26.

15. Henry Wikoff, *The Reminiscences of an Idler* (New York, 1880), quoted in M. J. Heale, "The Role of the Frontier in Jacksonian Politics: David Crockett and the Myth of the Self-made Man," *Western Historical Quarterly* IV, no. 4 (October 1973), p. 407.

16. A letter to G. W. McLean, January 17, 1834, in the Library of Congress contains a clear expression of Crockett's attitude.

17. Letter to Carey and Hart, February 23, 1834, in the Boston Public Library, by permission of the trustees of the library.

18. *Register of Debates,* vol. X, p. 3550.

19. Letter to John Wesley Crockett, January 10, 1834, in the Beinecke Rare Book and Manuscript Library, Yale University.

20. From a copy of the Area Research Center, Forest R. Polk Library, University of Wisconsin-Oshkosh, of an April 1936 auction announcement from the American Autograph Shop, of a page from Octavia Claudia Walton Le Vert's *Album of Memories.*

21. The tour is summarized in David Crockett, *An Account of Col. Crockett's Tour to the North and Down East, in the Year of Our Lord One Thousand Eight Hundred and Thirty-four* (Philadelphia: E. L. Carey & A. Hart, 1835), which was probably the work of William Clark, a Congressman from Pennsylvania on Crockett's behalf. Unless otherwise noted, citations for this discussion are from *The Autobiography of David Crockett,* edited and

with an introduction by Hamlin Garland (New York: Charles Scribner's Sons, 1923), p. 149.

22. *Autobiography,* p. 159.

23. *Ibid.,* p. 175.

24. *Ibid.,* pp. 180–81.

25. *Ibid.,* pp. 183–85.

26. *Niles' Weekly Register,* vol. XLVI, June 7, 1834, p. 221.

27. *Register of Debates,* vol. X, p. 4133.

28. *Niles' Weekly Register,* vol. XLVI, June 21, 1834, pp. 295–96.

29. *Register of Debates,* vol. X, p. 4586.

30. *Ibid.,* p. 4588.

31. Curtis Caroll Davis, "A Legend at Full-length: Mr. Chapman Paints Colonel Crockett—and Tells About It," *American Antiquarian Society Proceedings* 69 (October 1959).

32. *Ibid.,* p. 171.

33. Letter to John Wesley Crockett, January 10, 1834.

CHAPTER TEN
THE LONG FALL

1. Shackford, *David Crockett,* p. 170, although he mistakenly puts home as Gibson County.

2. *Autobiography,* p. 191.

3. Letter to Nicholas Biddle, October 7, 1834, Nicholas Biddle Papers, Historical Society of Pennsylvania.

4. Letter to Nicholas Biddle, December 8, 1834, Gratz Collection, Historical Society of Pennsylvania. Shackford wrongly assumed that this letter referred to funds Crockett requested of Richard Smith in the Washington Branch in 1832 and used it as evidence that Crockett had wrongfully accepted money from Biddle.

5. Letter to Carey and Hart, December 8, 1834, in Houghton Library, Harvard University.

6. Nicholas Biddle to David Crockett, December 13, 1834, in President's Letter Book, p. 275, the Library of Congress.

7. Letter to George Poindexter, December 13, 1834, President's Letter Book, p. 279, the Library of Congress.

8. Letter to Nicholas Biddle, December 16, 1834, Nicholas Biddle Papers, Historical Society of Pennsylvania.

9. Letter to John P. Ash, December 27, 1834, University of the South Archives.

10. Adam Huntsman to James K. Polk, January 1, 1835, photostat in Tennessee State Library and Archives; original in James K. Polk Papers, Library of Congress.

11. *Congressional Globe,* February 14, 1835.

12. Schlesinger, pp. 190–91.

13. *Congressional Globe,* February 13, 1835, p. 241. The Whiggish *Register of Debates* carries a slightly different version: "There was nothing in the President's message pleased him so much as the recommendation of giving homes to poor settlers. He began to think the President was almost turning a Crockett man." Vol. XI, p. 1354.

14. The letter to James K. Polk on May 12, 1835, in *Correspondence of Andrew Jackson,* ed. John Spencer Bassett (Washington: Carnegie Institution of Washington, 1931), vol. V, p. 345, is representative of his view, expressed in a series to Tennessee friends and supporters.

15. Letter to John P. Ash, December 27, 1834.

16. Letter to Carey and Hart, January 12, 1835, New-York Historical Society, Manuscript Department.

17. *Tour,* p. 173.

18. The whole is reproduced in *ibid.,* pp. 203–14.

19. Shackford, *David Crockett,* citing a letter to Carey and Hart, January 16, 1835, which I have been unable to locate, pp. 186–87.

20. *The Life of Martin Van Buren* (Philadelphia: Robert Wright, 1835), p. 13.

21. *Ibid.,* pp. 80–81.

22. Edgar Allan Poe, "Autography," *Graham's Magazine* XIX, no. 6, (December 1841).

23. John Seelye, "A Well-Wrought Crockett or, How the Fakelorists Passed Through the Credibility Gap and Discovered Kentucky," in Lofaro, ed., *Davy Crockett,* pp. 21–45.

24. *Davy Crockett's 1835 Almanack of Wild Sports of the West, and Life in the Backwoods* (Nashville: Snag & Sawyer), p. 2.

25. Schlesinger, pp. 277–78.

26. Shackford, *David Crockett,* p. 198.

27. Letter to Carey and Hart, August 11, 1835, VF., Manuscripts Division, Maryland Historical Society Library.

28. Folmsbee and Catron, "David Crockett: Congressman," p. 78.

29. Davis, p. 151.

30. Letter to Carey and Hart, August 11, 1835.

31. *Ibid.*

32. Davis, p. 143. Crockett had been thinking of Texas for some time before the election.

33. Letter to George Patton, October 31, 1835, in Shackford, *David Crockett,* p. 210.

34. Davis, p. 145.

35. Shackford, *David Crockett,* p. 313n.

36. Letter to Margaret and Wiley Flowers, January 9, 1836, the so-called last letter, copy in the Daughters of the Republic of Texas Library,

San Antonio. The letter exists only in typescript, which was punctuated by the person who made it.

37. *Ibid.*

38. *Papers of the Texas Revolution: 1835–1836*, ed. John H. Jenkins (Austin: Presidial Press, 1973), vol. 4, item no. 1782. In his letter to his daughter and son-in-law on January 9, Crockett says he has taken the oath, and he may have verbally or in his heart. He signed on the fourteenth.

39. *Ibid.*, no. 1740, James Gaines to Lieutenant Governor Robinson.

40. *Spirit of the Times* (New York), April 9, 1836.

CHAPTER ELEVEN
A TIME TO DIE

1. Jeff Long, *Duel of Eagles: The Mexican and U.S. Fight for the Alamo* (New York: William Morrow & Co., 1990), p. 31.

2. James, *The Raven*, p. 181.

3. *Ibid.*, pp. 163–70.

4. *Ibid.*, p. 183.

5. Capsule biographies of Travis appear in Walter Lord, *A Time To Stand: The Epic of the Alamo* (Lincoln: University of Nebraska Press, 1978); and Long, *Duel of Eagles.*

6. James, *The Raven*, p. 201.

7. Letter from J. C. Neill to Sam Houston, January 14, 1836, *Papers of the Texas Revolution*, vol. 4, no. 1783.

8. Sam Houston to Governor Henry Smith, January 17, 1836, *Papers of the Texas Revolution*, vol. 4, no. 1813. Houston to Philip Dimmitt and James Collinsworth, March 15, 1836, *Papers of the Texas Revolution*, vol. 4, nos. 2307 and 2328.

9. James Bowie to Governor Henry Smith, February 2, 1836, *Papers of the Texas Revolution*, vol. 4, no. 1989.

10. *Ibid.*

11. William Barrett Travis to Henry Smith, January 29, 1836, in *Official Correspondence of the Texas Revolution, 1835–1836*, ed. William Campbell Binkley (New York: D. Appleton-Century Co., 1936), vol. I., pp. 362–63.

12. Most standard histories rely heavily on a memoir by one Dr. John Sutherland called *The Fall of the Alamo* (San Antonio: Naylor Company, 1936). Sutherland claimed to have been a physician at the Alamo and one of the final messengers for Travis, which is why he escaped. Thomas Ricks Lindley in "The Revealing of Dr. John Sutherland" (Daughters of the Republic of Texas Collection, 1989) convincingly demonstrates that Sutherland was probably not at the Alamo and that his account is a fiction.

13. Long, pp. 131–32.

14. Lord, p. 84.

15. Travis to Governor Henry Smith, February 13, 1836, copy in Baker Texas History Center, University of Texas.

16. Lord, p. 85.

17. *Ibid.*, p. 91, citing Fannin letters to Robinson on February 14 and 21, 1836.

18. Travis, February 24, 1836, *Papers of the Texas Revolution,* vol. 4, no. 2168; original in Texas State Archives.

19. Travis to Sam Houston, February 25, 1836, *Papers of the Texas Revolution,* vol. 4, no. 2177.

20. John Sowers Brooks to his mother, March 2, 1836, from Fort Defiance in Goliad, *Papers of the Texas Revolution,* vol. 4, no. 2218.

21. Based on the recollections of Señora Candelaria, a Mexican woman who had entertained various of the principals in her house and claimed to have nursed Bowie in his final hours, and Susannah Dickinson, wife of artillery commander Almeron Dickinson, who with her daughter was in the Alamo. Maurice Elfer, *Madam Candelaria: Unsung Hero of the Alamo* (Houston: Rein Company, 1933). Mrs. Dickinson's recollections were published in various newspapers; clips are on file at the Daughters of the Republic of Texas Library.

22. Fannin to Robinson, February 28, 1836, quoted in Lord, p. 122.

23. James, *The Raven,* p. 224.

24. José Enrique de la Peña, *With Santa Anna in Texas: A Personal Narrative of the Revolution,* ed. and trans. Carmen Perry (College Station: Texas A & M Press, 1975), p. 44.

25. De la Peña, p. 53. Dan Kilgore, in *How Did Davy Die?* (College Station: Texas A & M Press, 1978), reopened this debate, but for many years after the Alamo, it was a given that Crockett had been captured and killed.

26. De la Peña, p. 53. He goes on to say that he turned his head away but heard that General Sesma was among the murderers.

27. *Ibid.*

28. Lord, p. 213.

29. *Ibid.*, pp. 207–8. Lord does not believe Señora Candelaria was present, but the Texas State Legislature awarded her a pension as a survivor a few years before her death in 1899. Long, pp. 338–39. Susannah outlived her daughter and managed to retire from prostitution.

30. Lord, p. 167.

31. *Ibid.*, p. 182.

32. Long, pp. 299–301.

33. S. H. Stout, "David Crockett," p. 12.

34. Shackford, *David Crockett,* p. 239.

35. Bounty Book, Texas Research Library, Austin. Interview with Mrs. Matilda Crockett Fields, n.d., in the Crockett miscellaneous file, Daughters of the Republic of Texas Library.

36. Josephine A. Pearson, "The Tennessee Woman Trecker—Elizabeth—Widow of David Crockett," *Tennessee Historical Magazine,* n.d.

CHAPTER TWELVE
THE LEGENDARY HERO

1. James, *The Raven,* p. 258.
2. *Ibid.,* p. 389.
3. Bernard de Voto, *Mark Twain's America* (Boston: Little, Brown & Co., 1932), p. 92.
4. Derby, pp. 550–54; "Biography of Richard Penn Smith," *Burton's Gentleman's Magazine and Monthly Review,* September 1839; and Richard Boyd Hauck, *Crockett: A Bio-Bibliography* (Westport, Conn.: Greenwood Press, 1982), pp. 51–52, for the reference to Longstreet.
5. Schlesinger, p. 297.
6. Buffalo Bill (Hon. W. F. Cody), *Story of the Wild West and Camp-Fire Chats* (Chicago: Charles C. Thompson Co., 1902), p. 157.
7. *Davy Crockett's 1837 Almanack of Wild Sports in the West, Life in the Backwoods & Sketches of Texas* (Nashville: Published by the heirs of Col. Crockett, 1836).
8. *The Autobiography of David Crockett,* p. 318.
9. Remini, *Henry Clay,* p. 565.
10. *Crockett's 1850 Almanac Containing Rows, Sprees, and Scrapes in the West, Life and Capers in the Backwoods, Adventures on the Ocean, etc.* (New York: Fisher & Brothers).
11. Compiled from several editions of Crockett almanacs. The quote is from *The Idle Hour Book or Scrapiana* (New York: Turner & Fisher, n.d.).
12. *The Crockett Almanac 1839: Containing Adventures, Exploits, Sprees & Scrapes in the West, Life and Manners in the Backwoods* (Nashville: Ben Harding).
13. Richard Dorson, ed., *Davy Crockett: American Comic Legend* (New York: Spiral Press for Rockland Editions, 1939), p. 82.
14. *Davy Crockett's 1837 Almanack.*
15. Dorson, p. 22.
16. *Ibid.,* p. 20.
17. *The 1840 Crockett Almanac* (Nashville: Ben Harding).
18. Dorson, p. 55.
19. *Davy Crockett's 1836 Almanack of Wild Sports in the West, and Life in the Backwoods* (Nashville: Published for the author).
20. Charles K. Wolfe, "Davy Crockett Songs: Minstrels to Disney," in Lofaro, ed., *Davy Crockett,* p. 163.
21. *Ibid.,* p. 167.
22. Garland, "Introduction" to *The Autobiography of David Crockett,* p. 3.

23. Leonard Grover et al., *Davy Crockett & Other Plays,* vol. IV of *America's Lost Plays,* ed. Isaac Goldberg and Hubert Hefner (Princeton: Princeton University Press, 1940), p. 135.

24. *Ibid.,* p. xvii.

25. Reported in the *Austin City Gazette,* March 18, 1840, and elsewhere.

26. Frank Thompson, *Alamo Movies* (East Berlin, Pa.: Old Mill Books, 1991), p. 61.

27. Dan Kilgore, *How Did Davy Die?* (College Station: Texas A & M Press, 1978).

28. "How the West Was Really Won," *U.S. News and World Report,* May 21, 1990.

29. *Niles' Weekly Register,* September 7, 1833.

BIBLIOGRAPHICAL NOTE

It is appropriate to begin with Crockett's printed works, virtually all of which were written in collaboration with ghostwriters, and all of which, with the exception of the Martin Van Buren polemic, have been reprinted in a variety of forms. I will list the date and publisher of the first edition of each: *A Narrative of the Life of David Crockett of the State of Tennessee* (Philadelphia: E. L. Carey & A. Hart, 1834); *An Account of Colonel Crockett's Tour to the North and Down East, in the Year of Our Lord One Thousand Eight Hundred and Thirty-four* (Philadelphia: E. L. Carey & A. Hart, 1835); *The Life of Martin Van Buren, Hair-Apparent to the "Government," and the Appointed Successor of General Jackson* (Philadelphia: Robert Wright, 1835); and *Col. Crockett's Exploits and Adventures in Texas* (Philadelphia: T. K. & P. G. Collins, 1836). Richard Penn Smith wrote *Exploits*, while the ghostwriters for the other works are named in the preceding text and so are not identified again here. During his legislative career, Crockett had several speeches and circular letters published on his behalf: An 1824 Circular to "Fellow-Citizens of the counties of Humphreys, Perry, Henderson, Carroll, Madison, Gibson, Dyer, Tipton, Haywood, Hardeman, and Fayette"; *Address of Mr. Crockett, to the voters of the Ninth Congressional District of the State of Tennessee; Together with His Remarks in the House of Representatives,* January 5, 1829 (Washington: Gales and Seaton); "A Sketch of the Remarks of the Hon. David Crockett," in *Speeches on the Passage of the Bill for the Removal of the Indians Delivered in the Congress of the United States, April and May, 1830* (Boston: Perkins & Marvin, 1830); *Speech of Mr. Crockett, of Tennessee, on a Bill Proposing to Construct a National Road from Buffalo to New Orleans"* (Washington: Duff Green, 1830); and "David Crockett's Circular: To the Citizens and Voters of the Ninth Congressional District in the State of Tennessee," 1831. I have found the facsimile edition of *A Narrative of the Life of David Crockett of the State of Tennessee,* with annotations and introduction by James A. Shackford and Stanley J. Folmsbee (Knoxville: University of Tennessee Press, 1973) to be the most useful of a shelfful of editions of this classic. *The Autobiography of David Crockett,* edited and with an introduction by Hamlin Garland, (New York: Charles Scribner's Sons, 1923) contains most of the *Narrative, Tour,* and *Exploits,* along with a noteworthy introduction.

There is no central collection of Crockett manuscripts (which in any event are not numerous), books, or government documents, but significant amounts of such material, including newspaper clippings, ephemera, and personal observations by a number of people who knew him reside at the Daughters of the Republic of Texas Library at the Alamo; the Barker Texas History Center at the University of Texas at Austin; the Tennessee State Library and Archives in Nashville, which houses the collection of the Tennessee Historical Society; and the University of Tennessee Special Collections. Copies of all Crockett resolutions to the House of Representatives are found in the National Archives. Significant letters are located at the Library of Congress, including Nicholas Biddle's letter book; Houghton Library, Harvard University; the Historical Society of Pennsylvania; the Maryland Historical Society; the Boston Public Library; the Maine Historical Society; the New York Public Library and the New-York Historical Society; the Wilson Library Manuscripts Division, the University of North Carolina at Chapel Hill; the North Carolina State Archives; the East Carolina Manuscript Collection of the J. Y. Joyner Library, East Carolina University; the Lilly Library, Indiana University; the Pierpont Morgan Library; the Chicago Historical Society; the Huntington Library; the Buffalo and Erie County Historical Society; the Beinecke Rare Book and Manuscript Library, Yale University; the Jessie Ball duPont Library Archives and Special Collections, University of the South; the Alabama State Archives; and the Area Research Center, Forrest R. Polk Library, University of Wisconsin at Oshkosh.

Government documents consulted include Tennessee county record books for Carroll, Gibson, Greene, Jefferson, Lawrence, Lincoln, and Weakley counties; U.S. Census reports for Lawrence County, 1820, Gibson and Weakley counties, 1830; *Journal of the House of Representatives of the State of Tennessee* and *Acts of the General Assembly of the State of Tennessee; Gales & Seaton's Register of Debates in Congress; Journal of the House of Representatives; The Congressional Globe; Biographical Directory of the United States Congress, 1774–1989, Bicentennial Edition; Congressional Directories;* Muster and Payroll Records, the War of 1812; *Papers of the Texas Revolution,* ed. John Jenkins (Austin: Presidial Press, 1973); and Civil Action no. 8231, *Walt Disney Productions* v. *Morey Schwartz, Hannah Schwartz, and Davy Crockett Enterprises, Inc.,* filed May 6, 1955. *The Historical Atlas of United States Congressional Districts: 1789–1983* (New York: Free Press, 1983) by Kenneth C. Martis was useful for locating Crockett and his contemporaries.

Newspapers and news magazines containing significant information on the life and legend are: the *Jackson Gazette*, the *Jackson Southern Statesman*, the *Nashville Whig* and the *National Banner and Nashville Whig*, the *Nashville Republican*, the *Memphis Advocate*, the *Knoxville Register*, the *Austin City Gazette*, the *Houston Telegraph & Texas Register*, the *New York Sun*, the *New York Mirror*, the *New York Evening Post*, the *New York Traveller*, the *Spirit of the Times and Family Journal*, the *National Intelligencer*, the *Washington Globe*, *Harper's New Monthly Magazine*, *Niles' Weekly Register*, *Burton's Gentleman's Magazine and Monthly Review*, and *Graham's Magazine*. For more current portraits, I have turned to the *Baltimore Sun*, the *New York Post*, *The New York Times*, the *San Antonio Light*, the *San Antonio News*, *The Wall Street Journal*, *Entertainment Weekly*, *Harper's*, *Life*, *The New Yorker*, *People*, *Saturday Review*, *Time*, *Texana*, and *TV Guide*.

Versions of Crockett's autobiography and various biographies, of variable authenticity, began to appear in his lifetime, with the anonymous *Life and Adventures of Colonel David Crockett of West Tennessee* (Cincinnati: For the Proprietor, 1833), republished under the name of the author, James Strange French, *Sketches and Eccentricities of Colonel David Crockett of West Tennessee* (New York: J. & J. Harper, 1833). Others include: John S. C. Abbott, *David Crockett* (New York: Dodd, Mead & Co., 1874); Walter Blair, *Davy Crockett—Frontier Hero: The Truth as He Told It—The Legend as His Friends Built It* (New York: Coward-McCann, 1955); William F. Cody, *Story of the Wild West and Camp-Fire Chats, by Buffalo Bill, (Hon. W. F. Cody): A Full and Complete History of the Renowned Pioneer Quartette, Boone, Crockett, Carson and Buffalo Bill* (Philadelphia: Historical Publishing Co., 1888), as well as a 1902 edition published by Charles C. Thompson of Chicago; Edward S. Ellis, *The Life of Colonel David Crockett* (Philadelphia: Porter & Coates, 1884); Mrs. J. Stewart French and Zella Armstrong, *The Crockett Family and Connecting Lines* (Bristol, Tenn.: King Printing Co., 1928); Richard Boyd Hauck, *Crockett: A Bio-Bibliography* (Westport, Conn.: Greenwood Press, 1973); Stewart H. Holbrook, *Davy Crockett: From the Backwoods of Tennessee to the Alamo* (New York: Random House, 1955); *Davy Crockett: Gentleman from the Cane*, ed. James C. Kelly and Frederick S. Voss (Washington, D.C., and Nashville: National Portrait Gallery & Tennessee Museum, 1986); *Davy Crockett: The Man, the Legend, the Legacy, 1786–1986*, ed. by Michael A. Lofaro (Knoxville: The University of Tennessee Press, 1986); Enid L. Meadowcroft, *The Story of Davy Crockett* (New York: Grossett & Dunlap, 1952); Constance Rourke, *Davy Crockett* (New York: Harcourt, Brace & Co., 1931); James Atkins Shackford, *David Crockett: The Man and the Legend*, ed. John B. Shackford (Chapel Hill: University of North Carolina Press, 1956) and "The Autobiography of David Crockett: An Annotated Edition" (Ph.D. dissertation, Vanderbilt University; 1948); Miles Tanenbaum, *Hunting Davy Crockett: A Guide to Crockett Studies*

(Nashville: Tennessee Department of Conservation and Tennessee State Museum, 1986).

Useful articles include: Walter Blair, "Six Davy Crocketts," *Southwest Review,* July 1940; Texas Jim Cooper, "A Study of Some David Crockett Firearms," *East Tennessee Historical Society's Publications* 38 (1966); Curtis Carroll Davis, "A Legend at Full-length: Mr. Chapman Paints Colonel Crockett—and Tells About It," *Proceedings of the American Antiquarian Society* 69 (1960); Stanley J. Folmsbee and Anna Grace Catron, "The Early Career of David Crockett," *East Tennessee Historical Society's Publications* 28 (1956), "David Crockett: Congressman," in no. 29 of the same (1957), and "David Crockett in Texas," in no. 30 of the same (1958); M. J. Heale, "The Role of the Frontier in Jacksonian Politics: David Crockett and the Myth of the Self-made Man," *Western Historical Quarterly,* October 1973; Robert M. McBride, "David Crockett and His Memorials in Tennessee," *Tennessee Historical Quarterly* 26 (1967); S. H. Stout, "David Crockett," *The American Historical Magazine* VII (January 1902); and Phillip Thomas Tucker, "Motivation of United States Volunteers During the Texas Revolution, 1835–36," *East Texas Historical Journal,* 1991. Useful journals, in addition to other numbers of the above, are *Journal of American History* and the *Tennessee Historical Quarterly.*

The legendary Crockett is portrayed in almanacs, novels, plays, films, and television programs. The novels include: Dee Brown, *Wave High the Banner: A Novel Based on the Life of Davy Crockett* (Philadelphia: Macrae-Smith, 1942); James Wakefield Burke, *David Crockett: The Man Behind the Myth* (Austin: Eakin Press, 1984); William Alexander Caruthers, *The Kentuckian in New York; Or, the Adventures of Three Southerns* (New York: Harper & Bros., 1834); and James Strange French, *Elkswatawa; or, The Prophet of the West: A Tale of the Frontier* (New York: Harper & Bros., 1836); Irwin Shapiro, *Yankee Thunder: The Legendary Life of Davy Crockett* (New York: Julian Messner, 1944), one of a score of children's books on the order of Billie L. Matthews and Virginia Hurlburt Hendrick, *Davy's Dawg* (Dallas: Long Publishing Company, 1989) of dubious accuracy; and Meridel Le Sueur, *Chanticleer of the Wilderness Road: A Story of Davy Crockett* (New York: Alfred A. Knopf, 1951). The almanacs appeared in forty-five editions under different titles and publishers. Copies and microfilms are found in a number of collections, including those of the American Antiquarian Society, the Barker Texas History Center, the Daughters of the Republic of Texas Library, and the Beinecke Library at Yale University. Episodes are collected in *Davy Crockett: American Comic Legend,* ed. Richard Dorson (New York: Spiral Press for Rockland Editions, 1939; reprint, New York: Arno Press, 1977), and *The Crockett Almanacks: Nashville Series, 1835 to 1838,* ed. Franklin J. Meine (Chicago: Caxton Club, 1955). Significant plays are: James Kirke Paulding, *The Lion of the West: The Kentuckian, or a Trip to New York,* rev. John Augustus Stone and William Boyle Bernard, ed. James N. Tidwell (Stanford, Calif.: Stanford University Press, 1954), with *The Letters of James Kirke Paulding,* ed. Ralph M. Aderman (Madison: University of Wisconsin Press, 1962), also being useful; Frank Murdock, *Davy Crockett; or Be Sure You're Right, Then Go Ahead* in *America's Lost Plays,* vol. IV, ed. Isaac Goldberg and Hubert Hefner (Princeton: Princeton University Press, 1940); and Edwin Justin Mayer, *Sunrise in My Pocket, Or the Last Days of Davy Crockett: An American Saga* (New York: Julian Messner, 1941). The most significant TV programs and films devoted to Crockett are Walt Disney Productions' "Davy Crockett, Indian Fighter"; "Davy Crockett Goes to Congress"; and "Davy Crockett at the Alamo," released as a film, *Davy Crockett, King of the Wild Frontier* (1955), and the film *Davy Crockett and the River Pirates,* including "Davy Crockett's Keelboat Race" and "Davy Crockett and the River Pirates" (1955); *The Magical World of Disney,* beginning in 1986, aired "Guardian Spirit," "A Letter to Polly," "A Natural Man," "Rainbow in the Thunder," and "Warrior's Farewell." Other film biographies are: *Davy Crockett—in Hearts United,* directed by Charles K. French (New York Motion Pictures, 1909); *Davy Crockett,* directed by Hobart Bosworth (Selig Polyscope, 1910); *Davy Crockett Up-to-Date,* directed by W. E. Browning (United Film Service, 1915); *Davy Crockett,* directed by Dustin Farnum (Pallas, 1916); and *Davy Crockett, Indian Scout* (United Artists, 1948). Music from Crockett's time is found in *Crockett's Free-and-Easy Song Book: A New Collection of the Most Popular Stage Songs* (Philadelphia: J. Kay, Jr., & Bro., 1837).

The Alamo is remembered in: Walter Lord, *A Time to Stand: The Epic of the Alamo* (Lincoln: University of Nebraska Press, 1978); Jeff Long, *Duel of Eagles: The Mexican and U.S. Fight for the Alamo* (New York: William Morrow & Co., 1990); José Enrique de la Peña, *With Santa Anna in Texas: A Personal Narrative of the Revolution,* trans. and ed. Carmen Perry (College Station: Texas A & M University Press, 1975); Dr. John Sutherland, *The Fall of the Alamo* (San Antonio: Naylor Co. 1936); and Thomas Ricks Lindley, "The Revealing of Dr. John Sutherland," a manuscript in the DRT Library; Dan Kilgore, *How Did Davy Die?* (College Station: Texas A & M University Press, 1978); Thomas Lawrence Connelly, "Did David Crockett Surrender at the Alamo?" in *Journal of Southern History* 26, no. 3 (1960), predates by eighteen years Kilgore's assertions about Crockett's death; Amelia Williams, *A Critical Study of the Siege of the Alamo and of the Personnel of its Defenders* (Ph.D. dissertation, University of Texas, 1931); Maurice Elfer, *Madam Candelaria: Unsung Hero of the Alamo* (Houston: Rein Co., 1933). Films are thoroughly catalogued in Frank Thompson, *Alamo Movies* (East Berlin, Pa.: Old Mill Books, 1991), with the most significant efforts in recent years being *The Alamo,* directed by John Wayne (United Artists, 1960); *The Last Command,* directed by Frank Lloyd (Republic Pictures, 1955); and *The Alamo: Thirteen Days to Glory,* directed by Burt Kennedy (NBC, 1987).

Contemporary references to Crockett or his times are found in Thomas Hart Benton, *Thirty Years' View*, 2 vols., (New York: D. Appleton & Co., 1856); *The Correspondence of Nicholas Biddle Dealing with National Affairs, 1807–1844*, ed. Reginald C. McGrane (Boston: J. S. Canner & Co., 1966, reprint of 1919 ed.), which does not include letters pertinent to Crockett, obtainable only from the President's Letter Book in the Library of Congress; J. C. Derby, *Fifty Years Among Authors, Books, and Publishers* (New York: G. W. Carleton & Co., 1884); James D. Davis, *The History of the City of Memphis* (Memphis: Hite, Crumpton & Kelly, Printers, 1873); Margaret L. O'Neale Timberlake Eaton, *Autobiography of Peggy Eaton*, ed. C. F. Deems (New York, 1932); John Filson, *The Discovery, Settlement, and Present State of Kentucky* (1784); Timothy Flint, *The Life and Adventures of Daniel Boone, the First Settler of Kentucky* (1833); Benjamin Franklin, *Autobiography*, ed. Leonard W. Labaree (New Haven: Yale University Press, 1964); *Correspondence of Andrew Jackson*, vol. V, 1822–38, ed. John Spencer Bassett (Washington, D.C.: Carnegie Institution of Washington, 1931); Amos Kendall, *Autobiography of Amos Kendall*, ed. William Stickney (his son-in-law) (Boston: Lee & Shepard, Publishers, 1872); Augustus Baldwin Longstreet, *Georgia Scenes* (Augusta, Ga.: *State Rights Sentinel*, 1835); Pat B. Clark, *The History of Clarksville and Old Red River Country* (Dallas: Mathis, Van Nort & Co., 1937); Harriet Martineau, *Society in America* (London: Saunders & Otley, 1837), and *Retrospect of Western Travel* (London: Saunders & Otley, 1838); Josephine Seaton, *William Winston Seaton of the National Intelligencer: A Biographical Sketch* (Boston: James R. Osgood & Co., 1871); *Correspondence of James K. Polk*, vol. I, 1817–32, ed. Herbert Weaver (Nashville: Vanderbilt University Press, 1960); Benjamin Perley Poore, *Perley's Reminiscences of Sixty Years in the National Metropolis* (Philadelphia: Hubbard Brothers, Publishers, 1886); Alexis de Tocqueville, *Journey to America*, ed. J. P. Mayer, trans. George Lawrence (London: Faber & Faber, 1959), and *Democracy in America*, ed. J. P. Mayer, trans. George Lawrence (New York: Harper & Row, 1966); and *The Autobiography of Martin Van Buren*, ed. John C. Fitzpatrick, in *Annual Report of the American Historical Association for the Year 1918* (reprint, Washington, D.C.: Government Printing Office, 1920).

Secondary sources include: Herbert Aptheker, *American Negro Slave Revolts* (New York: International Publishers, 1969), and *Nat Turner's Slave Rebellion* (New York: Grove Press, 1968); Ralph C. H. Catterall, *The Second Bank of the United States* (Chicago: University of Chicago Press, 1902); W. J. Cash, *The Mind of the South* (New York: Alfred A. Knopf, 1941); Bernard De Voto, *Mark Twain's America* (Boston: Little, Brown & Co., 1832); Richard Drinnon, *Violence in the American Experience: Winning the West* (New York: New American Library, 1979), and *Facing West: The Metaphysics of Indian-Hating and Empire Building* (Minneapolis: University of Minnesota Press, 1980); John Mack Faragher, *Daniel Boone: The Life and Legend of* an *American Pioneer* (New York: Henry Holt & Co., 1992); Daniel Feller, *The Public Lands in Jacksonian Politics* (Madison: University of Wisconsin Press, 1984); Daniel Walker Howe, *The Political Culture of the American Whigs* (Chicago: University of Chicago Press, 1979); Richard Hofstadter, *Anti-Intellectualism in American Life* (New York: Alfred A. Knopf, 1963); Marquis James, *The Life of Andrew Jackson* (Indianapolis: Bobbs-Merrill Co. 1938) and *The Raven: A Biography of Sam Houston* (New York: Blue Ribbon Books, 1929); Vernon Louis Parrington, *The Romantic Revolution in America: 1800–1860,* vol. II of *Main Currents in American Thought* (New York: Harcourt, Brace & Co., 1927); Francis S. Philbrick, *The Rise of the West, 1754–1830* (New York: Harper & Row, 1965); Robert V. Remini, *The Election of Andrew Jackson* (Philadelphia: J. B. Lippincott Co., 1963), *The Age of Jackson* (New York: Harper & Row, 1972), and *Henry Clay: Statesman for the Union* (New York: W. W. Norton & Co., 1991); Michael Rogin, *Fathers and Children: Andrew Jackson and the Subjugation of the American Indian* (New York: Alfred A. Knopf, 1975); Arthur M. Schlesinger, Jr., *The Age of Jackson* (Boston: Little, Brown & Co., 1945); Alexander Saxton, *The Rise and Fall of the White Republic: Class Politics and Mass Culture in Nineteenth-Century America* (London and New York: Verso, 1990); Richard Slotkin, *Regeneration Through Violence: The Mythology of the American Frontier, 1600–1860* (Middletown, Conn.: Wesleyan University Press, 1973), and *The Fatal Environment: The Myth of the Frontier in the Age of Industrialization, 1800–1890* (New York: Atheneum, 1985); Frederick Jackson Turner, *The Frontier in American History* (New York: Henry Holt & Co., 1920); Dale Van Every, *A Company of Heroes: The American Frontier, 1775–1783* (New York: William Morrow & Co., 1962), and *Ark of Empire: The American Frontier, 1784–1803* (New York: William Morrow & Co., 1963); and Howard Zinn, *A People's History of the United States* (New York: Harper Colophon, 1980).

INDEX